Ask the Chief

Ask the Chief
Backbone of the Navy

J. F. Leahy

Naval Institute Press
Annapolis, Maryland

This book has been brought to publication by the generous assistance of Marguerite and Gerry Lenfest.

Naval Institute Press
291 Wood Road
Annapolis, MD 21402

ISBN 978-1-59114-441-0
All photos courtesy of the U.S. Navy
ISBN 978-1-61251-231-0 (eBook)

First Naval Institute Press paperback edition published 2012.
Library of Congress Cataloging-in-Publication Data
Leahy, J. F., 1946–
    Ask the chief : backbone of the Navy / J. F. Leahy.
        p.   cm.
    Includes bibliographical references and index.
    ISBN 978-1-59114-460-1 (alk. paper)
    1. United States. Navy—Petty officers. 2. George Washington
(Aircraft carrier) I. Title.
    VB308.L43 2004
    359.3'38—dc22

                                                    2003025423

Printed in the United States of America on acid-free paper ∞

19 18 17 16 15   8 7 6 5 4

Contents

Preface

I never made chief. Like many young and immature sailors, I suppose at the time I thought it unimportant. I know better now.

It's not that I didn't have the opportunity. I actually had more chances than the average sailor. I first spent four years on active duty during the Vietnam War. I progressed from seaman recruit to radioman second class in just under three years, and I spent my fourth Navy year with Mobile Construction Battalion One in Vietnam. In 1970, as my enlistment drew to a close, I fidgeted impatiently as I sat across from Chief Bagdigian, the battalion career counselor. His was not an easy job, dodging mortar and rocket fire in a stifling bunker while trying to convince young sailors to ship over. He listed all the benefits of reenlistment while in a war zone: automatic promotion to first class, extra points on the chief's exam, choice of duty stations, even a tax-free bonus. I listened, but declined politely, determined to go home, away from the insanity of war and destruction. A few weeks later, I tossed my white hat into the back bay of the Philadelphia Navy Yard as I walked out the main gate and up Broad Street. I knew—as only youth can know—that the world was my oyster.

Well, if not an oyster, perhaps a clam. Older, wiser, but mostly coveting the monthly drill pay, a few years later I affiliated with the Coast Guard Reserve. Things went well there, too. I'd picked up RM1 in the Coast Guard, and during my last active-duty period at Coast Guard Radio New Orleans, I completed my evaluations for chief petty officer. In one action-packed, two-week period, I participated in the events associated with not one but two hurricanes menacing the Gulf, the search for a crashed Air Force fighter, and a sinking Honduran freighter. For a high-speed Morse operator guarding the 500 kHz distress frequency, life doesn't get more exciting than that. But other priorities intervened: my family was growing, and my civilian career required extensive international travel. And so, reluctantly, I left the Coast Guard and the sea services forever. Or so I thought.

I pondered all this as I lay aboard the USS *George Washington* (CVN-73) one sultry evening in July 2002. It was well past taps. I was sleepy and I was hungry, and I couldn't decide which appetite to appease first. We were in the North Atlantic, somewhere off the coast of Africa. I was comfortable in my small, darkened rack in the forward chief petty officer's quarters on the nuclear carrier's third deck. I'd pulled the blue privacy curtain when I had turned in, so that I might review my writer's notes without disturbing my eighty-five shipmates in the "goat locker," the sailor's traditional and usually apt name for CPO quarters. I debated whether to roll over and sleep, hoping that no alarm or drill would disturb me until reveille, or to get up, dress by the dim red light of my flashlight, and head aft to the mess for a midnight snack. Well, I thought, I can sleep anytime. Indeed, for the last few weeks I had been propping my pillow on the bulkhead of the forward ammunition hoist. Once I overcame my uneasiness about 500-pound bombs passing within inches of my head, the rattling of the elevator just served to remind me that I was among sailors again, and at a ripe old age, too. I can't recall a happier time in my life.

Quietly, I rolled out of my rack to the deck. It wasn't much of a drop, for my old friend Command Master Chief Mike McCalip, taking into consideration my age and girth, had assigned me the lowest of the three-tiered bunks.

I retrieved my clothes from the foot of the bed and dressed, then climbed the ladder to the second deck, headed aft, and descended to the CPO mess. *George Washington,* like all carriers, is a twenty-four-hour operation. The lights were dimmed in recognition of the hour, and only a single mess cook ("food service attendant," in today's jargon) tended the rotating hot-dog cooker, the popcorn wagon, the sandwich line, and the ever present steaming coffeepot. Leaving the coffee for the watchstanders, I grabbed some popcorn and, nodding to the mess cook, retreated to the far corner and opened my notebook. Alone for the moment—always a rare treat on a busy aircraft carrier—I buried my head in my notes, and prepared for the next day's work.

"Hey, are you the writer that's talking to chief petty officers? Master Chief McCalip tells me you're an old radioman—I am, too. I'm Senior Chief Perry, by the way, but call me Chuck. I just came off watch—but what brings you here at this late hour, anyway?"

I looked up to see a lanky, affable senior chief petty officer walking toward my table. He sat across from me, and, between mouthfuls of popcorn, I began to explain. Several years previously, I had been honored to have Master Chief Petty Officer of the Navy John Hagan write the foreword for *Honor, Courage, Commitment: Navy Boot Camp,* my book about the Navy's Recruit Training Command, Great Lakes. "Why not write a book about the people who really keep the Navy afloat? " he had asked me then. "Get out there in the fleet and talk to the chiefs. And don't make the mistake that most writers make—just let them tell the story in their own words. Chief petty officers are lots of things, but they're never shy. You'll have enough material for ten books by the time you're finished."

And so, as I explained to Senior Chief Perry, at the invitation of Capt. Martin Erdossy, *George Washington*'s skipper, I'd boarded the carrier at Pier 11 in Norfolk as she departed for a six-month deployment in support of Operation Enduring Freedom. Mike McCalip, whom I'd known and respected for years, had arranged for me to live and work among the ship's chief petty officers. Whenever sailors are stuck for an answer—if the anchor gets fouled, or the paint won't dry—someone usually shrugs and says, "Well, let's ask the chief." I had done just that, filling dozens of audio tapes and two reporter's notebooks with comments and stories, concerns and observations related by the 350 chief petty officers of the ship's company and embarked air wing. Before boarding, I had already received nearly two hundred detailed replies to a single posting on a bulletin board serving active and retired chiefs, and after leaving *George Washington,* I planned to visit several other commands to improve my understanding of the world of chief petty officers. Captain Erdossy had promised to put me ashore "somewhere this side of the Suez Canal," and I had another week or so of interviews before I left the ship to return to my job as a university professor in Ohio.

"A radioman turned writer, huh?" Senior Chief Perry replied. "Well, I guess I've heard everything now. Must be from all those years pounding on a teletype machine. They call us 'information system technicians' now, but we're just old RMs in disguise. In fact, we still wear the four sparks on our rating badges, even though none of us have touched a telegraph key in years. I came on active duty in 1964 and stayed till 1968, got out for a while, then came back in to finish my thirty years. They tell me I'm the oldest sailor on the *George Washington* these days. Lots of people suspect that I went to sea with Noah—but I really first went to sea on *Noa.* That's the USS *Noa* (DD841), I mean. We were a *Gearing*-class destroyer, homeported at Mayport, Florida. Who knows—maybe we worked each other back then. Our voice call sign was 'Steel Head' and our call sign was NBBS. The Navy is a small place, isn't it?"

I nodded, and pushed aside the popcorn as we began to reminisce. Our first tours had overlapped, and we had many common memories. We talked of a radioman's life: of transmitters that wouldn't stay on frequency and receivers that on the midwatch mysteriously tuned themselves to Wolfman Jack or other stateside disk jockeys. We talked about the infamous dead zones in mid-ocean and elsewhere, where the ether sucked the life out of radio signals, and of irate officers hammering on the radio shack door as we tuned desperately to every frequency in the spectrum, trying to raise a shore station—any shore station!—through the pounding, crashing static. We compared notes on the dreaded zero-hour changeover, when all circuits would go silent as new encryption codes were installed for the day, and how unit pride, and tyrannical chief radiomen, made us dread being the last station to come back on line. Mundane things, of course, but to a radioman, the heart and soul of our rating.

Fists rapping happily on the mess table, we were comparing notes on telegraph keying techniques when we attracted the attention of Master Chief Ben Barrett. "Well, I'll be damned," he said. "I thought Morse code went away years ago." Sure enough, although now the leading chief petty officer for combat systems, Ben himself had spent nearly twenty-four years as a radioman, and soon he too added to the conversation as we sat in the dimmed lights of the quiet mess. We talked of radiomen, real and mythical, who could nod off on watch, yet spring to instantaneous action whenever their call sign beeped through their earphones. Radiomen who could hear and decode the faintest of signals, buried beneath static and noise of Russian, Chinese, and Cuban jammers. Men and women who could tend a dozen teletype circuits at a time, and still cross the aisle to help you if you got behind on your own machines. Sailors who would brave the wildest weather to climb the tallest mast to tweak "just a little more gain" out of a corroded antenna. We laughed and joked and told sea stories, and the young mess cook looked on, bemused, perhaps, that in an age of e-mail, satellite TV, and instant phone calls home, three old sailors could find simple enjoyment in rapping code signals on the table. For Chuck and Ben, I suppose, it was just another late night in the mess. For me it was, well, magical.

But even magical moments must end, and I soon bade good night to my new friends. I returned to the forward berthing area and turned in, but the urge to sleep had left me. Still basking in the glow from my chance encounter with my fellow radiomen, my mind drifted back to other chiefs, to other radiomen whom I had known over the years. Chief petty officers who had guided me, instructed me, and sometime even rescued me from my own stupidity. Chiefs like RMC Black at Naval Facility Lewes (if he had a first name, he never made it known to his strikers), who took a chance on a young, undesignated seaman and managed to find a billet for me in his radio shack. Fresh from boot camp, I had saluted him as I crossed the quarterdeck on my first day aboard. After he stopped laughing, he asked me what I wanted to be when I grew up. I owe my long career in telecommunications, and years in the intelligence community, to that chance meeting. I thought of Chief Jack D. McCoy, leading radioman at

Roosevelt Roads, Puerto Rico, who taught me that being a hotshot radioman and a good petty officer were not necessarily the same thing. And I thought of others, too, and not just radiomen; of Seabee chiefs, who taught me that "Can Do" was more than an empty motto, and that everyone, blackshoe and Seabee, was a rifleman first, when a battalion went off to war. I though of chiefs like Martin Zeller and Al Nelson, Debbie Reilly and Mike Lucas, whose presence graces my earlier book and who endured the freezing cold and blowing snows of Recruit Training Command, Great Lakes, to turn modern kids into stable, trustworthy sailors. Great chiefs, every one of them.

But as I lay there, the faint red glow of the night battle lamps reflecting off the bulkhead, I was overtaken by a profound and lingering sadness. For at that moment, I realized that for all that these chiefs had done for me—for every time they had bailed me out, covered my watch, discounted my immaturity, or helped me in ways that I could not count—I had never said thanks. And that moment of sadness was deep and profound and very real, as only the realization of lost opportunity can be. Many years have passed, and perhaps they have, too. But others have taken their place—others whom they had trained and inspired, rebuked and instructed, guided and, yes, even loved.

This, then, is their story, told in their own words. Big decks riders and small boy sailors, blackshoes and Airedales, active, reserve, and retired, it matters not. They are chief petty officers in the United States Navy. And belated, imperfect, or incomplete as this book may be, it's my way of saying thanks.

I am who I am because of each of you.

Acknowledgments

Special thanks are due to those who made this book happen:

Capt. Martin Erdossy, USN, and Capt. Dennis Watson, USN, commanding officer and executive officer, USS *George Washington* (CVN-73), for hosting me during my own "Journey into the Mess."

Capt. Dana Potts, USN, and Capt. Mark Guadagnini, USN, commander and deputy commander, Carrier Air Wing Seventeen, for providing full access to the members of their squadrons and subordinate commands.

Capt. O.W. Wright, USN, and Capt. Mary Kolar, USN, commanding officer and executive officer, Recruit Training Command, Naval Training Center, Great Lakes, for their wonderful hospitality in inviting me back to RTC and granting access to the chief petty officers in their command.

Master Chief Petty Officer of the Navy Terry Scott, Master Chief Petty Officer of the Navy (Ret.) Jim Herdt, and Master Chief Petty Officer of the

Navy (Ret.) John Hagan for their gracious assistance, wisdom, and insight, which they freely provided to me while I was writing this book. As a writer, I'm grateful for their assistance. As an American citizen, I'm even more grateful for the contribution that they and their predecessors have made to the United States Navy.

Command Master Chief Mike McCalip of USS *George Washington,* for once again shining the light and allowing me to see the Navy as few outsiders ever get to see it. This book would not have happened without the eager cooperation of one of the Navy's premier chief petty officers. Thanks, Mike.

Command Master Chief Scott Benning, Carrier Air Wing Seventeen, for permitting me to experience, up-close and personal, life among the Navy's aviation communities. Climbing the outboard ladder to the flight deck during flight operations was an experience I'll never forget, Scott.

Command Master Chief Bennie Pierce and the members of the chief petty officers mess aboard USS *Normandy* (CG-60) for inviting me to share again the life of those who sail "closest to the water."

Thanks, too, to MMCM(SS) Greg Peterman (Ret.) and the cadre of active, reserve, and retired chief petty officers who muster daily at www.goatlocker.org, the premier Web site serving the chief petty officer community. The plankowners were unfailingly kind and resourceful, and have immediate access to a wealth of primary sources of information regarding the life and lore of chief petty officers. Knock three times and uncover—they'll be glad to help you, too.

A very special thank-you to Chief Aviation Electronics Technician Eric Oitzman, my mentor, escort, and good friend aboard USS *George Washington,* who made sure that I was in the right place, with the right tools, at the right time, every time. I couldn't ask for a better shipmate.

And, finally, to my son Michael T. Leahy, who served as a key researcher for this book and who transcribed hundreds of hours of audio tapes, deciphered notes, managed the data collection element through the Internet and the libraries at Ohio State University and Franklin University, and who was always cheerful, always helpful, and always available when I needed help or encouragement. Thanks again, Mike.

Ask the Chief

One

What Is a Chief Petty Officer?

Hear the voices of three chief petty officers of the United States Navy:

> "I was out on the USS *Simpson,* a sister ship to USS *Cole,* right before *Cole* got hit. We were intercepting and boarding Iraqi tankers. They were in such bad condition that you could see President Bush's thousand points of light, right through the hull. I looked around for some leadership advice—and remembered at that moment that I was the leader. Now, there's a sobering thought for you."

> "The average age on the flight deck is about nineteen. And at nineteen, you are invincible, you know? Nothing bad is going to happen to you—it's going to happen to the other guy. Well, I'm the guy who breaks the news to you—and I'm not gentle about it—that if you don't pay attention to what I'm going to tell you, you are going to die. Right here, right now, on this 4-acre flight deck. Today."

"As an independent duty corpsman, I am responsible for the four hundred sailors on USS *Normandy*. My boss is the navigator; no medical help there. We often steam independently, away from the rest of the battle group. People don't usually get hurt when the seas are calm and the winds are light. No, it's when you can't launch boats or recover helicopters that things get hairy. I'm a senior chief hospital corpsman—what you see is what you get. I'm all there is."

What exactly is a chief petty officer? According to the U.S. Navy,

Chief Petty Officers are enlisted members, in pay grades E-7 through E-9, who lead and manage the sailor resources of the Navy they serve. They are responsible for, have the authority to accomplish, and are held accountable for:

Leading sailors and applying their skills to tasks that enable mission accomplishment for the U.S. Navy

Developing enlisted and junior officer sailors

Communicating the core values, standards and information of our Navy that empower sailors to be successful in all they attempt

Supporting with loyalty the endeavors of the chain of command they serve and their fellow Chief Petty Officers with whom they serve.[1]

"Leading, Developing, Communicating, Supporting." Every chief petty officer knows that definition by heart, and each chief practices those traits every time he or she crosses the quarterdeck of a ship or station. That's what chiefs do; that's what chiefs have always done.

Chiefs *are* what chiefs *do*. And just what is it that chiefs do? Ask any sailor, from the greenest recruit to the most distinguished admiral, and he or she will gladly tell you. Perhaps he'll recall for you a special chief petty officer in his life, someone who got him back on track when he had temporarily misplaced his internal compass. Ask another, and she might tell you that a chief is the only one who will willingly get out of his or her rack at oh-dark-thirty to rescue a young and stupid sailor from the clutches of the local gendarme in a god-forsaken port halfway around the world. She might mention, too, that a chief is that sailor who will go into harm's way, risking life and limb, to clear debris from a flight deck so that circling pilots, low on fuel, can land safely. Yet another sailor might chuckle at the memory, and tell you that a chief is the one sailor who will stand up, respectfully but forcefully, and counsel a young division officer or an experienced department head: "With all due respect, sir, what you are suggesting just plain won't work." Or he might recall, with no little chagrin, that a chief is the person who will read a young sailor the riot act, questioning his legitimacy, sanity, intelligence, metabolism, and common sense, in language no mother should ever hear, and then, at captain's mast the next morning, say: "Well, sir, he's a darn good sailor, one of the best, and I'm sure that we don't want to hold a little mistake against him, now do we?" And the captain, if she's wise in the ways of the Navy and the world, will see the little wink, and know that her ship and sailors are in good hands.

Chiefs *are* what chiefs *do.*

Young sailors, fresh from the rigors and terror of boot camp, may think that the chief petty officer position has been around forever. Consider the leathery faces and work-scarred hands in any chiefs mess at sea, and you might be forgiven for thinking that the members of that mess have been around forever, too. And it won't be long before someone reminds you that "officers run the Navy—but the chiefs run the ship."

So who, then, was the first chief petty officer? Records are scarce and open to interpretation, but Chief Warrant Officer Lester Tucker has researched the issue extensively for the Naval Historical Center. He states that "during the Revolutionary War, Jacob Wasbie, a Cook's Mate serving on board the *Alfred,* one of the first Continental Navy warships, was promoted to 'Chief Cook' on June 1, 1776. Chief Cook is construed to mean Cook or Ship's Cook, which was the official rating title at that time. This is the earliest example of the use of the term 'Chief' located to date by the author."[2]

Tucker's research is meticulous and valuable, but, as he points out, names can be misleading. Sometimes the term *chief* had functional rather than positional meaning, similar to our use of the word *leading* today. Yesterday's chief carpenter might well be today's leading damage controlman; yesterday's chief apothecary could be today's independent duty corpsman. It may be an oversimplification to trace the concept of today's chief petty officer—one charged with the training and leadership of sailors in a wide range of duties—to a single colonial ship's cook. If we look elsewhere, though, we'll soon find the spiritual, if not etymological, ancestors of today's chief petty officers. For a cadre of petty officers—junior to the most junior officer aboard ship, yet senior to all other sailors—did exist, even before colonial times, and it is to this group of sailors that we look for antecedents of the modern chief petty officer. These fine sailors were ship's masters-at-arms.

Surprisingly, there is no written record of masters-at-arms in the British Royal Navy until 1694, although certain trusted sailors had always been given responsibility for the ship's guns during battle. These individuals were called "masters of the armory," and were responsible for musketry, cutlasses, and other small arms, as well as supervision of the ship's main armament. In August 1694 the Admiralty determined that the senior lieutenant on each warship would henceforth be installed as the first lieutenant. The first lieutenant, among his other duties, would be responsible for the good order and discipline of the ship's crew. The first identified officer to hold this billet in the Royal Navy, one Lt. Henry James, found it difficult to maintain discipline aboard ship, given the Royal Navy's practice of "press ganging" or taking unwilling landsmen to sea for extended periods of time. Indeed, most seamen were recruited from the lowest classes of society, and often went to sea only to avoid imprisonment, transportation to the colonies, or hanging. The mess decks of British men-of-war were rough and rugged places, and Lieutenant James nominated sturdy, reliable men as his assistants. Naturally, many were those already trusted with access to, and care of, ship's armaments. Thus was born the community of masters-at-arms. The Royal Navy held them responsible for maintaining good order and discipline, as well as for training the crew in hand-to-hand combat. The master-at-arms in the Royal Navy also had other names—even today, the assistants in that branch are known as regulating petty officers (or, colloquially, "crushers") responsible for enforcing ship's regulations and maintaining good order below decks.[3]

The newly founded American Navy copied many practices from the British. The concept of a ship's master-at-arms was twice mentioned in the

Naval Regulations of 1775, and during the Revolution the master-at-arms was generally considered to be the senior "enlisted man" aboard any ship. It was not until the Civil War, however, that a formal role for masters-at-arms was dictated. By 1865 *Naval Regulations* stated: "The Master-at-Arms will be the Chief Petty Officer of the ship in which he shall serve. All orders from him in regard to the police of the vessel, the preservation of order, and obedience to regulations must be obeyed by all petty officers and others of the crew." During this period, the badge of the master-at-arms, worn on the right sleeve, displayed three chevrons, an eagle, and three arcs, quite similar in appearance to that of an army master sergeant of the period. Indeed, it was the basis for today's CPO insignia, which has three chevrons and a single arc or rocker, and which came into use shortly before the turn of the twentieth century.

During the draw-down and reorganization of naval ratings following World War I, the formal rating of master-at-arms was disestablished, and tasks performed by the master-at-arms were assigned collaterally to other senior petty officers. Given the disciplinary and morale issues prevailing during and at the end of the Vietnam War, however, the rating was reestablished in 1973.

Today, the master-at arms serves as a force protection/antiterrorism specialist for Navy ships and commands, and also assists in maintaining good order and discipline at sea and ashore. Master Chief Gregory Ciaccio is the master-at-arms aboard the USS *George Washington* (CVN-73). Chief Will Scheer is his primary assistant. I caught up with both of them just a few hours before the *George Washington* battle group was about to pass through the narrow, and potentially dangerous, Straits of Gibraltar.

Master Chief Ciaccio:

We MAs were around forever, but then we were abolished as a separate force in the 1920s. Mostly, I think, that was because the chiefs were angry that we were always the senior petty officers on board; in fact, the whole idea of chief petty officers started with masters-at-arms. In a way, that role is now filled by command master chiefs. But when they reinstituted MAs, we became the senior rating in the Navy, even above boatswain's mates. Fortunately, when they initiated the command master chief program, we got away from all the hostility about senior ratings, and I think that's a good idea. We're more like what a first sergeant is in the Army, as far as good order and discipline goes.

While many things have changed since colonial days, the reliance upon the master-at-arms force as the ship's experts in small arms and close-in defense certainly has not.

Master Chief Ciaccio:

We're also the naval infantry; we're here to fight for our ship. If you look at the history of masters-at-arms, that's what we've always done. Not only are discipline and good order our responsibility but, even back in history, we've always done antiterrorism. We're the people that were with John Paul Jones, we're the people that went against the Barbary pirates, we're the people that would go overboard and fight with a cutlass and a musket. The weapons have changed, but that's what we still do. In 1973 Congress told the Navy to reinstitute master-at-arms as a separate rating. If you go to the hall of heroes in the Pentagon, you'll find MAs all over there; they were awarded the Medal of Honor. It's our ship, let us fight for it.

Most chiefs, like those quoted at the beginning of this chapter, take their leadership role very seriously. And none articulates that responsibility better than Master Chief Ciaccio.

Master Chief Ciaccio:

When I think of our role here, I always recall a movie that I saw, and something that a guy said that struck me. It was the movie *Anzio,* and in the movie, Peter Falk played Cpl. Jack Rabinoff, who was badly wounded previously and discharged, but managed to get back in the military. He was a terrific soldier, a natural, and he knew how to take care of his unit. And this officer said something to him, and he offended the officer, I guess, because the officer was from a higher social stratum, and the officer pretty much wasn't listening to him. So Falk's character said, "You can do anything you want with me, you can put me on report, or whatever. But I'm going to take care of everybody," and he said it from the heart. And that's my job as a master chief: to take care of everybody. That means my chiefs, my petty officers, my seamen, the new guy, the captain, the CMC, the mess cooks; my job is to take care of everybody. And I truly believe that that is my job. Sometimes I see them going the wrong way, and I open my big mouth, and sometimes it works real well, and sometimes I hurt somebody's feelings. We need to do the right things: we need to keep our people alive, fulfill our missions, and take care of sailors. That's what we do—Leading, Developing, Communicating, and Supporting. If we aren't caring about our people, then it all ends right there; it's a nonstarter. I think that sometimes people make decisions for the wrong reason. They worry "How's it going to look?" My job is to take care of the chiefs, the chief's job is to take care of the sailors. I always say to my people, "If you make me lead, I'm going to make you sorry." Because that means that everybody below me, from chiefs to third-class, is failing somewhere. Take care of business: Developing, Communicating, and Supporting. Leading is a fallback position; if you take care of the other three, leadership happens.

A great deal has been written about the all-volunteer force, and the mind-set of today's young enlisted soldiers and sailors. Sometimes it falls to the senior enlisted to remind their juniors that, after the events of September 11, 2001, this is, indeed, "the real thing."

Chief Scheer:
Most of the younger sailors, I think, still haven't bought in to the fact that this is a war patrol. Now, our guys, the masters-at-arms force, it's different with them. We had to do a battle-focusing as we were preparing to get under way. We laid it out straight for them; we are done with the calm period, and we're out here to get down to brass tacks. Even though we hope that nothing happens to us, the potential

for something bad to happen is there. Sailors on the mess decks, generally, I suspect, feel the same way. Maybe they didn't fully understand
it, until after the captain came on and spoke about the threat, or after
we went to the hangar bay the other night and heard the admiral
speak. The guys that have been on cruises before, I'm sure they understood. But the junior sailors on the mess decks, to be honest, I don't
think they really had a clue until it was really brought into focus by
the admiral and the captain's words.

Sometimes, even the most experienced chief petty officers find themselves
reflecting on the gravity of the situation, and the heavy responsibility they
have undertaken.

Master Chief Ciaccio:

If you're honest with yourself, you're going to question yourself a lot of
times. I don't care if you're the captain, the admiral, the CMC, whoever—
you will. When I hit the rack last night, I was dead tired, but I lay there
worrying—about our ammo, our equipment, our guys. Do they know
everything they need to know, is there anything else I need to tell them? I
was dead tired, but it was hard to get to sleep. If there's one thing that I
could fix—if someone handed me a pot of money—it would have to go
into weapons. We need more and better small arms, ammo, and equipment to fight as naval infantry. But whatever we have, that's what we're
going to fight with. And if that comes down to a fork, then I'll go down to
the mess decks and get a fork, and stick somebody with it.

Chief Scheer:

I agree with Master Chief Ciaccio. If I could fix only one thing in the
Navy, it would be the way we think about force protection. I would use
that money on the ships, especially our main assets like the carriers, to get
the personnel, the weapons, and the training in order to do our job effectively. We are working very hard to get this exactly right, because if we
fail, the results are unthinkable. And every day is an uphill struggle,
because there are so many frustrations involved; you have the different

type commanders, and the fleet commanders that aren't on the same page. And most of these problems are based on manning. We were told before we got under way we were going to get an additional assistant master-at-arms. Well, nobody ever shifted the money to get the billet filled, so consequently, we're making it work with what we've got. I've got really good, gung-ho people down there, but we could always use more.

As with all good leaders, most chief petty officers understand that a full appreciation of the "big picture"—being able to walk a mile in the other guy's shoes—is critical in today's military.

Master Chief Ciaccio:

I think some of the best things we've done in the Navy are the warfare pins, because it forces you to learn what the other guy is doing. If you aren't playing along with the ship, if you're being parochial, then you're ruining everything, and you're just making it impossible. Now, I don't think that they really thought that I was going to go up to CIC and be able to stand a watch for somebody; I don't think I should go up to Radio and take a watch; I certainly don't think that I should go down to Reactor and run a nuclear power plant. I don't think I'm competent to do those things. But getting my surface warfare qualifications makes me understand what the other people do, and what I can do to help make that happen, and that's important. That's what makes a team a team. I like to think I am a team builder, and that my team always takes care of me, and they always do. What makes a team is discipline, training, and shared values. Making that happen is what leaders do.

While force protection is certainly a vital role, perhaps the real test of leadership for today's Masters-at-arms is in maintaining good order and discipline aboard ship. In that role they function closely with the division and department chief petty officers. Many minor breaches of discipline can be handled by a quick word in the passageway between the master-at-arms and the offender's chief. But USS *George Washington* is, indeed, a floating city, and unfortunately, more serious violations do occur.

Master Chief Ciaccio:

You have to remember that while we have fifty-six hundred people on board, most of them are young adults; if they were our age, they might not be quite as much trouble. They tend to do things that young people do, although they are obviously more disciplined than the average person on the street. But they are still young, and they may do things that they might choose not to do later in life.

Chief Scheer:

A lot of people talk about gender integration in the Navy now. Gender integration aboard ship just adds another wrinkle to the job, to tell the truth. I've got fantastic first-class female petty officers who work down in my shop. And quite honestly, it [angers them] to see other females who shrug off their duties, or use pregnancy or whatever to take them off sea duty, when they are out here putting it on the line every day. And of course, when you put male and female sailors on board the same ship, humans will be humans, and opposites do attract. Yes, we've had sexual assault cases—and yes, that stuff happens here. This is especially true when you are dealing with sailors between eighteen and twenty-four years of age. Now, I wish I could say that those are the only people who get in trouble on board this ship, but that's not true. There's no color, there is no gender, there is no pay grade, it happens up and down across the board; people get caught in compromising situations regardless of who they are.

Some may think that chief petty officers are a breed apart. But all have come through the ranks: there are no directly procured petty officers serving in the Navy at present, although during wartime some special billets were created for especially skilled or talented individuals recruited directly from the civilian community.

Master Chief Ciaccio:

I became a chief in 1986. At the time I was a special agent in the office of the secretary of defense, assigned to Secretary Weinberger. I pinned with people at the EOD base at Indian Head; there's a large chiefs mess there. And when a CPO selectee comes to me today, I always write the same thing in everybody's charge book. It's a quote from Bull Halsey: "There are no great men, there are only great challenges, which ordinary men, like you and I, are forced by circumstances to meet. There are no great men." Often we think that we are not up to the task—it's too hard, I don't know how to do this, it's not my forte, whatever. But you know what? There's nobody else. In about forty-eight hours we are about to go some-place really dangerous, and I don't know that I'm their best leader. I've done this a long time, I've done a lot of things that might tell you that I can do this real well, but still, maybe I'm not the best leader. But I am the leader—because I'm here. "There are no great men." Just me and my guys, and I make them believe that they are great men, but I'm not so foolish as to think that I am. But as a team, we're unstoppable.

Chief Scheer:

And that's what we do every day as chiefs. Now, among officers, I some-times think ROTC guys are a little more receptive to the role of Navy chiefs—more than guys from the Academy or wherever. They realize right up front that they don't know it; that they don't have a clue. And because they don't know it, and they know that they need us, they are a little more apt to allow us to take them under our wings, and develop them into successful officers. I'm not trying to stereotype anybody; I've worked with excellent Academy officers who are receptive to the enlisted community as well. But sometimes the Academy guys are a little less receptive. That may have something to do with the way they are treated as midshipmen, I really don't know. But I do know that the role we play as chiefs is vital. We're the link between the wardroom and the deck plates. And I don't think that our peers in any of the other branches feel that importance, that "connectivity" as much as we do here.

Master Chief Ciaccio:

We're different from the other services, I think, because sailors live so close, and we're away a lot. Most services say that they deploy frequently, but not like sailors. And you need somebody whom you look at differently; remember that the Navy always had a class system, and that's where officers and chiefs and the khaki uniform comes in. It's maybe not as obvious today as when I first enlisted in 1964, but it's there. Officers are different than enlisted, and we, the chiefs, are the link between the two. We wear the same uniform, basically, that the officers do, but we've been down there—down on the mess decks. Sometimes you are talking to an officer and you say, "Sir, what's happening here is the normal adaptation process for a young person becoming a sailor; things will work out." Or you say, "Ma'am, this is not the normal adaptation, and this young person may not make it unless he makes a very quick turn. We really need to take a good look at that, and at some point we may want to cut our losses here. This guy may have enlisted, but he hasn't joined."

There's a big distinction between enlisting and joining. I often say that some people on board here are sailors, and some are just employees, and there's a world of difference. I'll tell anybody who asks, you had better be here and prepared to fight fires and do whatever you have to do. I am terrified of fires, but I've been a repair party leader, and I'll go into that fire, because that's what I have to do. I am much more afraid of fire than of engaging an enemy with an M-16; I figure that I know more about those weapons and how to fight than the other guy, and I'm going to win. But fire, that's a law of physics that I'm fighting there. Everyone is afraid of something, but, once again, "there are no great men." Just because I'm afraid of fire doesn't mean that I'm not going to do the job; in fact, if I'm afraid of something, I am going to do it, because it's the only way I can live with myself. "There are no great men." Out here, the fire department ain't coming.

When I set up the force protection barriers for this ship, I set myself out where I'm in visible danger. My force protection officer, he's up with the captain; my chiefs might be with my machine gun teams. I wear a Rhodesian mercenary chest pouch, so that I can most effectively carry my weapons and lots of ammunition. And we train our people to use their weapons out to their maximum effective range, because we want to kill aggressors all the way in so that they'll say to themselves,

"Hmm, that may not have been a good idea, attacking the USS *George Washington.*" I put myself out there where I am liable to be killed, and I do that intentionally, so that my people look and say, "Hey, here's this fifty-five-year-old guy, and he's out here with us. I don't mind fighting and dying next to this guy." And they won't lose heart. Now, I'm not a SEAL, mind you. I'm a Walrus: I'm old, gray, long in the tooth, and I'm very territorial. And I can get really, really nasty, if you piss me off.

Two

In the Beginning

Throughout the age of sail, masters-at-arms continued as the primary leaders on the lower decks. Their rule at times was draconian; life at sea aboard a man-of-war was not a gentle excursion. Seamen of the era, no doubt, would have been more comfortable in a dockside grogshop than in a fancy drawing room.

The early colonies were maritime communities. After the Revolution, the colonies—now states—were continually threatened by Britain and other established European powers. By 1797 the Continental Congress, recognizing the threat to the young nation's security, directed the construction of several vessels, which became the foundation for our modern Navy. Although the ships themselves differed in size and armament, jobs aboard were not dissimilar. In addition to masters-at-arms, a ship's captain usually appointed additional petty officers to serve at his pleasure—that is, they could be removed or reassigned depending on performance and circumstances. These petty officers were responsible for the more highly skilled tasks aboard the vessel, and usually included clerks (the only rating that required the ability to read and write), boatswain's mates, coxswains to look after the ship's boats, sailmaker's mates, gunner's mates, carpenter's mates, armorers, stewards, and coopers. Use of the term *mate* as part of the rating usually indicated the presence of a commissioned or warrant officer in a leadership role. The gunner's mates, for example, reported to, and were directed by, the ship's gunner, usually a junior officer. The remainder of the crew were able seamen, ordinary seamen, and midshipmen. With minor changes, similar manning structures continued until the Civil War period.[1]

Much has been written about the precedence of certain ratings over others during this period. Indeed, one very good way to stir up emotions in a chiefs mess even today is to bring up the question (especially in the presence of boatswain's mates!) of which rating takes precedence over others on ceremonial occasions. Unfortunately, deductions concerning leadership among nonofficers during this period are based upon circumstantial evidence. Up until the Civil War, one could infer the precedence of ratings based upon the sequence in which ratings were listed on ship's rosters and the differences in pay of various petty officers, as well as the order of names as they appeared on muster rolls. Nevertheless, it has been naval tradition that "petty officers of the line"—that is, those with direct responsibilities for the safe navigation and war-fighting capabilities of the ship—should take precedence over those with staff responsibilities. Within the line ratings, boatswain's mates, followed by quartermasters, signalmen, and gunner's mates, had "pride of place" over most other ratings aboard ship. Precedence within a rating was spelled out in the *Navy Regulations* of 1863, which stated: "Precedence among petty officers of the same rate, if not established particularly by the commander of the vessel, will be determined by priority of rating. When two or more have received the same rate on the same day, and the commander of the vessel shall not have designated one of that rate to act as a chief, their precedence shall be determined by the order in which their names appear on the ship's books." That wording was shortened in the 1865 regulations to read simply, "Precedence among Petty Officers of the same rate shall be established by the Commanding Officer."

By January 1884 only three ratings carried the title *chief*. All were in the line divisions: boatswains, quartermasters, and gunners. Within a year, the Navy had developed a rating structure with three grades of seamen and three of petty officers. Oddly, the three "chief"-level ratings were positioned at the first-class petty officer level, a situation that has caused confusion for historians, and for chief petty officers researching their "genealogy," ever since. Other ratings were awarded the level of chief, including masters-at-arms, apothecaries, yeomen, ship's writers, schoolmasters, and band masters, and were also pegged at the first-class level, but listed in a special branch separate from the line or seaman's branch. Machinists, who were becoming increasingly important as the fleet moved toward total reliance upon steam, were listed as first-class petty officers in the "artificer branch," a skill grouping that exists today in British and Commonwealth forces.

Today, chief petty officers celebrate 1 April 1893 as the "birthday" of their rate. With the establishment of yet another pay scale, the rate of chief petty officer was established above the rate of petty officer first-class, but below the rank of warrant officer. Even now, grizzled old chief petty officers, wise in the way of the Navy, often ask CPO selectees to identify the first chief petty officer of the modern era. Like winding the dogwatch and carrying steam to the engine room, this is an impossible task. Most first-class petty officers in 1893 were automatically retitled as chief petty officers. Schoolmasters—who, despite their title, were not seagoing academics but were employed aboard training ships and resembled our current recruit division commanders— remained at the first-class level. Ship's writers evolved into a rating structure that included first-, second-, and third-class petty officers, and the carpenter's mate rating showed billets at third-class through chief petty officer levels. With the release of the 1893 lists, the Navy had nine ratings with representation at the chief petty officer level:

Chief master-at-arms
Chief machinist
Chief yeoman
Chief boatswain's mate
Chief carpenter's mate

Apothecary
Chief quartermaster
Chief gunner's mate
Band master

Before the establishment of the chief petty officer grade, and for many years thereafter, commanding officers could promote petty officers to acting appointments in order to fill vacancies in ships' complements. Men thus "frocked" served various lengths of time under acting appointments, generally six months to a year. If service was satisfactory, the captain recommended to the Navy Department that a man be given a permanent appointment for the rate in which he served. Otherwise, the commanding officer could reduce a man to the grade or rate he had held before his promotion. The change in status from acting to permanent appointment was always a relief. Personality was removed from the equation; it would now take a court-martial and the bureau's approval to reduce a chief serving under a permanent appointment.

In 1920 the Navy standardized pay at all levels from apprentice seaman through chief petty officer. Base pay for permanent-appointment chiefs was $126 per month. Amazingly, these rates did not change until well after the outbreak of World War II. Congress established the current pay tables, listing grades E-1 through E-7, in October 1949.

Pay tables then remained constant for nearly ten years. In 1958, at the urging of the secretary of the Army, who was concerned about retention of soldiers at the highest levels, and with very limited backing by the Department of the Navy, Congress established additional pay grades at levels E-8 and E-9. The Navy, after some discussion, named these grades senior chief petty officer and master chief petty officer. To staff these billets, eligibility for promotion to E-8, the senior chief level, was restricted to chief petty officers with a minimum of four years in grade and ten years of service. To initially populate the E-9 community, a minimum of six years' service as a chief petty officer with a total of thirteen years' service was required. Service-wide examinations for outstanding chiefs were held in August 1958, with the first promotions becoming effective in November. A second group of chiefs from the February 1959 examinations were elevated to E-8 and E-9 six months later.

The current number of ratings for chief petty officers falls far short of the 207 rating titles found at the end of World War II. Many of those ratings were designated as "wartime emergency only," and, indeed, the specialty mark for many of them (a lozenge or diamond surrounding a centered letter) has not been used since the end of the Korean War. With reduced manning of many ships as part of the DD-X initiative and other long-range plans, rating compression continues to occur at all levels. At the present time there are 81 rating titles that apply to chief petty officers, 80 titles for senior chiefs, and 69 rating titles for master chiefs. But in a time when technology plays a substantial role in modern warships, two ratings have remained in continuous use since 1797: those quintessential sailors, boatswain's mates and gunner's mates.

THE VIEW FROM THE QUARTERDECK

As Master Chief Ciaccio pointed out (see chapter 1), the Navy has always had a keen appreciation for class, status, and the perquisites of rank. Through the efforts of Adm. Bud Zumwalt at the end of the Vietnam War, Adm. Mike Boorda in recent years, and many other broad-minded officers, the position and authority afforded to chief petty officers—and, indeed, to an increasingly well-educated and -informed enlisted force—has grown dramatically. It was not always so, however; the distance from the quarterdeck to the fo'c'sle was much farther than the dimensions of a ship's keel might indicate. Some of that attitude can be read between the lines of Lt. Norman R. Van Der Veer's "Short Talk with Chief Petty Officers," published in the 1908 edition of the *Bluejacket's Manual:*

1. Part IV of "The Bluejacket's Manual" is written as a general guide for Chief Petty Officers. It should be regarded more in the light of an index as to what Chief Petty Officers of different branches are supposed to know, and what qualifications they are supposed to possess, than as a book of information. In as much as every Chief Petty Officer is supposed to be an expert in his own branch, an effort to embody in one book all of the information that each Chief Petty Officer is supposed to know would result in a very large vol-

ume, as it would necessarily have to cover every detail of the naval profession. Consequently, this book is merely an index of the subjects that you are supposed to know; and it tells you where you may find the subject fully discussed.

2. Chief Petty Officers of each branch should therefore make a point of studying the subjects which relate to their particular specialty and should study them from the reference books mentioned. In doing this, Chief Petty Officers should not overlook the subjects that are laid down for them as a class, irrespective of their specialty.

3. This "Short Talk to Chief Petty Officers" will, of course, be more directly applicable to those who are just coming up for their rate than to those who have held the rate for a long time; for Chief Petty Officers of any length of service should be familiar with the duties and responsibilities of their position. However, as the same honor, dignity and demeanor are required of all Chief Petty Officers, it is hoped that this talk may be of some value even to those who are already rated Chief Petty Officers, by giving them the point of view of their senior officers, by telling them how their seniors regard them, how they desire to treat them, and, on the other hand, what degree of proficiency and what general demeanor they expect.

4. Take your own particular case, for example. It is quite probable that you entered the service a few years ago an inexperienced and irresponsible boy, without any knowledge of the Navy, of discipline, and probably without any knowledge of the special branch, or specialty, in which you are now to become a Chief Petty Officer. During the time you served through the lower ratings you were under instruction not only as to your individual duties, but also in the elements of discipline. While you were in the lower ratings, you were not supposed to be highly responsible: you were supposed to do what you were told, to acquire the knowledge requisite for the rating you held, to use that knowledge under the direction of your petty officers, and to behave yourself and comply with the rules of military discipline.

5. Then came a great change in your status; you were appointed a petty officer. When you received this promotion, it showed that your officers considered that you had a sufficient knowledge of the details of the duties of your rating, and that you were sufficiently disciplined to warrant your stepping up from a status in which you

merely did what you were told to a status in which with the knowledge of what was required to be done and how it should be done, you could be trusted with the duty of taking charge of a number of men and giving them orders, under the general direction of your seniors. Your duty was to follow up the work and assure yourself that it had been done properly. Instead of merely doing what your immediate petty officer told you to do, you, as a petty officer, had a larger field and performed your duty not by your own labor, but by directing a group of men under you; and such was your status whether you were engaged in cleaning ship, painting ship, coaling ship or drilling. In each case your excellence as a petty officer was measured by the amount and excellence of the work which was accomplished by the men under you, their practical knowledge, their proficiency, their thoroughness and their reliability. As time passed and as your experience increased, you were promoted from third class to second class, and, finally, to first class; with each promotion you added to your experience and knowledge, your duties broadened and your responsibilities increased; nevertheless, at all times you were more or less under instruction and under trial.

6. You have now come to the point where, having served through all the lower ratings, you are supposed to be an expert in your own branch. You have training and experience, and had you not succeeded in making your officers believe that you had proper regard for orders and for discipline, you would not now be coming up for Chief Petty Officer. When you are promoted to Chief Petty Officer, your status changes even to a greater extent than it changed when you were promoted from the ranks to petty officer. The change from petty officer, first class, to Chief Petty Officer probably carries with it a greater change in status than any other promotion in your whole career. Your uniform changes, your quarters and your method of living change; the treatment accorded you by your senior officers changes. All Chief Petty Officers welcome these changes as well as the corresponding increase in pay. But don't forget that these are not the only features of your life that change. Along with all these changes comes a very great change in your responsibilities as well as the absolute necessity for a different point of view. If you forget the changes of this nature, you altogether fail in your duties to the Government.

7. The aim of this little talk is to dwell upon this new point of view, this increased feeling of responsibility, this sense of duty which impels you to do

a thing not because you have to do it, but because it ought to be done, because it is your duty to do it.

8. The position of Chief Petty Officer is one of special honor. It shows not only that you have served successfully, but that your service has met with the commendation of your seniors, that you are proficient, trustworthy and reliable. The uniform of a Chief Petty Officer shows therefore not only that you are serving honorably now, but that you have served honorably for years, and have by your own successful effort risen to the top of the petty officers of your own branch. See to it that your entire demeanor is such as to elevate the standing of the uniform which you now wear. Make your life and your actions both on board ship and on shore such as to increase rather than to decrease the difference between the bluejacket's uniform and that of the Chief Petty Officer.

9. Your position is such that your senior officers wish to treat you as an officer. In order to be accorded this treatment you must adopt the point of view of an officer. This point of view can best be described by saying that you must cultivate a deep sense of responsibility, a high sense of duty, and live up to a high professional standard.

10. Standards.—The fact that you are a Chief Petty Officer is evidence that you know how things should be done. Do not neglect to do your duty properly, do not fall to a lower standard simply because you think you will not be spoken to or reported for not doing this duty properly. Such an attitude is not surprising in a recruit; there are times when it may even be overlooked in the lower ratings of petty officer, but, as Chief Petty Officer, you have passed that stage. You are constantly under the watchful eye of your juniors. Anything they see you do, they naturally think is all right. If, for example, they see that you are careless about your uniform or about saluting, regardless of the amount of instruction they may have received, their standard is lowered. If you are punctilious, the men under you will copy the precedent you have established. If your manner is military toward your seniors, you will find the enlisted men under you more easily brought up to standard. If the Chief Petty Officers are thorough, respectful, and have a high sense of duty, the tone of the whole ship will follow. If, on the other hand, enlisted men see that the Chief Petty Officers are unmilitary, that they violate orders and regulations

when officers are not around, they will feel even more than ordinarily justi-
fied in doing likewise. The tone of the ship, the tone of the service itself must
come more directly from the Chief Petty Officers than from any other group of
people in the Navy. You have the standard; live up to it, whether you are on independent duty, or on duty under officers; whether you are unobserved or directly
under the eyes of your seniors. Live up to the standard, and you will find that
those under you will be more inclined to do likewise.

11. Sense of Duty.—You know the standard; you know what to do; you know the rules
    of discipline; of military etiquette; you know the regulations and instructions per-
    taining to your own branch. The Government—not the officers over you—pays
    for your services. It pays you for doing things as you know they should be done.
    The sense of duty is that feeling that impels you to do these things not because you
    have to do them, but because it is your duty to do them. And in deciding whether
    it is your duty, be very liberal in your interpretation.

12. Sense of Responsibility.—It frequently happens that both commissioned officers
    and Chief Petty Officers see things that should be done, although it is clear it is
    not their duty to do them; such cases, for example, that would result in confu-
    sion were the officer or Chief Petty Officer in question to do them. If you are con-
    fronted with such a condition, take a point of view that you have reached a posi-
    tion of responsibility in the service; that something which should be done may
    have escaped notice; if this omission is clearly of such a nature that it is not your
    duty to remedy it, it is, nevertheless, your duty to call the attention of the proper
    person to such an omission. Sometimes lives are lost because some manifest dan-
    ger has not been pointed out. If you are in doubt as to whether it is your duty to
    look after something that you know should be done, the only safe rule is to do it.
    If you know that it is someone else's duty, call attention to it. Take the attitude that
    you are a part of the Navy, not merely a part of your department on an individ-
    ual ship; try to do a little more rather than a little less than a strict interpretation
    of your duty demands. Both your seniors and you, yourself, will be better pleased,
    and the service will benefit thereby.

13. Professional Work—As a Chief Petty Officer, you are an expert in your own
    department. There are no petty officers senior to you. Those below you will look
    up to you for information and instruction. Be sure the information you give out
    is absolutely accurate. If you are weak on any feature of your specialty, study it
    up. It is all down somewhere in black and white. Study the best methods; keep

up all improvements. Do not feel that because you passed an examination you have finished studying. Keep yourself fully informed, and be ready to impart your knowledge and skill to your subordinates.

14. Thoroughness and Reliability—An absolute essential of your rating is reliability. This does not mean merely that you are certain to return on time for duty. It means that you may be relied upon to do thoroughly and in the manner that it should be done whatever you are going to do, however important the duty, and however general your orders may be. It means that when you report the duty finished your report may be accepted without an inspection and your senior feels that the duty has been done and everything finished as well and as thoroughly as it would have been done, had he been there personally. If, for any reason, you find that you cannot carry out your orders in every detail, report any part of the order you were unable to carry out and why you were unable to carry it out.

15. Duties—Every Chief Petty Officer understands in a general way that he is the senior petty officer on the ship in his particular branch, that his duties are of a general nature in his department and that he is required to see his department and everything connected with it kept in shipshape condition. All this, however, constitutes but a part of a Chief Petty Officer's duties. As a Chief Petty Officer, you recognize these duties; but in paying due attention to the material, do not overlook your duties in connection with the personnel. Too many Chief Petty Officers wholly neglect the fact that, in all probability, the most important part of their duty is the training and instruction of their subordinates. As a Chief Petty Officer you are an expert in the details of your department. Unless you recognize that it is your duty to instruct your juniors and unless you do instruct them, and unless you endeavor to inculcate in them the knowledge of how things should be done, of how they should conduct themselves, you will have failed in your duties. Too often petty officers direct inexperienced men of lower ratings to carry out certain orders, and then think no more about it; later, when it is found that the work has not been done; or has not been thoroughly done, or has been done improperly, they lay the blame on the junior. In such a case it is clearly evident that the petty officer has neglected his duty. Remember always that you are an instructor, and that the instruction of your juniors is one of your most important duties; that it is your duty to instruct them not only in the details of the profession, but also in regard to their general conduct or demeanor on board ship. Not only is it your duty to instruct them, it is also your duty to enforce compliance with such instruc-

tions, and see that they are trained to do their duty properly, thoroughly, and to observe the rules and the regulations of the service.

16. Twofold Nature of the Duties—Duties in the Navy are twofold in nature. Not only must you be an expert in your specialty and be able to instruct others in that specialty; but in addition to this, do not for a moment forget the military side of your life. As a Chief Petty Officer it is more incumbent upon you to remember this than it would be were you in one of the lower ratings. For example, if you happen to be a chief machinist's mate, there is no reason why you should not be able to march a squad of men in a military manner, halt them, and face them smartly. Because you may be a chief yeoman, there is no reason why you should neglect boat etiquette, or neglect to salute your seniors. If you happen to be a chief pharmacist's mate, that is no reason why you should not know and observe uniform regulations, or orders concerning ship routine. Every Chief Petty Officer should take pride in knowing, in observing, and in requiring others under him to observe all of these details of ship life. Simply because you may not happen to be in the seaman branch, do not allow yourself for a moment to think that your duties do not extend to the military side of your profession.

17. Let Officers Judge your Proficiency—It frequently happens that, when the time draws near for a Chief Petty Officer to receive a permanent appointment, or when he desires a letter of commendation preparatory to taking an examination for warrant, he becomes very enthusiastic and eager to expound his points of excellence. Let your conduct as a Chief Petty Officer be such that instead of being forced to explain your points of merit, your officers will already know them. Let your officers be the judges of your proficiency. An officer knows no greater pleasure than that of being able to give an unqualified recommendation to a man who has served under him. Your letter ought to be based on your excellent work as a Chief Petty Officer rather than upon the excellent manner in which you plead your case when you come up for promotion.[2]

Most experienced chief petty officers would give similar advice to newly promoted colleagues, although, no doubt, the condescending tone reflected in Lt. Van Der Veer's comments might well be attenuated.

Chief Aviation Electronics Technician (AW/SW) Eric R. Oitzman,
USS George Washington (CVN-73):
I'd give a new chief about the same kind of advice I was given. Do your best

no matter what it is you are doing. Whether you are down in the bilges or a super secret guy in the Comm center, do your best on every assignment you're given, and look at your leaders, your division officers and department heads, and think to yourself, "Is that how I would do that? Why am I being asked to do that?" There's always a higher purpose of some sort. And absorb that, because it makes sense, and do it that way, and it will be successful, then emulate the things that you find successful. Success begets success. There are folks out here who have come out to this ship because of the reputation this ship has, the reputation for being a "together" command. Find those people and emulate them. That's what I'd tell a new chief.

Command Master Chief (AW/SS/SW/PJ) Michael McCalip,
USS George Washington:
   I'd echo some things that were said to me when I made chief, nearly fifteen years ago. There were some great things said about trust. I always knew that the CPO mess always trusted one another, and it does, but I got some good advice to continue to check, continue to verify. And in fact, one of the things I have in my Palm Pilot today is a note, "Trust and Verify," and so I look at that every day.

Chief Journalist (SW) Luis M. Luque, USS George Washington:
   I'd say to that young selectee that you have to look outside of yourself to understand why things are the way they are. Why is the chain of command so adamant about this or that rule? Why is the chain of command wanting me to stand this seemingly pointless watch? Why is the chain of command asking me to do this bizarre thing that I just don't understand? I would say that the key to understanding the chain of command is to stop looking at it from your own perspective. Whatever the task is, look at it from the chain of command's point of view. What if we let every sailor walk around with their hands in their pockets, and their shirts unbuttoned and tucked out, and their shoes untied, looking however they wanted to look, with their hair long, or whatever? Does that lead to a road of no discipline, and a "who cares, who gives a damn" attitude? Yes, it does. And you can extend that to a hundred different directions. The chain of command has reason for its decisions, for its actions, its rules. And people need to try and look at it from the other perspective, from the management side, rather than from their own.

Chief Religious Program Specialist (AW/SW)
Donna M. Norman, USS George Washington:

    I tell my staff—and I'd tell any selectee—that he or she has to become educated. Knowledge is power in the military. You can't just go around doing your job, sitting back and letting everyone else make your success for you. You have to be disciplined, you have to want to be promoted, and strive for it, and show initiative on a daily basis. As a female chief petty officer, I often mentor young women coming into the military right now. I tell them to be strong, be focused, that there is a time and place for everything, but you are on a military fighting ship. You are a sailor just like everyone else, and you have a job to do—a vitally important job. You should not expect to do anything more or less than what your counterparts are doing. But you should always be willing to prove yourself as an individual, not just as a female, because you want to be successful and you want to show that you have the material to be one of the best that this military has.

    Every chief petty officer is aware that following the directives of leadership—the chain of command, in Chief Luque's perspective—has a downside and risk, as well as reward. Even in peacetime, a sailor's lot is not an easy one. Long separation from home, difficult living and working conditions, all can take their toll on the drive and motivation of even the most dedicated chief petty officer.

Senior Chief Navy Counselor (SCW) Dolores I. Buie ,
USS George Washington:

    If someone asked me where I'd rather be, I suppose the politically correct answer is I would rather be home with my daughter. But the reality is, that what I am doing, the average American will not do. We go into harm's way—tomorrow morning, this ship is going to transit the Straits of Gibraltar, and who knows who is waiting up there on the cliffs to take a pot shot at us, you know? Certainly, it's frightening, because you don't know what tomorrow will bring. But I would not want to be anywhere else on the planet at this moment. I am needed here, on the *George Washington,* and I have five thousand or more sailors depending on me for the services my department provides. That's how we function together. It's not just me, it's all of us together. This may sound like a cliché, but somebody has to do it, and twenty-two years ago I raised my hand and signed up. I adapted to the environment, and this is something that, at this point in my career and in my life, I have freely chosen to do. When I talk to sailors here, I ask them, "Your family has been attacked—if you were on the streets of your hometown, what would you do about it? What if the terrorists came after your family?" "Well, I'm going to protect my family" is the usual reply. Well, that's what we're doing—we're protecting your family, and my family, and every American family by being out here. Somebody has to step up to the plate, and this is where I need to be. If someone had told me a couple of weeks ago, when we were pulling out of Norfolk, "You can stay behind and not go," well, I could never do that; I'd be missing something that I see as my obligation. I signed up for this, and here I am. If I don't do it, who will? We are willing to put ourselves in harm's way, and we have been doing it for thousands of years. And chiefs are the ones that take care of everybody else, because the reality is that there is no one else to do it. Every young kid on this ship looks to us—to the wardroom and to the chiefs mess—to make sense out of all of this and to bring them home to their families safe. And that's what we are about.

Civilians, or those not familiar with military service, often do not appreciate the critical role that senior enlisted play in day-to-day operations. "Officers run the Navy, but chiefs run the ship" is an oft-repeated cliché in the naval service. One question often posed by naval screening boards is, "If all the officers fell overboard, the chiefs would fight the ship and bring her safely home. If all the chiefs fell overboard, then what would happen?"

Chief Damage Controlman (SW) Terry Wylie,
USS George Washington:

If all the chiefs fell overboard, there would be a serious information gap. I describe my job as a translator, because officers and the blueshirts on the deckplates often speak different languages. Officers are on a different plane altogether. And a lot of them are completely disconnected from the deckplate sailor. They look to the chiefs to make that connection between the officer community and the deck. If all the chiefs fell overboard, it would be like having all the officers speaking French and the crew speaking German, and we would probably end up in Finland. And the chances of actually getting the mission done are next to nil, because the officer community is not intimately familiar with the inner workings of the enlisted. They don't know how things get done. They simply give orders, and expect that these orders will be fulfilled. We're the link, we really are.

Senior Chief Aviation Electronics Technician Mark T. Raab,
USS George Washington:

First, we have very few officers who could turn the ship around and get us home. This is no slander against officers, but they aren't trained to take the steps, the things that have to be done. They'd have to find folks to do that. But if the chiefs fell overboard, the ship would still work, I do believe, because our first-class and even junior petty officers, after a pretty intense period of adjustment, would be able to step up. But initially, this ship would go dead in the water, we wouldn't be able to get anything done. But just for a while.

CMC McCalip:

You know what? If we've done our job, our job as leaders and technical experts in our areas of responsibility, well, if every one of us fell overboard tonight, the hard-charging first-class petty officers, and their subordinates, and every other sailor on board this ship would pitch in and keep it going. Look at the USS *Cole*—in one instant, you lost seventeen people out of the damage control party of a small ship, including some really key people, a chief, and a former chief who had just commissioned as an LDO engineer. The people whom they trained and led saved that ship. If we all fell overboard? We'd keep right on launching planes and recovering them. That's what leadership by example is all about. And that's what chiefs do.

Three

Making Chief

"That's what chiefs do." Leadership—that strength of personality which combines technical ability with keen insight into human behavior—is at the core of the chief petty officer's world. And it is the attraction of exercising that leadership, the ability to make a difference in the lives of shipmates and the success of the unit's mission, that motivates many sailors to reenlist—"ship over," in Navy jargon—for the possibility of one day trading "crackerjacks" for the khaki uniform of the chief petty officer. Indeed, even in the earliest days of a sailor's career, the allure of the khaki uniform, with all that it signifies, is a major focus. Most begin to think seriously of their career options sometime after their first reenlistment; by the time they've reached petty officer first-class (E6), often enough the quest has become an obsession. And when the happy day comes, it is a career milestone.

Chief Aviation Machinist's Mate Jose R. Valero,
USS George Washington *(CVN-73):*

I remember when I first learned I made chief, about five years ago. When the selection list came out, I didn't see my name on it. I was an instructor at North Island, and one of the master chiefs came by and said, "Hey, you, Valero—have a problem with you." So I wondered what's wrong here, what have I done wrong? He pulled me out of the classroom and said, "You are not wearing the right uniform," and I was surprised, because I always prided myself on being squared away. I checked in the mirror, and I said, "What, did I miss a crease?" I was wearing my whites, and I figured, well, maybe my ribbons are wrong or something like that, but he said, "Valero, I want to see you in my office right now." And as soon as I stepped in there, there was a crowd of chiefs in there waiting for me, and I knew then that I had made it, and they all started congratulating me, and I felt real good, I've got to tell you. Once I got over the shock, I sat and thought about things for a while. I was glad I had made it, but scared, too, in a way. I guess it's a perception thing, maybe. My perspective of what I should do, how I should act, how I should contribute to the Navy. It used to be, when I was a blueshirt, everything was self-centered; it was sort of "every man for himself." I was out there to do the best job that I could do, to prove to all my fellow first-classes that I was the best. But putting on the chief's uniform changed all that. Suddenly I had this realization that now I have to actually go out there and pass on to others all the knowledge and skills that I have, so that they in turn could be up and coming as a chief. And that takes a totally different way of looking at things, you know?

Most chief petty officers share in the excitement that their shipmates feel when they are finally selected for promotion to chief. Division mates or those who share a common rating are, like proud parents, usually delighted by their shipmates' success. A great deal of good-natured ribbing generally accompanies the notification process. And Chief Valero wasn't the only chief selectee to have his "chain pulled" when being notified of his selection to chief petty officer.

Chief Norman:

I made chief in eight and a half years, which was possible then, but would be unthinkable now, I suppose. Even so, I didn't think that I had a chance to make it that year, I really was just trying to get some experience with the test and the selection process for the following year. But when the list finally came out, I got a call from a senior chief, one of my mentors, just as I was about to leave for a tour of duty at Keflavik, Iceland. She called me and told me someone had made a big mistake, and I thought, oh no, because I really wanted to go to Keflavik and I thought there was some problem with my orders. But then she laughed and said, "No, it's an even bigger mistake—they just promoted you to chief." And I was just totally blown away by all that. I flew up there in a trance, and when I stepped off the plane at Keflavik, I was greeted by a sign that said, "Welcome, RPC (slug) Norman." "Slug" is the way that members of the mess refer to selectees who haven't yet gone through initiation into the CPO mess. I found out that there were about fifteen or sixteen others who had made it, and we began our preparations to join the CPO mess that very day.

Senior Chief Aviation Boatswain's Mate (AW)
Michael A. Gentry, USS George Washington:

I was on the *Dwight D. Eisenhower* then, and I got a phone call from a master chief at AIRLANT named Marty Chappel. Now, Marty was one of those old-time guys. He called up and asked for my senior chief, who wasn't in, and he was playing a little game with me; he mentioned the name of everyone who had made it, except my name, and then finally he told me that I had made it on my first try. He ragged me pretty good—he called me a slug and all—but then he told me to go out and buy the uniforms, and that he knew I'd do a great job. It's an emotional thing for most guys; I don't know if you can explain it unless it happened to you, but it's a truly great feeling inside.

Chief Interior Communications Electrician Kevin R. Henry,
USS George Washington:

My first reaction was, "Are you sure?" I mean, there are a couple guys named Henry in the Navy, and I said, "Are you sure they got the right one?" We were at a joint command, and I had a good friend from the *Yellowstone* who was there, too, and our boss, an Air Force colonel, came around and congratulated him, and I was really proud and happy for my buddy. I was a little jealous for a couple minutes, too, and then the colonel turned and congratulated me as well, and, we were both grinning from ear to ear, and I'm still grinning ear to ear over it. I was just elated.

The Navy doesn't hand out promotion to chief petty officer at random. Indeed, there are a number of serious hurdles to overcome and hoops to jump through before an up-and-coming sailor can pin on the coveted anchor pins on 16 September, the Navy's traditional promotion day.

A sailor must have at least three years as a petty officer first-class, unless rated as an "Early Promote," a status reserved for the most outstanding sailors. In that case, a one-year waiver may be granted. In addition, he or she must have at least eleven years of active service. Altogether, 10 percent of the eligible candidates each year can be identified as "early promotes," although, given the draw-down and force reductions of the 1990s, it is extremely rare today to find a successful CPO candidate with fewer than twelve years' service.[1]

Chief Signalman (SW) Michael P. Swain, USS George Washington:
When I heard I had finally made it I was incredibly happy, because I had made first-class petty officer in just six years, so I had been sort of on a roll there. But then it took me a long while to make the next jump; I didn't make chief till I had about fourteen years in. Sometimes it gets a little frustrating, you either make it or you don't, and sometimes it's tough to figure out why the board acted the way it did. Your master chief and CMC might give you some general ideas as to what you could have done or should have done, but even that guidance is pretty general, and sometimes not all that helpful. But there was a great sense of relief, and I really felt good about the Navy and myself. And now that I look back, maybe the extra experience as a first-class petty officer helped make me a better chief when I finally did get promoted. I was

aboard the USS *Grapple* at the time—a salvage and rescue ship—and we had eight or nine chiefs in the mess. We had a master chief in charge of the divers, and he served as our CMC as well. Those were some of the most squared-away guys I ever met in the Navy. That was a great place to make chief, I must say.

Chief Swain's frustration at being listed as PNA ("Passed but not advanced") is shared by many experienced sailors. Even in the best years, less than 40 percent of candidates are promoted, and many, like Chief Swain, have completed the process several times. The selection process is thorough; candidates are evaluated on several criteria, including the following:

Performance evaluation: overall marks for the preceding five years
Career history: sea/shore rotation, leadership positions and performance during challenging assignments
Potential: surfaces early? newcomer? latecomer?
Personal initiative: demonstrated by command/community involvement, education, personal awards commendations, and so on.[2]

Command Master Chief McCalip:
I tell every first-class petty officer on this ship: study, study, study. You must make the cut on the tests to be board-eligible. Attend the Leadership Continuum course, and take those jobs and duty stations that will provide challenges and leadership opportunities that will make you competitive for CPO. Regardless of how good you think you are—or how good the command thinks you are—there's someone else out there in the fleet who has the edge on you. It might have been more challenging assignments early in his or her career or some really sterling achievements along the way. But if you study well, you'll do your best on the rating examinations, and that tends to even things out a bit.

Master Chief McCalip's points are well taken. In earlier times so-called practical factors—the ability to demonstrate mastery of specific craft skills—were a key discriminator as to who got promoted and who did not.

Demonstrated mastery of practical factors is still required, though in different format than sailors of an earlier era might remember. A bibliography is published each advancement cycle to provide each sailor with references to consult in preparation for the written test. Naval Leadership Continuum for POIs is required for eligibility for the test. Warfare qualification is required if a sailor is on a sea rotation at a command with an active warfare program.

The CPO advancement test is administered once each year, usually in mid-January. After the tests are scored, a cut-off score is identified, based on projected manning requirements for the coming year. A "board eligible" list is then generated and released. Candidates prepare a "package," with updated service records including watch, station, shipboard, and warfare qualifications; correspondence courses; off-duty education; recent awards; and copies of the most recent annual evaluation. Today, one of the most important elements of a sailor's package is "enlisted warfare qualification." Today's sailor must qualify as either a surface, air, or submarine warrior, or obtain similar qualifications in a specialty field before consideration by the board. In 2002, of nearly five thousand CPO selectees, only one sailor was selected to advance who did not have a warfare qualification. His was a special case—he had been on recruiting duty, and previous to that in a precommissioned ship—and at these commands, there is no enlisted warfare program available. A rare exception was granted, and he competed on an equal footing with his peers. No doubt, his sense of elation was no different than what his peers experienced.

If a sailor passes the test and qualifies as board-eligible, but does not get selected, the command will hold a career development board to review his career and service record. One of the responsibilities that chief petty officers take most seriously is to identify and develop their juniors, and to provide opportunities for them to be competitive for selection to CPO. An unsuccessful applicant can retest the following year.

Experienced chiefs know that the evaluation board consists of a captain who serves as president, a junior officer who serves as recorder, and, most important, master chief petty officers who serve as board/panel members and are familiar with or of the same rate as the petty officers under review. Most senior and master chiefs will help a potential selectee "fine-tune" his or her personal file to reflect the best current practices in a particular rating. The chief of naval personnel establishes a maximum quota for each rating and gives the number of selection possibilities to each panel. Each panel must fill the quota with the best qualified candidates competing for advancement, but must not exceed the quota. However, if not enough candidates are "best qualified," the panel may leave part of the quota unfilled.

Passing the test and being selected are only the first steps in becoming a chief petty officer. "You may be an E-7, but you're not a chief until you're accepted in the chiefs mess" is a familiar refrain throughout the Navy.

Chief Scheer:
I made it two years ago. I was sitting around the supply office, with a buddy of mine, SK1 Levorse. I was president of the first-class mess, and he and I were just sitting in there just chatting and trying to figure out when the list was likely to come out. Now, we had this damage control chief aboard, who was originally from Scotland, and he opens up the door, and says in a Scottish accent, "Levorse and Sheer . . . in the mess!" And we go down there, and there are seven of us, and on a frigate, that's just about unprecedented. But I still don't know what's going on, and we get down there, and the captain is down there waiting for us, too. Now, I figured this wasn't too good, because as a master-at-arms, I was always getting chewed out for one thing or another, so I figured, well, here we go again. But we stood there, and when he told us, "Congratulations!" well, first, it was total disbelief. "Would you mind checking that list again, Sir, you've got to be kidding us . . ." It was a just a fabulous moment. But then as soon as the skipper left the mess, all hell broke loose. We were about to get welcomed to the chiefs community—big time. But even back then, I loved chief initiations.

One of the first tasks assigned to Will Scheer, as to every CPO selectee, was the development of a chief petty officer's charge book. Selectees are tasked with routing the charge book to every chief petty officer in the mess. This practice dates back at least sixty years, and there are earlier, informal records indicating

that newly selected CPOs kept private notebooks with information passed
down to them by other, more experienced chiefs. The student guide to the chief
petty officer indoctrination course provides a concise history:

> During World War II, Commanding Officers were authorized to advance and pro-
> mote deserving and qualified sailors to chief petty officer, without reference to
> outside commands, nor approval by the Bureau of Personnel. Under wartime
> conditions, determination of "deserving and qualified" could be difficult for the
> Commanding Officer. The situation also presented challenges to the sailor who
> aspired to attain a Chief's rating. How to best prepare and to plan and track
> preparation? How to best display your qualification? From these dilemmas sprang
> the original charge books.
>
> Chiefs began to direct first class petty officers to prepare themselves to assume
> the additional responsibilities by recording all the details of those responsibili-
> ties. Professional libraries on ships were generally nonexistent or poorly stocked.
> Much had to be learned directly from conversations with the chiefs themselves
> and taken down to be studied later. In addition to the technical aspects of the var-
> ious ratings, chief petty officers also talked to the first class aspirants about lead-
> ership, accountability, supporting the chain of command, and other professional
> subject matters, often using personal experiences to illustrate how something
> should (or should not) be done. The collection of notes and study material even-
> tually came to be called by some a Charge Book, perhaps because the petty offi-
> cers who kept them were their "charges" (entrusted to their care) for professional
> development or perhaps because the entries included charges (authoritative
> instructions or tasking of a directive manner).[3]

Unfortunately, over time, the original intent of the charge book became
diluted, and it often became a vehicle for sophomoric pranks or degrading
personal comments. A document that, like a high school or college yearbook,
should have become a treasured memory often was debased and became a
source of embarrassment, not pride, in later years. As part of an overall return
to Navy tradition, from about 1995 onward, new emphasis was placed on
returning the charge book to its rightful place in the journey toward full
membership in the CPO mess. The CPO indoctrination course continues:

"Today's Charge Book then is a great tradition which has its roots in a magnificent period of our history. We have preserved it and have returned it to its original purpose. Today's Charge Book is not entertainment, and it is not a vehicle for hazing, however mild. It is valid and valuable and must be so treated by all concerned. Even better, when CPO initiation season is over, it becomes a treasured keepsake and the repository for the accumulation of the most precious photos and mementos of our career."[4]

Chief Fire Controlman (AW/SW) Shahid "Mario" Ahmed,
USS George Washington:

> At one time, before I became a chief, I had heard horror stories about how charge books were treated. I feel like I became chief and became initiated by choice at the right time, because that was the point when MCPON and the higher leadership were saying, "Hey this is hazing, stop the funny stuff. Let's go about initiating people objectively, where they learn something from what we do." And I benefited from that a lot. Most of the time, when I put my charge book around, some of the chiefs who got initiated the old way wrote generic sentences, like "be good, take care of your people," things like that. But as you got to know them during initiation, they became your friends, and whatever they wrote later was more meaningful. I've heard horror stories about people writing nasty stuff in other people's charge books, but in my charge book, everything was positive. Many advised me to not forget where I came from. And, you know, I use that to my advantage, as a tool. Most of the time, I'd be talking to my people: "Why did you do this, why did you fail to finish your assignment, how come you are late, how come you are tardy, why can't you make an appointment on time?" And they give me funny stories, and I tell them, "Don't forget, I was in your place, I was a blueshirt at one time. I don't forget where I come from. If I can do it, you can do it better, because you are the generation that is smarter than everybody."

Chief Norman:

> Well, my charge book got stolen and held for ransom, right after I started routing it. It was a group of junior officers that did it, and it cost

me a lot in fines on initiation night, because they had photographic evidence. There are two kinds of people when you route your charge book. There are those who just want to harass you, and there are chiefs who really take the time and sit down and talk to you about what it means to be a chief. And I think the ones that took the time to sit down with me, to explain what it means to be a chief petty officer—what about the organization is so special, and why becoming part of that will be a lifetime experience—I think that meant more to me than the ones who cycled me for twenty minutes, or made me come back three or four times, and made me shine their shoes or whatever. I got more out of just sitting and talking to someone whose counterpart I was going to be in the chiefs mess, and to this day, I still go back and read the things they said in the charge book. You go back afterward and read what they said—they really see something in you when you are going through the initiation that maybe you don't see in yourself.

Chief Valero:

Let me tell you one thing about my book: my charge book made it through the first week of initiation, and then it vanished! I tried to figure out what the heck happened, and right before I put on my anchors, I got word from one of the senior chiefs that my charge book was in Japan. So I said, What is it doing in Japan? I discovered that there were a few other chiefs in Japan who knew me from before, and they wanted to have a hand in my book. I didn't get my book back until well after I got pinned.

Regardless of what pranks might have been played with a selectee's charge book, most find meaning in the inscriptions placed there by senior members of the mess.

Chief Valero:

They all said congratulations to me for being chosen as a member of this exclusive community, and they did impart the tasking ahead of me. They cautioned me that one word out of my mouth, and it usually gets carried as dogma, so I had to be very cautious as to what I said, and how I said it. I didn't believe that until a little farther down the road, when I said jokingly to one of the petty officers, "Oh, sure, you can take off work," and sure enough, he disappeared for the rest of the day and I had to answer to the skipper as to why this guy wasn't around. I learned my lesson from then on.

Senior Chief Gentry:

They talked about how sacred the mess is, how if you need advice or guidance you always come here for it first. And they talked about the real meaning of the fouled anchor, which maybe some of us didn't really appreciate until the creed was read after our initiation. But the biggest thing was that we're here to help and train you, and we're not going to let you fail.

Master Chief Aviation Maintenance Administrationman
(AW) April D. Beldo, USS George Washington:

The one that I most remember is, "Don't forget where you've been, don't forget where you came from, and never, ever let your people down." And I really believe that even now; if it weren't for the people that worked for me, I would not be where I am today. Trust me, I didn't get here because I am so good! All these people helped me over the years to get to where I am today. So that's one of the biggest things, to not forget where you came from and never forget the people that helped you get to where you are.

Even the simple task of routing the charge book to members of the mess—and in some commands there could be five hundred members or more—has value to some selectees.

Chief Aviation Electronics Technician (AW) Julia M. Grodski,
USS George Washington:

Oh, yes, I learned not only from the written pages in the charge book, but I learned to go up to darn near anybody and stick out my hand and say

"Hi, my name is Julie." I was the shyest person you ever met when I first came into the Navy. And I just had to get over that. I had been less shy as my naval career went on, but at that point it was time to abandon it all and say, "Here I am." I still have my charge book, and I still go back and read it. I have pulled it out on some really bad days, when I question whether I'm doing any good at this job. I pull out that charge book, and I say, "Okay, that's right." And I remember that I resolved myself to do this, and these other chiefs went through the exact same thing, and I'm not alone. I have the mess. And no matter what problem I face, I can take it to the mess and find someone who has been through the same thing, and that's a neat feeling.

The importance of the charge book as a continuity vehicle—a method of conveying the collective wisdom of the chiefs community to its newest members—has been recognized at the highest levels. Master Chief John Hagan, when serving as the eighth Master Chief Petty Officer of the Navy, wrote:

One of the most useful tools of the process is based on an old one: CPO charge books. At a memorable CPO anniversary dining-in, instead of delivering a conventional speech, Admiral Stan Arthur (then the Vice-Chief of Naval Operations) read excerpts from the "Memory Book" of his father—Chief Machinist Mate Holland Arthur. The first entry included Recruit Arthur's thoughts on the train ride from his Illinois home to Recruit Training Command Great Lakes in the '20s. The chiefs listened with awe and pride. Many sailors kept such a record; memory books were a combination journal, scrapbook, and diary of their Navy experiences to take home and share with family. During World War II, CPO hopefuls often carried a more formal logbook, recording the wisdom and advice collected from chiefs in preparation for advancement into the Chiefs' Mess. For many years after the war, the contents of a charge book were seldom worth preserving. They were nothing more than government issue log books, sporadically carried by selectees, eventually becoming the center of much negative activity, some of it egregious and outrageous. Today's reinvigorated charge books tap the roots of these early traditions of pride in accomplishment and knowledge. CPO initiates now build a book or box (or both), some of which are so creative they qualify as genuine works of folk art and instantly acquire status as family heirlooms. The

traditional CPO charge book has changed, evolving in strength from the old tradition, as the chiefs' mess directed it.[5]

Many newly minted chief petty officers find that life changes drastically
the moment they are selected. Announcement of selectees is usually made
in early July, with formal installation scheduled for mid-September. But the
moment word is received aboard ship, treatment and perceptions—by juniors, seniors, and self—are utterly changed.

Master Chief Beldo:

That's exactly the way it is. All of a sudden you're not in Kansas anymore. Yes, I did get treated differently immediately. As an AZ1, I had to
take suggestions to the CPO, and the CPO said yes or no, and he might
talk it over with the master chief, and they made a decision. The next
day when I became a CPO, before I could ever ask a question, it was,
"Well, what do you think, Chief Beldo?" And I'd say, "Well, I'd like to do
it this way." And that's the way things would get done. It was like day
and night.

Senior Chief Perry:

Master Chief Beldo is right. Definitely. A lot more doors will open for
you. You walk into disbursing as a blueshirt, and it's "Hey, pal, line
forms to the right." You walk in there the next day as a chief, and it's
"Hey, Chief, what can I help you out with?" It's like that everywhere.
You walk down a passageway now, and sailors will say, "Here comes a
chief, step aside." But you know, a lot of times we old-time chiefs will
just step aside and let those sailors do what they have to do. They are
busy, they are working, and I'm just going up to my shop. I know what's
going on; that's been me on the other end of that swab in the past.

Chief Electronics Technician (AW/SW) Doug Helderman,
USS *George Washington:*

Oh, it was a huge, huge change, and it happens overnight. On Tuesday,
you're just another blueshirt walking through the passageway, and the
next day, well, now when you walk down the passageway it's "Good

morning, Chief. Hi, Chief. How are you today, Chief?" Because you are
the chief. Your knowledge level has changed only by what you learned
in initiation—take off your shirt, and you're still the same guy underneath it.

Chief Aviation Ordnanceman (EOD/AW) Doug Farris,
Naval Training Center, Great Lakes:

I think that, for myself at least, respect for the mess, and who we are,
helps me uphold an image of professionalism. I'm the inert-ordnance
certification officer for the Explosive Ordinance Team here—I just
interacted the other day with the Kenosha County sheriff's department,
up in Wisconsin. When I went up there to X-ray this piece of suspected
ordnance, I had tremendously more respect given to me as Chief Ferris
than I used to have as Petty Officer Ferris. When you interact with civilians, and wearing khakis, then you are the visible subject-matter expert.

Master Chief Beldo:

Senior Chief Perry hit it right on the head about the uniform making
things happen. And you know what's even funnier: as a chief, they'd get
something for me faster than they did when I was an AZ1. As a senior
chief they get it for me even a little faster. As a master chief, they bring it
to me; I don't have to go get it! This is wonderful. I didn't think it could
get any better, but now I don't even have to go get stuff, it's "We'll bring
that right up to you, Master Chief!"

Four

Initiation

Master Chief Beldo and her shipmates have identified the major shift in responsibility and authority that occurs when a sailor is promoted to chief petty officer. There is a newfound respect for his or her technical competence, as well as for his or her assumed leadership abilities. Artifacts of life change, too: those selected to be chief petty officers wear a different uniform, eat and sleep in different quarters, and are accepted into a fraternity that differs both in substance and in appearance from anything similar in the other military services. Some might wonder what makes Navy chiefs different from senior enlisted in other services. In the Army, a soldier in the field might learn of his promotion to sergeant first-class, yet wait weeks until he returns to base to purchase his new rank devices. An Air Force technical sergeant, newly promoted to master sergeant, may celebrate her good fortune at the base senior enlisted club, and yet the promotion is usually commemorated only among friends or close associates. The new master sergeant certainly will assume greater responsibility and authority, but, aside from the new "rocker" on his chevrons, there's little to suggest a major life transformation or capstone event. But in the sea services, the Navy, Coast Guard, and, to a lesser extent, the Marine Corps, the transition is vastly different.

Command Master Chief (AW/SW/SCW) Scott A.
Benning, Carrier Air Wing Seventeen:

In the Navy, promotion to chief petty officer is more than moving up a single pay grade. It's a graduation to a new level. You're now the technical expert, of course, but you're the expert in leadership, too. There is certainly a great sense of pride. I think the change in uniform, the change to khaki, emphasizes that the chief joins with the junior officers as the leaders of the ship or squadron. It's an outward sign of what has happened inside you, what you've been able to accomplish, and what you'll be able to do in the future.

Chief Henry:

Initiation into the mess, that's the difference. That's what it is all about. I've worked with members of the other services, and some actually went through initiation into a CPO mess because they were at a Navy base. They actually have a set of CPO anchors, believe it or not. I had one guy, an Air Force master sergeant, who, when I routed my charge book, took out his wallet and pulled out his card. He wasn't aware that I was coming, so it wasn't staged at all, but he opened up his blouse pocket and showed me that he still wore a Navy anchor there, underneath the flap of his uniform. When you have sergeants from the other services and they want to take part in our initiations—they voluntarily take part—and they have the same values we have, I think that speaks volumes as to what it all means. Their officers may not have understood why it was so important, but the sergeants did, every one of them that went through it with us.

Master Chief Storekeeper (SW) Antonio Decena,
USS George Washington (CVN-73):

It's easier now to make chief, I think, but harder, lots harder, to do the job. That's why the mess is so important—you have resources here you can tap. For some reason, sailors are much more sensitive than ever before. People say you can learn leadership from a book, but I don't think that is so. You learn by watching what the other guys in the mess do. And that's why we as chiefs are different from anyone else, aboard ship or in the field. Because we know that we can rely on one another, to teach and be taught by each other. And the wardroom never knows it's happening.

As Chief Henry points out, and Master Chief Decena amplifies, chief petty officers have a sense of separateness much greater than that of other services. Theirs is a sense of identity separate from, but in addition to, their loyalty to country, to the Navy, or to the ship or command. No longer is a chief simply a member of his rating family (boatswain's mate, torpedoman, and so on); he is now part of the CPO community. And the valence that holds the CPO community together is much greater than that which binds the chief petty officer to other communities of which he or she may be a part.

One of the characteristics of any military service, and especially of the CPO community within the sea services, is a sense of group cohesion. Cohesion, of course, plays an important role in everyday life. The Army, in particular, has extensively researched the impact of group cohesion on morale and unit success, particularly in dealing with the stressors of combat. Research at the mental health facilities of the First Armored Division at Wiesbaden, Germany, and elsewhere shows that group cohesion can have both positive and negative implications for a military organization. When exercised positively, it can be rewarding, building trust and allowing friendships to develop among individuals in the same unit. Units tend to work more efficiently and effectively under conditions of high group cohesion, and there are indications that soldiers serving in highly cohesive units are at reduced risk of subsequent development of post-traumatic stress disorder (PTSD). Unfortunately, highly cohesive groups can be quite stressful as well, with increased aggression toward those who are perceived as not being "team players." The workplace can become less productive, members tend less to rely on others, and soldiers may have to develop coping mechanisms to deal with the dynamics of the group.[1]

To a degree perhaps greater than in the Army, separate communities have always been a characteristic of the sea services. The basic distinction between officer and enlisted has certainly been stronger than in the other armed forces. First enshrined in the distance between quarterdeck and fo'c'sle, and now portrayed as the distance between wardroom and the deckplates, this "level consciousness" has expanded to include a sense of separateness between chief petty officers and their "blueshirts." For the past forty years, one avenue to build cohesion and to signal the transition from blueshirt to khaki has been a two-day initiation before the effective date of promotion. While members of CPO messes afloat and CPO associations ashore have always held out a welcoming hand to their newest members, over a period of time formal (or not so formal) initiation rituals began to develop. Ceremonial initiation was not unknown in the 1950s and early 1960s, but by 1964 it had begun to take on a semi-standardized form.[2] Unfortunately, with the formalization of initiation came incidents of abuse. One very senior command master chief explains:

CNOCM(SW) Thomas Sheppard, command master chief,
Naval Air Training Command:

> Based on conversations that I have had with retired chiefs (some from the old sailors' home in Gulfport) my best guess is that the drunken revelry that the initiation became famous for emerged during the Vietnam era. I have had some retired master chiefs around here tell me some outrageous stories of initiations in Vietnam. I suspect they are close to true, and it fits with the culture of the time. A conscript force, many very young chiefs, and the flower-power generation all combined to create the "Animal House" style of initiation. I have talked to World War II retirees and earlier with mixed results; some say they had no initiation, while others say yes, they did have one and it did include a pig trough.

It would be crass for an author to disclose private rituals described by others in confidence. But, as Master Chief Sheppard points out, much of the initiates' natural inhibitions were offset by copious consumption of alcohol, and specific rituals were designed to instill a sense of humility into the neo-phytes ("slugs"). The motivation for and psychological soundness of these rituals are open for debate. Indeed, groups such as fraternities, sororities, clubs, and fraternal associations that seek to instill high levels of cohesiveness sometimes resort to coercive, rather than cohesive, techniques to ensure compliance with group norms. Many groups have the idea that if accession to the group is difficult or painful, members who complete the initiation process will prize membership more highly. Sometimes these rituals cross the line into unacceptable hazing practices.

Hazing, unfortunately, does have a long history within naval service, both in the U.S. Navy and the Royal Navy, where, as noted earlier, many of our customs and traditions originate. Indeed, the well-known naval author, Capt. Edward L. Beach Sr., for whom Beach Hall at the Naval Academy was recently renamed, recounts hazing incidents that occurred while he was a midshipman at the Naval Academy before the Spanish American War. While the Navy went so far as to expel some of the hazing midshipmen (one of whom returned, years later, to become secretary of the Navy), enforcement of the antihazing policy was at times spotty, and less than wholehearted.[3]

Chief petty officers who experienced initiation into the mess, particularly in the period 1980–97, frequently recount similar stories.

Chief Norman:

> I was initiated into the mess in 1995, before all the changes were made. My sponsor, who is now a master chief, had a videotape of her own initiation, which she refused to show me until after I had finished my own. After I had finished my own, I understood why. I went through a lot less than she did, years before. I went through a lot that I'm thankful that the slugs that are coming through now aren't going to see. I learned a lot during the initiation because there were good parts, too, but there were times when it did get out of hand, alcohol was still allowed, and, to be honest, it really did cross the line into hazing. We didn't say anything when I came through, but I still have scars on my hands where I was told to squeeze a pair of anchors without the frogs on them. And you know you do it, because you want to be accepted

into the organization. That doesn't happen anymore, though, and I'm glad, because the focus is now on what the chiefs mess really is—it's on discipline, on training, heritage, on teaching the first classes who are coming into this organization what it means to be a leader of this caliber in the U.S. Navy.

Senior Chief Buie:

I was initiated in Japan. A lot of squadrons were in Yokosuka, so it was pretty big. So we had to deal with the ships as well. Because I was on shore duty at the time, it's not just the shore duty personnel; you had to go out to the ships, and you'd do some pretty strange things. But our association was pretty good. I have to agree with some of the criticism, though. Some of it, I think, was cruel. Some of the things I wouldn't dare mention; I would never want to see someone go through that again. I understand the logic behind the humbling, but some of the things were really borderline. I saw people get hurt, get sick. It should not have been done, maybe, the way it was. But instead of crossing that line now, we've just drawn a different line altogether. So they are not getting a lot of the things that we should have held onto, as far as "why" we are doing this training. Now, it has become more like a sit-down dinner. There are so many things you can't do, and you are focusing so much on that, and that's not what it's about. A lot of changes have been made, but some of it I think they need to bring back.

Chief Information Systems Technician Mary E. Williams,
USS George Washington:

I was initiated in 1999. When I went through, it was a transition between old and new style. Sure, it was ugly at times, but it was helpful, too, and there were lots of things that I learned then. But there were moments when I asked, "What's the logic behind all this?" Now, I've always been someone who can get the job done, but during initiation, I learned how to ensure that other people get the job done and how to motivate people to get results. I knew how to motivate myself, but I had to learn how to motivate others so that the group and the mission succeed. And one of the things that really surprised me was the immediate acceptance from the other members of the mess. Now, working with the chiefs in my rating before, we were a close-knit community, even when I was a first-class petty officer. But the change after I pinned on my anchors was amazing. Even when we were first announced as selectees, even though we still hadn't gone through the six or seven weeks of initiation, that acceptance was there already.

Many observers would agree that these events, and those described by countless other CPO selectees, would certainly constitute hazing. That mild to moderate hazing has been a part of naval culture for years is undeniable; indeed, many of the Navy's most cherished and time-honored rituals involve a significant element of hazing. "Plebe Summer" at the Naval Academy, the Shellback ceremony marking a ship's transit of the equator, the Golden Dragon festivities when crossing the international dateline: all are enshrined in the folk memory of the Navy. Indeed, journalistic integrity requires the writer to disclose—with no small degree of pride—that his shipmates, recognizing both his girth and mirth, once appointed him as the "Royal Baby" in King Neptune's court during his own naval service in the late 1960s. However, events in the 1990s—beginning at the notorious Tailhook convention in Las Vegas in 1991, and fueled by revelations of excesses in such ceremonies as "blood pinning" among SEALS and other special units, focused public attention upon such practices. By 1997 Secretary of the Navy John Dalton felt compelled to outline specific guidelines regarding hazing in the Naval Service:

> Hazing is contrary to our Core Values of Honor, Courage and Commitment. Adherence to Core Values by our Sailors and Marines is central to the Navy's ability to meet its global mission. These values have served the sea services well during war and peacetime. They are our guiding principles for treating every Sailor and Marine with dignity and respect, and as a valued member of the Navy and Marine Corps team. Hazing degrades and diminishes the ability of victims to function within their unit. It destroys members' confidence and trust

in their shipmates and is destructive to a unit's cohesion and combat readiness. Every member of the Department of the Navy must be afforded the opportunity to be a productive and contributing member free of hazing and its ill effects. Hazing is not part of our "time honored traditions" and it has no place in the modern Naval Services. Hazing will not be tolerated by any member of the Navy or Marine Corps. Sailors and Marines are our most valuable resources. DON leadership has a responsibility to create and maintain an environment free from hazing.

Military customs and traditions have long been an integral part of the Navy and Marine Corps. Although in the past some hazing has occurred in conjunction with ceremonies, initiations or rites of passage, these activities, if properly supervised, can be effective leadership tools to instill esprit de corps, unit cohesion and respect for an accomplishment of another Sailor or Marine. While most ceremonies commemorate the many selfless feats of bravery of our military men and women, they also commemorate significant events. These feats and events form the basis upon which our Core Values of Honor, Courage and Commitment were founded. Graduations, chiefs' initiations, "crossing-the-line" ceremonies, and others are only meant to celebrate and recognize the achievements of individual Sailors or Marines or those of entire units. Service members must be able to work together, building up, encouraging, and supporting their shipmates. Hazing behavior that is degrading, embarrassing or injurious is unprofessional and illegal. Commanders must be aware of all ceremonies and initiations conducted within their organizations and take proactive steps to ensure that these activities do not violate this policy.

[Therefore], it is Department of the Navy policy that:

Hazing is prohibited and will not be tolerated.

No service member in the Department of the Navy may engage in hazing or consent to acts of hazing being committed upon them.

No commander or supervisor may, by act, word, deed, or omission, condone or ignore hazing if they know or reasonably should have known, that hazing may or did occur. It is the responsibility of every Sailor and Marine to ensure that hazing does not occur in any form at any level. Every service member has the responsibility to make the appropriate authorities aware of each violation of this policy.

Commanders or individuals in supervisory positions are responsible for ensuring that all ceremonies and initiations conducted within their organizations or commands comply with this policy.

Supervisory personnel shall ensure that service members participating in command-authorized ceremonies, initiations and other activities are treated with dignity and respect during these events.

Reprisal actions against any victim or witness of hazing incidents are strictly prohibited.[4]

Every sailor is trained to follow orders, even if not all were convinced that a strict crackdown was necessary.

Chief Scheer:

Well, in my opinion, and a lot of others, any guy who refuses to go through initiation is not a chief. He might think he is, he might say he is, but he's just an E-7. And there's a world of difference.

Master Chief Barrett:

I've been in ship's messes where we've had guys who didn't go through initiation. And, as a matter of fact, it was on board this ship—I think it was last year or the year before—we had a guy we had to reinitiate, because he missed it at a previous command. And he was already wearing khakis, so we said, "Better late than never." In the 1980s we used to get Class A messages from commands that said, "And by the way, this guy did not go through initiation, or what have you." They probably wouldn't do that today, though.

Senior Chief Gentry:

Some things we did we took to extremes, and a lot of people felt there was no purpose to making us eat balut (a Philippine delicacy consisting of partially fertilized duck egg) or whatever. I don't necessarily agree with that. It's not that I just want to see others go through what I went through, but every initiation now, each year, attitudes of the selectees seem really bad. "You can't do this to me, you can't do that to me." It's vital that we teach some humility, break people down a little, and there's nothing more humbling than making someone do something that they absolutely refuse to do, because there may be a situation where you have to swallow your pride and do something that you don't like to do or don't want to do. As long as we don't violate safety, well, if I'm on the flight deck and there's someone who may be senior to me, or who has more information than I have, and I'm too bullheaded to bend, then I could cost someone their life, and one of the things that I learned at initiation is that if you trust these people, and do what they tell you to do, then there is a lesson there.

Master Chief Sheppard:

But you know, if you look up rites of passage in the encyclopedia it says all rites of passage have three parts: symbolic death, mystical transformation, and finally rebirth. In Bill Moyers's interviews with Joseph Campbell, "The Power of Myth: The First Storytellers," he talks about the need for rituals and rites of passage. These are used to teach conformity, and that is exactly what we are trying to do (even if most of us cannot articulate it). We are trying to get the next generation of chiefs to accept our values.

Master Chief Sheppard understands both the academic and practical sides of initiation rituals. Indeed, most reports of CPO initiation do include clearly identifiable elements of traditional rites of passage, such as "symbolic death," "mystical transformation," and "rebirth." For instance, on the evening preceding promotion to CPO, most messes gather their initiates (slugs) at dusk. As the light fades, initiates are directed to burn, bury, or "deep six" their round white "Dixie cup" hats, which, with the associated crackerjack uniform, constitute the universally recognized, and sometimes derided, symbol of the enlisted sailor. As the hat burns, they are told that they are now in limbo—they are not yet chiefs, yet they cannot, in conscience, return to the junior ranks. They are, for the moment, men and women in limbo. They are warned of the rigors of the events to follow, and, like those unfortunates cited by Chiefs Scheer and Barrett, are warned that they will be ostracized by those already initiated, if they don't pass the tests ahead.

Following the white hat ceremony, selectees were usually escorted to the CPO mess or association (there are legal differences between CPO messes afloat and CPO associations ashore, but they have little bearing on the initiation process). It was during this second element—mystical transformation—that hazing excesses took place. In a process similar to fraternity initiation, neophytes underwent "trial by fire," including a kangaroo court composed of senior members of the ship's mess. The judge (often the oldest, if not the most senior, member present) would generally accuse the neophyte of impersonating a chief petty officer, with fines, imprisonment in a makeshift brig, and administration of balut or "truth serum" (a vile concoction of various consumables) following. While protocol varied from mess to mess (although particularly entertaining variations, developed at a single location soon propagated throughout the fleet), most messes caused the candidate to perform physical exercises, often to the point of nausea, or required stunts, some of which, if gone awry, could be dangerous to the participants. All of these, of course, were fueled by frequent libations, requiring the neophyte to generally prove his or her worthiness to join the "august company of chief petty officers."

It is a characteristic of human nature that those who successfully complete an initiation ceremony often downplay the significance of the humiliations played out upon them. Chief petty officers are no exception.

Senior Chief Perry:

Well, I'm an oldtimer. Everybody now looks back at our initiations and says, "Well, that was degrading" and stuff like that. But all of that was to get to know you. It's to get to know your fellow chiefs. You'll get a lot more work done if you get to know your fellow chiefs. And it teaches you a lot. As a blueshirt, I might not be able to get something done, but as a chief, I call down and say, "Hey, Chief, I need this," and I know I have it. And if a fellow chief—even if it's someone I don't know all that well, and he is in California, and I'm in Norfolk—calls me up and says, "Hey, Chuck, I need 10 pounds of lobster," well, there will be a plane flying in, and I'll have it there, no problem. You don't worry about money, you don't worry about anything like that. He needs it, you have it, you give it. But as far as initiation goes, I thought it was fun. I took it as, hey this is fun. Sticks and stones, you know?

Command Master Chief (SW) Buck Hickman,
Electronic Attack Squadron 132:

There are some traditions that we've pushed away from now, that part of me wishes we still had. I don't know if that's my way of saying, "It happened to me, it ought to happen to these guys too." But I also remember when my dad made chief. I was young, but I remember them throwing him on the lawn after the initiation process, all bruised up and drunk. I was very thankful that I didn't go through that. When my own initiation was over, at Pensacola, I remember my dad, who had probably had two or three beers too many at the time, telling me that "this was nothing." And I could tell the guys today, this was nothing, but they get a lot more training than I ever got. My training, when I made chief, consisted of delivering lunch every day to the master chiefs and the chiefs in the conference room—they'd pay for it, we'd bring it and entertain for an hour.

Now there is so much training; now there's more focus on teaching that young chief how to be me, the things that I did and I learned. You go to different duty stations around the world, and they each put their own little spin on it, as to what they do. The classes now that they give, most of the time, are by master chiefs, people who have been doing it for a long time. Back when I made chief, there was a whole lot of yelling, a whole lot of screaming, and I took the humiliations that they gave out, it was a great shock when it hit me. Now, you still get some of that, not a lot, but when it is all said and done, the young chief is pulled aside and asked to "explain what just happened." And sometimes they understand, and sometimes they don't. So I'll explain, "This is why I did this, this is what I was trying to show you. You just didn't get it." But I'm jealous of what the guys are getting now, I really am.

Master Chief Barrett:

I always liked the old initiations; they got wild sometimes, but no one got hurt. The chiefs community is different now, all the way. The whole purpose of initiation, while there's some training in there involved too,

is often just the initiation of a new member to a certain club or fraternity. This guy has got to know that their E-6 and below days are over,
and they are now going to be a part of this organization. And hazing or
harassment, or whatever you want to call it, was all part of the game, to
make it stick indelibly in their minds, to let them know that they are
on a different team now.

The third element, rebirth, traditionally takes place early on the morning of 16 September, the usual date for promotions in the sea services. That
is when the initiates, dressed in clean, pressed uniforms, formally receive
their hat and anchor pins, usually from the hands of a loved one. It is an
emotionally charged moment for all.

Chief Oitzman:
The day I got pinned as a chief petty officer was, for me, the most
exciting thing that has happened in my career. In fact, it's one of the
most exciting and emotional moments of my entire life.

Chief Valero:
The most exciting thing was making chief! I knew then that I would be
in a position where I could actually influence change—and to me, that
was really gratifying.

Master Chief Barrett:
Even afterward, it takes a while to really absorb what it's all about.
Nobody does right away. There's a lot of things that are said in the
mess, and what's said in the mess stays in the mess, that kind of thing.
If you get a guy who doesn't want to be initiated, then right away, he is
kind of an outsider. We figure that he is here for a different purpose, he
doesn't want to be a chief, he wants to be an E-7. E-7 is just a pay
grade. Being a chief is an honor. And right away, you know that everybody is going to put him in a bad light. If he is going to be any good,
then he is going to have to make up some lost time.

The CPO community itself recognized the dangers inherent in unscript-
ed, and often unrehearsed, initiations. Beginning in 1997, and continuing

today, the hazing component of CPO initiation has been converted to a "journey into the chiefs mess."

The ninth Master Chief Petty Officer of the Navy, Jim Herdt, neatly summed up current thinking in the guidelines issued for the 2001 initiation cycle:

> Every year is filled with expectation and hope as the results of the CPO Selection Board results are announced. There is great expectation and hope, of course, among those that have their records considered by the board for selection. They anxiously await the announcement hoping that their name will be found among the long lines of selectees' names. Working and serving diligently throughout their careers, they hope that they will be among the honored who will make the final journey through the months of August and September preparing to become a member of the most honored and trusted of all fraternities, that of the chief petty officer's mess. Meeting their expectations of that journey in which they will learn and prepare are solemn responsibilities that must be met by all seasoned chief petty officers. Failing to meet their expectations is a failure of the highest order. . . .

> No guidelines can be written that will entirely supplant either good common sense or the deep abiding respect that CPOs hold for Sailors in their charge. Likewise, writing a "cookbook" for the journey would unnecessarily limit the intelligent and innovative approach to this task that have been hallmarks of CPO mess for years. Accordingly, it is the responsibility of the Command Master Chief, and the Command Master Chief alone, to ensure the intent and the guidelines for the journey in their command meet all existing requirements and that all activities are constructed from a common sense perspective delivering a value-added product to the journey. My words in these guidelines have been very carefully chosen and should be carefully considered when read. The items listed under "Don't" are not open for interpretation. The words "may" and "should" may be interpreted as recommendations to be considered and hopefully adopted. The words "shall" and "will" must be considered as mandates that will be adhered to unless requested and approved by higher authority.

Master Chief Herdt listed several steps that commands should take to welcome the newly appointed chief petty officers, including instruction in naval heritage and mess etiquette, and inclusion of families in appropriate activities. He also specifically prohibited a range of activities, including the following:

Inappropriate or sexually or explicit jokes or skits (such as cross-dressing)

Verbal abuse

Physical abuse

Videos of training or the graduation events

Lone rangers (everything is group participation)

Activities not tied to the values inherent in CPO Creed

Forced feeding (There shall be no feeding at all; an easy rule of thumb, "Nothing in the mouth and nothing down the gullet.")

Vulgarity entered into or damage/defacement inflicted upon the charge book

Use of any prop that may cause injury

Drinking during any part of the training exercises or before or during the graduation

Officer participation during transition process until pinning ceremony. (only exception is when CO/XO/Flag are invited by CMC to observe)

Participation of other services as selectees without fleet or force approval

Repercussions for nonparticipation

All night activities (activities must secure at taps)

Master Chief Herdt concluded: "The Navy as an organization and I personally have the greatest trust and confidence in each CPO's ability and judgment to make this journey memorable and valuable. Each of you make the Navy run! Let the Journey to the CPO Mess begin!"[5]

Master Chief Waldrup:
I think things are better and worse now. The worst is that there's not the closeness in the mess that there may have been, back in the 1980s. I think we lost some things that may not have been necessary, or politically correct, but that—from my point of view, because I experienced it—showed me that as a chief, there is nothing you can't do. And initiation helped us realize that you can do it, physically, mentally, and psychologically. I went through the hard initiations where you ate things, but none of it ever hurt you. Sure, you were scared, but you either overcame it or you didn't.

And now you don't quite get that sense anymore, that you can do anything that you need to do. The good thing is that now we're emphasizing
the history of the Navy, and the history of being a chief. We're doing
some good training on the really hard things, such as "You have a sailor
die—what do you have to do?" And we don't lay out the steps, the slugs
have to figure it out for themselves. We didn't have that, and I think
that's a good thing to be doing these days. When I was initiated, most of
it was designed to help us be part of a team—we're going to make you a
part of our mess. They proved that you can overcome anything, and
when you were done, you felt a part of the group. It was teambuilding—
that's what it was really all about.

Chief Mess Management Specialist (SS) Darryl Martin,
Naval Training Center, Great Lakes:

I think the message of chiefs' initiation is the same message that has
been sent this year, last year, twenty years ago, forty years ago. It is the
message that we are a fraternity, that there is strength in numbers, and
that if you trust your fellow chiefs, you can't go far wrong. Everything
else is just window-dressing. That's the message of initiation.

Master Chief Boatswain's Mate Robert W. Heinrichs,
USS George Washington:

I think that the changes made recently are right on target. My initiation
served me nothing, it didn't make me the master chief that I am today.
The process needed more orientation to what's really needed, and what
you can expect as a chief. I think all those other things were all humiliation, and being able to handle humility. Well, humility is one of the things
that my mentor, Master Chief Charles Inhger, modeled to me. Now, I
have trouble with humility myself, but I still say that the changes that the
last few MCPONs made are right on target. Fellows that don't understand
it—well, they haven't been to the right places to understand the changes
we're making. If they see what's happening at Battle Stations in boot
camp, at Service School Command, at the Senior Enlisted Academy—
that's where you learn why we're making the changes we are—including
the changes in CPO initiation.

Five

The Chief Petty Officers Mess

At the completion of every initiation ceremony, the initiates, as well as all current and retired chief petty officers present, stand, and in the most solemn moment of the ceremony, recite together the CPO Creed:

> During the course of this day you have been caused to humbly accept challenge and face adversity. This you have accomplished with rare good grace. Pointless as some of these challenges may have seemed, there were valid, time-honored reasons behind each pointed barb. It was necessary to meet these hurdles with blind faith in the fellowship of Chief Petty Officers. The goal was to instill in you that trust is inherent with the donning of the uniform of a Chief. It was our intent to impress upon you that challenge is good; a great and necessary reality which cannot mar you—which, in fact, strengthens you. In your future as a Chief Petty Officer, you will be forced to endure adversity far beyond that imposed upon you today. You must face each challenge and adversity with the

same dignity and good grace you demonstrated today. By experience, by performance, and by testing, you have been this day advanced to Chief Petty Officer. In the United States Navy—and only in the United States Navy—the rank of E-7 carries with it unique responsibilities and privileges you are now bound to observe and expected to fulfill. Your entire way of life is now changed. More will be expected of you; more will be demanded of you. Not because you are an E-7 but because you are now a Chief Petty Officer. You have not merely been promoted one paygrade, you have joined an exclusive fellowship and, as in all fellowships, you have a special responsibility to your comrades, even as they have a special responsibility to you. This is why we in the United States Navy may maintain with pride our feelings of accomplishment once we have attained the position of chief petty officer. Your new responsibilities and privileges do not appear in print. They have no official standing; they cannot be referred to by name, number, nor file. They have existed for over 100 years, chiefs before you have freely accepted responsibility beyond the call of printed assignment. Their actions and their performance demanded the respect of their seniors as well as their juniors. It is now required that you be the fountain of wisdom, the ambassador of good will, the authority in personal relations as well as in technical applications. "Ask the Chief" is a household phrase in and out of the Navy. You are now the Chief. The exalted position you have now achieved—and the word exalted is used advisedly—exists because of the attitude and performance of the chiefs before you. It shall exist only as long as you and your fellow chiefs maintain these standards. It was our intention that you never forget this day. It was our intention to test you, to try you, and to accept you. Your performance has assured us that you will wear "the hat" with the same pride as your comrades in arms before you. We take a deep and sincere pleasure in clasping your hand, and accepting you as a Chief Petty Officer in the United States Navy.[1]

Chief Sonar Technician (SW) James Reynolds,
Naval Training Center, Great Lakes:

It was awesome, standing there at the initiation ceremony as we recited the Creed. I looked around at all those squared-away chiefs, and I thought, well, in today's Navy, the chief sets the standard, and is then held to that same standard. When I first came in, the image of the average chief was, well, a little heavy, maybe, carrying a coffee cup, and you never saw the chief unless you were getting your butt chewed out. We have to be there, we are setting the standard, and the other folks follow us—we have to be fit, to set the example, to be the standard for them to follow.

Chief petty officers by definition are leaders. But that leadership is not exercised in a vacuum. "You have joined an exclusive fellowship and, as in all fellowships, you have a special responsibility to your comrades, even as they have a special responsibility to you." The focus of that fellowship is the chief petty officers mess.

Chief Helderman:
I've often seen the chiefs mess come together to solve a problem. I did it recently for one of the operators. I went to his chief in the mess, and said, "Hey, this is what we are up against." And once, one of my counterparts had a tough problem, and he and I discussed it in the mess, we pulled a couple of other chiefs in, said, "What have been your experiences with this? How have you dealt with this? How can we work around it?" This was a junior chief; he had just picked it up a year or so ago, and he had no idea how to overcome this situation. I had been a chief for a while; it was a little easier for me, so I kind of mentored him. Now, it just happened to be a warrant officer he was having the problem with. And the warrant officer had been a chief just a year or so before, so it was a pretty sensitive kind of thing. But the mess backed the young chief, the warrant backed off a little, and the chief got stronger. That's how the mess works, and it helps all of us in the long run. Now, the entire mess obviously won't corral around him, but his peers who work with him, and his friends, will definitely rally around him and support him in whatever way he needs.

Command Master Chief (AW) Miguel A. Sanchez,
Helicopter Squadron 15:
I tell you, coming into the mess was a bit of a shock. The uniform

transition is a big part of it, sure, and the separation when it comes to berthing and messing is there, too. But one day I was AD1, the next day I was the ADC, and when I said things, people listened. One day it was, "Well, that's just Mike, complaining again." And the next day I could mention something around the table in the chiefs mess, and bang—the next thing you know your problem has been fixed. It came as a shock, sure, but it was a good shock.

Master Chief Heinrichs:

This is my second carrier, and the chiefs on the *George Washington* do a pretty nice job making this mess livable and hospitable. I made chief on the first carrier, and it was pretty much the same. You could put any six blueshirts in a room, and at the end of the day they are friends. It's even better with chiefs. Put six of us into a room, and we'll break down into a leader and some followers, but we'll be friends and we'll find out things about each other that would take six civilians three months to find out about each other. It doesn't matter if they are with the squadron, ship's company, riders, or whatever; there's an instant bond. We're chiefs, and this is our home.

"The mess is our home." Nothing is more important to a sailor than a good meal and a warm, dry place to sleep, relax, or just hang out. Indeed, for centuries, groups of sailors would join together, either voluntarily or by watch assignment, in ad-hoc dining clubs. These ship's messes—the word derives from the Latin *mensa,* meaning "table"—long precede the cafeteria-style food service found on most ships today. And, while there is no proven etymological link between the concept of "mess" as a dining arrangement and "mess" as disorder or disarray, it takes no great leap of imagination to envision what dinnertime must have been like on the lower decks of a pitching, rocking warship, caught in a North Atlantic gale.

It had long been the custom in the Royal Navy for sailors berthed in the same areas to join together as messmates. "Messmates before shipmates, shipmates before a landsman, a landsman before a dog" was an old Royal Navy adage. The colonial American Navy adopted this custom, like many others, and since sailors with similar responsibilities usually berthed together, the concept of ship's messes further strengthened the bond between sailors with common interests. Seamen messed with boatswains and coxswains; stokers with trimmers and firemen.

Rivalries and tensions were not unknown among the various messes on large warships. These tensions were aggravated by the system of food preparation then in use. Each mess would nominate one or two members as designated "messmen" (later messcooks, and even later, food service attendants) who would draw supplies and transport them to the galley, where a full-time cook would supervise meal preparation. Space on the galley range was limited, and since each mess was responsible for its own cooking gear, "first come, first served" was usually the rule. After the food had been prepared, the messmen would hazard the trip back to the berthing and messing spaces, often across weather decks awash with rolling waves. Safely back in the mess, the mess cook would turn over responsibility for the equitable distribution of the day's meal to the senior member of the group. This "killick of the mess," so named for the anchor of office worn on the cuff of his sleeve, would ensure that every man received his proper allotment of the day's meal. Dinner was usually served on a chain-supported table, and the mess members sat on their sea chests, or other convenient articles, as the killick—often with soup ladle in hand—maintained some semblance of order and discipline. At the end of the meal, the second messman would clear the table, clean the pots and pans, and return them to the galley to be ready for the next meal. The inconvenience of moving steaming hot containers of food from galley to berthing areas, while navigating heaving decks and near vertical ladders, was offset by the camaraderie and fellowship among members of a particular mess.[2]

Given the draconian discipline prevalent in those times, and the necessity of maintaining strong leadership, it is no surprise that senior members of the ship's company found it desirable and even necessary to berth and dine together. Not only were their facilities less spartan than the fo'c'sle, but dining together gave them the opportunity to relax for a few moments, secure in the knowledge that their tablemates understood and appreciated the stresses of everyday life at sea. The sailmaker might comment to the carpenter about the condition of the spars and masts that he noticed in his day-to-day work aboard ship; the master at arms and the apothecary might discuss the physical state of particular crewmen, and the impact of illness upon the ability of ship's company to call away at a moment's notice to board an enemy or repel boarders on their own ship. Thus was born the chief petty officers mess, as we know it today.

Much has been written about the sacredness of the chiefs mess afloat. Young sailors are warned of the dire consequences of wandering in uninvited. Most messes are located behind closed doors, and it's the rare sailor who has not stood nervously before the sign: "Knock three times, uncover, and do not enter until invited." Newly frocked chief petty officers are reminded that the CPO mess is a tangible symbol of the strong, effective bond among members. During the CPO initiation season special pains are taken to remind initiates that they are about to enjoy special privileges, but that with those privileges comes a unique set of obligations. Most seasoned veterans understand that membership in the chiefs mess comes with obligations that are not subject to personal interest, but to the CPO community itself. Today's chiefs mess exists to provide a venue to improve cohesion, as well as a place for training in "chiefness." It serves as a visual reminder of the separateness of the community, typifies the perks commensurate with newly accepted responsibility, and provides a place to discuss common problems and seek solutions from the collective wisdom of the entire group.[3]

At sea, separate messing for chiefs is set aside when space is available. Should personnel of the other armed services visit or be attached to an afloat command, they are accorded the same privileges as naval personnel in the equivalent pay grade. The senior member (usually the command master chief) acts as mess president and presides over the mess, maintaining good order and ensuring compliance with all governing rules and regulations. Most messes are quite comfortable; even the smallest ship provides appropriate space for embarked CPOs to grab a bite to eat and relax for a few moments. And they are very welcoming places.

Chief Grodski:

I've felt accepted in every chiefs mess I've ever walked into. When I checked on board this ship, not knowing anybody, I just walked down here to the third deck and into the chiefs mess and there was instant camaraderie. That special bond is one of the great things about being a Navy chief. I kind of have fun with it, because, you know, you walk up to somebody, you still half expect "Navy chief" to mean a male. You still say chief, and think of a crusty old guy. So as a female, when you walk up to people sometimes and say, "Hey, I'm a chief, too," it kind of shocks some people, but I have a lot of fun with it. And I know if I were in need, or stuck, or needed a ride, a fellow chief is someone that I can trust. Absolutely.

Chief Air Traffic Controller (AW) Leslee A. McPherson,
USS George Washington *(CVN-73):*

Even with over three hundred chiefs in this mess, I felt no shyness about going and sitting at whatever table has an empty seat. Sure, sometimes you'll have a table of master chiefs sitting there together, but that's usually after they have just come from an LCPO meeting or something, and then they all come in together for lunch. And sometimes they just naturally eat together. But no, there's no segregation by grade level or anything like that. It depends on the person. I'm very flamboyant and outgoing, and I'll go sit anywhere.

Chief Postal Clerk (SW) Carmen B. Butler, USS George Washington:

In the mess, if I have a problem and I see my department's master chief, I know I can go to him immediately. And, depending on what the issue is, I can go to one of the other female chief petty officers that I'm comfortable with, if it's that kind of problem. I think we female chiefs are particularly close-knit—for one thing, there are fewer of us, and for another thing, we all berth in the same space, whereas the guys are spread out a bit more. But this is the first place I'd look for a solution to a problem, definitely.

Senior Chief Hospital Corpsman (SW) Larry Gilbert,
USS George Washington:

That's exactly what we do. Guys come to me, especially if they have medical issues with their sailors. They'll sit down and say, "Hey, I don't

mean to interrupt dinner, but can we sit down and talk?" And if it's
something confidential or sensitive, we'll go off in one of the other
compartments in the chiefs mess and talk it over. I'd say pretty much
the majority of stuff gets solved right here. Sure, there are a lot of
chiefs on board, but when you need to find somebody and fix something, it's not all that big.

Chief Helderman:

There are some messes out there that don't work as well together as
this one, I suppose. If you get one or two bad apples in there, it can
decay a small mess. If you get a guy in there who is acting erratically or
immorally, then, no, the mess won't rally around him. Chiefs are
expected to carry a particular level of morality, and if they break that
level of morality, you kind of lose faith in them. Now, you've lost my
trust. And it's difficult to support somebody in that situation. But what
the mess will do is to step in and help the guy's division, help take care
of his responsibilities; they'll help his blueshirts handle things for him
in his absence due to his negligence. There's loyalty to the Navy, and to
the ship, but especially to the mess, and to the individual shipmate, too.

Command Master Chief McCalip:

We still refer to the chiefs mess as a brotherhood, even though we've
got our brothers and sisters in there. The mess is what makes for
"chiefness"—I think of it as one body. Not a body where everyone
agrees with everything, but one united group of sailors that makes
hard things easier sometimes. It's the chiefs mess that makes the
impossible happen, when we come together as one. Man, I could talk
about chiefness for hours, because every time I turn around and see
another chief, I have a different thought. We're a dynamic group, and
within the group, sure, there's going to be some controversy. But controversy is healthy, it makes you grow. The neat thing about a chiefs
mess is the loyalty that you find there; fifteen minutes after you've had
a disagreement and you finally come to a conclusion, you're all going
to march off in one direction. You won't find one guy going off and

whispering in the XO's ear that the chiefs mess is moving in ten different directions. You just don't find that. And, even more important, you don't find seamen talking on the mess decks about the big argument the chiefs had today, and we're not going to have to put out the effort today because the chiefs can't get their act together. Knowing when to stand alone, and knowing when to rely on the collective wisdom found in the chiefs' mess—that's a real sign of mature leadership.

Leadership. Almost anyone recognizes leadership when they see it, but finding a working definition is often difficult. Leadership is best defined as being engaged, open to the flow of communications upward and downward, and being willing to make whatever effort is necessary to accomplish the mission. It is the ability to guide others, to motivate and inspire, to meet a common goal. Leadership requires the agreement of those being led, and to get that buy-in, leaders need a plan of action. Leadership, effectively practiced, allows the division, department, or command to function at peak levels with maximum cooperation and enthusiasm. There are two kinds of leaders: those who lead by example, and those who simply issue orders. Leading by example is by far the better choice. Leadership is a combination of motivating, coordinating, facilitating, and recognizing; it is a way for people to motivate others and encourage others to reach their potential. Strong leaders exhibit self-control and believe in themselves, the other members of the mess, and in the sailors with whom they work.

Chief petty officers acknowledge, as part of their Creed, three specific leadership objectives:

To develop subordinates into future leaders

To develop division officers

To use fellow chief petty officers' experience and wisdom to solve day-to-day problems[4]

Every chief petty officer cherishes the memory of other chiefs who have exhibited the characteristics of great leaders, and have guided them in their naval careers.

Chief Norman:

I have a mentor, Master Chief Becky O'Brien. She was my first-class, then she transferred and later was my chief, and I even remember when she was going through chief's initiation. And up to this day, we keep in contact. She was probably the hardest person on me in the military—there were days when I hated this woman!—but she saw something in me that maybe I didn't see in myself. She'd push me to the point where I just wanted to scream. And she'd say, "I'm not giving you anything you are not capable of doing." She would assign me jobs, and she'd always give me tasks that were just a little bit above what I was really capable of doing. She never let me slack for even one minute; not on my professionalism, my military bearing, my uniforms, nothing. Now, she could cuss out a Marine and drink a Seabee under the table, but she was not going to take anything from me that wasn't perfect. And I was pinned with her anchors when I made chief, and I still have her senior chief anchors that she mailed to me when she made master chief. And the other thing is that she really clued me in as to what it's like to be a woman, and a woman chief, in the Navy.

Senior Chief Gilbert:

My first mentor was Master Chief Coleman, back in Great Lakes. I was there at Dispensary 237. I was a young kid, wild back then, but he brought me in and took care of me. He was hard on me; when I stepped out of line, he corrected me. He had been in the Navy for a lot of years, and he always used to try to show me how I could be success- ful in the military and in the civilian world, if I chose to go that route. Educate myself, never close the door on education, and always do something with my life. He was always trying to better himself. I was so impressed with him; he was from Mississippi, if I remember right, and he came in the Navy at a different time, back when there was lots of tensions between groups of sailors. He had two master's degrees that he always used to show me. "See—you can do this; you can make it in the Navy." Sure, you're scared, you're nervous, but he'd show me all the decorations, all the awards that he got for being out to sea and for being in Vietnam, and he was always looking to better himself. I'll never forget him.

Unfortunately, human nature being what it is, not every person in a leadership position exhibits good leadership. But even then, they can serve as a model of behaviors not to adopt. As one famous and perhaps apocryphal fitness report has it: "The only good thing about Chief Neversail is that he can be used as a bad example!"

Chief Grodski:

I had a chief who had a curtain in the back of the shop, and he'd go back there, put his feet up, sleep all day, and say, "Wake me up if anything explodes." I also had a female chief who was timid. I don't know how she made it to be a chief, frankly. That gave me a goal as a female chief, because she was useless to me. It made more work for me to circumvent her and get things done.

Senior Chief Hospital Corpsman (AW/SW)
Tiburcio G. Estampador, USS George Washington:

I've worked for bad chiefs, too. The worst are, in my view, the procrastinators. They know about what's going on, what's wrong, and still don't act on it. Not being proactive in solving the problem, instead they wind up being the problem themselves. I think those are the things that I hate to see in the chiefs community. The department head might want something done, but it only happens when the junior sailors realize that it has to be done. If you don't influence the junior troops to do the right thing, nothing right will ever get done.

Senior Chief Raab:

I had an experience as a very junior third-class, on the *Carl Vinson*. At that time we were on a deployment, out in the Hawaii area. The test equipment that I was maintaining was failing miserably. It was well beyond what we could troubleshoot. At the same time, USS *Ranger* was in port at Hawaii with us, and I came up with the idea to go over to

Ranger, troubleshoot what we had by comparing it to readings on their gear, and see if we could isolate the problem that way. We were a good distance away—it took ferry rides and bus rides to get over there—but we managed, and the senior chief at the time liked the idea, so he tasked me with making it happen. I was just a young AQ3 at the time. The rest of the shop was on liberty, but I was working anywhere from ten to fourteen hours a day, and I had no liberty, and this was the first time I had been to Hawaii. And, after eight days of this, and everyone going and partying every night, I took an afternoon off to go to the USS *Arizona* memorial, and you know, that senior chief in his drunken state proceeded to chew me up one side and down the other for not being a team player. And that right there was something that I've never forgotten, fifteen years later.

Master Chief Aviation Ordnanceman (AW/SW)
Carl J. Barton, USS George Washington:

Some of the worst were the ones that led from their chair, and some that just yelled and screamed, and didn't give a rat's behind what you had to say. I try to always be with my people, whether they're down in the magazine doing their job, or on the flight deck, and I don't have a false sense of pride so that I don't recognize that things do change all the time, and better and more efficient ways of doing the job come up. And I always listen to new kids when they've got something to say, because, hey, I'm old and things change, and there are better ways of doing things, and I'm always willing to listen. But I've worked for a number of people that just did not want to listen to anything you had to say.

Chief Personnelman (AW/SW) Major Bynum Jr.,
USS George Washington:

Where I was stationed before, there was a fire at base housing. And everyone went over there and cleaned and helped out. A couple of months later there was an awards ceremony, and our boss received a Navy commendation for what we did over at the housing area. And we just sort of looked at him and said, "Okay, here's a guy who's looking out for himself. He's not looking out for his people." I don't look for any praise, but it's nice at least to get credit for things that we do.

Despite the human foibles and occasional failings of individuals, most chief petty officers are comfortable and competent when leading sailors and applying their skills to accomplish the Navy's mission. There are four leadership roles contained in the chief petty officer's mission statement:

Command focus, being part of the chain of command, and being seen as the commanding officer's representative on the deckplates

"The subject matter expert of last resort," who, no matter the complexity of a problem or casualty, knows the answer, and gets things done

A valued member of a peer group (CPO mess), which is seen as the repository for technical and military knowledge, as well as the center for tradition and folk history of the command and of the Navy

An enlisted member who has a different relationship with the officer cadre than the traditional relationship between the blueshirts and the wardroom[5]

Most chiefs, in addition to identifying their personal mentors, can quickly name other chiefs who typify these roles.

Master Chief Barrett:

I once had a chief named Andy Miller, and he was a card. He never took on anything halfway. If he was going to do something, it was all or nothing. He would jump in with both feet with everything he did. Anything in his life, that's just the kind of person he was. But he also had—I wouldn't say a temper—but he just didn't put up with a lot of shenanigans. He was a no-nonsense kind of guy, and everybody knew that. People could do their job, or they could choose not to. But if they chose not to, the consequences always bit them, and they always knew it. It wasn't uncommon for him to be working on a Saturday, when we were in port, if things weren't up to par. He only had to do it once or twice, and pretty soon everything was running smoothly, and he always had a lot of great success with that. People would do what he asked, because they wanted to. But you always run into those that won't, and so there was a certain fear factor about this guy—not that he would hurt anyone, but he laid it on the line.

Chief Estampador:
The person who influenced me most was Master Chief Thomas, aboard the USS *John F. Kennedy.* He was a hard-charging master chief. Now, I know people said he was too rough, but I learned a lot of things from him. He's now retired. From him, I learned the importance of doing the right thing for the right reasons. I learned what it means to take care of your people—not just the easy words that people write in charge books. All the nice fancy equipment we have in our labs can't do a thing. It's the people who run it that make the difference. That's always stuck in my mind. Personnel make this the greatest Navy in the world. Not the money, not the ships, not the gear. The sailors.

In the early 1990s the Navy commissioned an extensive study of the characteristics that distinguish superior commands. One prime indicator of efficacy, easily identified, was the chiefs mess. Chiefs in superior commands demonstrated these identifiable leadership behaviors:

They promoted success of the command as a whole. Although they had a strong sense of ownership and took responsibility for their own division, they were able to look beyond their own immediate job to help the entire command. "When the ship sinks, everyone's feet get wet, so let's keep the ship afloat" seems to be the mantra of effective CPO messes afloat and ashore.

They upheld standards of behavior, dress, hygiene, and fitness. They were much less likely to turn "Nelson's eye" toward deficiencies or violations, even of the smallest rules of conduct or discipline. These chiefs played a key role in the enforcement of standards. Because they were out and about, they were able to see for themselves whether job performance and military bearing met the Navy's and the command's standards. When something was not up to standards, they gave feedback and acted to correct it. But most important, they modeled, on an ongoing basis, those behaviors and attitudes they wished to reinforce among their subordinates.

These chiefs talked daily to other divisions/departments when planning work schedules to prevent conflicts. They took a crow's-nest view of activities and managed their individual work centers accordingly.

They provided other divisions/departments or even other commands with assistance when requested or, often enough, when needed but not explicitly solicited.

They led by taking personal responsibility for their divisions. They exercised substantial influence upon their juniors, developing and communicating an overall plan, appealing to the self-interest of their subordinates, and presenting logical reasons and information for decisions, based upon their positional and personal authority.

They were master communicators, who passed the word both up and down the chain of command, and avoided gatekeeping, information voids, or other pitfalls that would keep them from successful team building.

They showed a distinct sense of pride, as exhibited by slogans such as "First and the Finest," "Ready, Aye, Ready," or the like, and they performed in such a way as to build a sense of common purpose. They paid attention to how new people were welcomed into the division, and provided rewards and recognition for individual accomplishment.

These chief petty officers supported and developed their division officers. They understood the difficulties inherent in that position and the problems that can arise in the relationship between chief petty officers and division officers. Chiefs in superior commands were sensitive to this and supported and developed the division officer. One way they did this was by suggesting to the division officer what should be done to solve problems. They also tactfully let the division officer know if he/she was charging off in the wrong direction. When disagreements occurred, they did not undercut him or her by saying so in public or allowing the crew to criticize him or her.

Finally, these chiefs formed a tight-knit team with the other chiefs in the mess. They used that bond to build trust and cooperative spirit to keep the command team moving forward.[6]

Great chiefs messes are composed of great chiefs. And if there's one great chief petty officer that stands out in a sailor's mind, often enough it's the very first chief whom they met out of boot camp.

Chief Wylie:

For me, it was MLC John Seller. I've lost track of him since he retired and went to Florida. He was my first chief, and if there's one term that could describe him, I would call it tough love. He was the kind of chief that when you toed the line with him, there were no ifs, ands, or buts about it. You knew where you stood at all times of the day, and in case there was any confusion, he was willing to straighten it all out for you. But he generally cared about us. At all levels. Whether at home, or at work, or at sea, it didn't matter; he knew us, knew what we were thinking, what we were doing, and what made us tick. And he kicked me in the butt when I needed to be kicked in the butt; he picked me up off the deck when I needed to be picked up off the deck. He did all of the right things, and I can't say enough good about the man.

Master Chief Heinrichs:

My first master chief was Master Chief Charles Inhger. We just buried the man three months ago. Oh, I was the cock of the walk back then. We had a real leadership problem on that ship, there was only one chief in that department, so it was easy for me to rise. And then this new master chief reported aboard. I had never dealt with a master chief before. He was having a conversation in the passageway one day, and I came up and interrupted him. And he fired me, just like that. He said, "Who do you think you are? You're fired, you're now the berthing and head cleaner." And I had never been fired before. That went on for about two weeks, and then we got into a head-to-head conversation, and he hired me back. He took me under his wing, and I made rate with him. He transferred up to Great Lakes and he retired there, and he passed away three months ago after being retired for just three years. But before he retired, his son came aboard this ship as a CPO—he's since transferred. But he was the best person, the best chief, that I ever met. People just swarmed around him. I've stored so many of his characteristics, his one-liners, but I can't do the eye contact the way that he used to do it. He made contact in a way to befriend people; he was tough, but he was the kind of good old country boy that everyone loved.

Senior Chief Perry:

The first chief I ever worked for was a chief radioman named Thorp. I have no idea what his first name was—back then, I don't think chiefs had first names, it was just Chief Thorp. I went aboard USS *Noa* (DD-841) at Mayport, and they said, "Okay, you have the midwatch tonight." I was so green I had to have somebody take me down to show me my rack, to start checking me in. I went on the midwatch, got off watch the next morning, and went and hit my rack. I got up, and found we were floating. We were on our way for a nine-month cruise in the Mediterranean. I went back up to radio, and I said, "Where are we going?" He said, "We are on our way to the Med, and it doesn't make any difference where in the Med to you, because you are going to copy code for three hours straight every day until I think you are ready to sit on a live circuit." And when he talked to you, you listened to him. I guess a lot of the guys didn't understand that he was only trying to teach you something.

Later, there was a guy named Thompson, the same way. Whatever he wanted, he got, and he could chew you out, and after he got done

chewing you out, you would be saying thank-you to him. He just had
that way. He didn't scream and holler, but when the man lowered his
glasses, and looked over the top of his glasses, you had better be moving. You just had it in your mind, you'd better be moving because
something is wrong. He is hunting for someone.

Six

Chiefs and Junior Officers

"Effective chiefs understand the difficult role of the division officer and the problems that can arise in the relationship between Chief Petty Officers and division officers. Chiefs in superior commands are sensitive to this and support and develop the division officer. One way to do this is by suggesting to the division officer what should be done to solve problems. They also tactfully let the division officer know if they think he/she is charging off in the wrong direction."[1]

Many might find it strange that chief petty officers are held responsible for the development of the officers who lead them. In civilian life, juniors rarely are responsible for the growth and training of their superiors. Nonetheless, in the Navy, more so than in the other services, chief petty officers are responsible for the successful introduction of junior officers into the role of command.

Senior Chief Buie:

> Every successful officer, I think, has had a mentor at some point in
> their career. It's usually a senior enlisted person, and they will tell you
> about some chief who took the time and showed them exactly how
> things should be done. Oh, you have some that are successful and have
> forgotten along the way, but successful officers always refer back to
> their chiefs, and they listen. Sometimes you have to yell and scream
> and close the door, but they always listen. They might not take on
> board everything that you say, but they know that in order to function
> they've got to listen.

Chief Oitzman:

> The first thing they need, really, is blind trust in their chief. When they
> come out of the Academy, with whatever they learned there, they have
> to know that regardless of personality quirks, they have to learn from
> their chiefs, and they have to have that blind trust. And you get these
> young guys who come out of flight school and whatnot, and they've
> got the world by the tail. They think they don't need any help getting
> where they are going. But it's the chief petty officer who signs off that
> plane for flight, it's the chief petty officer who makes sure the techni-
> cian is doing it right, it's the chief petty officer who trained the guy on
> the steering wheel at the helm of the ship. They have to know that
> there's foreknowledge. Yeah, and it's a humbling thing for them some-
> times. They've got all that confidence that sometimes falls over into
> arrogance when they come out of their various schools. And when they
> get on board, they realize that they don't have everything all lined up in
> a row. And they also don't understand that they just can't say it, to
> make it happen. They can send all the files and memos and e-mails in
> the world; that's not going to make anything get done. Chiefs make
> things happen.

All chief petty officers know that the final decisions at sea rest with the
commanding officer, delegated through his wardroom. But there is an old
adage, oft repeated: "Officers run the Navy; Chiefs run the ship."

Master Chief Storekeeper (SW) Aloysius Nelson,
Naval Training Center, Great Lakes:

Chiefs used to have a lot more power back ten or fifteen years ago. Leadership has changed. And what I mean by that is not that the chiefs have changed, per se, but the chain of command doesn't let us do what we need to do as CPOs. The chief used to run the ship, and I don't think that's the case right now. Officers get their fingers into things that maybe they shouldn't.

Senior Chief Mess Management Specialist (AW/SW)
Jesus R. Garcia, Naval Training Center, Great Lakes:

Back when I got ready to make chief, there was a big push to get officers to do things that we traditionally thought of as chief's responsibility. And it got to the point where we all said, collectively, "Hey, I don't have the say on anything anymore, so what's the point?" You had officers working on things like liberty policy for E-3 and E-4, and the chiefs were no longer allowed to make those decisions. The XOs wanted to have tighter control, and they worked through the wardroom. The paradigm shifted about fifteen years ago, and it's been a battle to get it pushed back to the other side.

Chief Mess Management Specialist (SS) Darryl Martin,
Naval Training Center, Great Lakes:

Here's a quote I picked up somewhere, and which I carry with me all the time. I even posted it on the bulkhead on my last sub, and the COB and everyone else seemed to appreciate it. "Commissioned officers who want to advance and win the respect of the enlisted Navy follow two principles: 'Chiefs run the Navy,' and 'Smart officers listen to their chiefs.'" Officers run the Navy, true, but we run the ships. And that's a fact.

Senior Chief Aviation Support Equipment Technician (AW)
Tracy Padmore, USS George Washington *(CVN-73):*

I take new officers aside, and, as directly as I can, I tell them the way it is. I say, "Listen, I know you are senior to me, and I have been in the

military long enough to know that if someone in the military gives me
an order, sure, I may discuss it with you, but when the decision is done,
I'm going to follow orders." That's the code we live by. I'm going to let
him know that he's got to attend the division officer meetings, and that
he's going to put out the info that I give him, and he's going to bring
back the info that we need to give to the troops. He's really going to be
a figurehead until he's learned enough from me, to go out there, and
work with the troops and make decisions that he needs to make. See,
lots of these junior officers are twenty or twenty-one years old, and
they are a lot more closely related to my enlisted guys, my airmen and
third-class, than to the first and chiefs. And if they bring that attitude
across, that's not going to fit well into our mission. So I tell him, "Hey,
you're the division officer; you'll attend all the meetings and represent
the division, and I'll support you, but when we discuss things, I'll tell
you how things are, and how they should be. And, if you're smart,
you're going to trust me and go with my opinion, because if you don't,
chances are you might be right, but odds are you might be wrong, too."

There is a story, perhaps apocryphal, recounted by the journalist and
author John Reese, and often circulated by chief petty officers:

Admiral William "Bull" Halsey was being honored in Los Angeles shortly after the
end of World War II. As is Naval tradition, a line of sideboys, all active duty or
retired chief petty officers, lined his path. As Halsey approached one grizzled veteran, the journalist saw them wink at each other. Approached later, Halsey was
asked about the wink. Halsey commented: "That man was my Chief when I was
an Ensign, and no one before or after taught me as much about ships or men as
he did. You civilians don't understand that. You go down to Long Beach, and you
see those battleships sitting there, and you think that they float on the water, don't
you?" The journalist nodded. "You are wrong," replied Halsey, "they are carried to
sea on the backs of those Chief Petty Officers!"[2]

Halsey wasn't the only admiral to recognize the importance of chief
petty officers in the development of his own career. Adm. Mike Boorda, the

most beloved of all CNOs, whose premature and tragic death in 1996 stunned and saddened sailors worldwide, had himself been an enlisted sailor for much of his career. At the commissioning of USS *Chief*, a minesweeper named in honor of all chief petty officers, past and future, Admiral Boorda remarked:

The title Chief raises so many memories for all sailors. Every one of us who has served for any length of time can tell you about his or her special chief, indeed, most of us have more than one—a salty individual who took care of them, who taught them all the important things, who set the example, who cared about them and was not afraid to show it in so many ways. We officers have our special chiefs too. Usually somewhat older than we, always wiser in the ways of the Navy than we could possibly be as we started out on our careers. Ready with advice, with counsel and with the know how to make it happen, to get it done, no matter how difficult. And through it all, those great chiefs were and are also great teachers. They know, as only Chief Petty Officers can know, that getting the job done today is important, but that the task of helping a new officer become a real pro, a true naval officer in the finest sense of the term, is part of the job. It's a key part, a critical role that Chief Petty Officers have been playing for over one hundred years now. Our Navy depends upon them, and the chiefs know that and they thrive on the challenge.

I am a lucky man for I have served as a new seaman, a petty officer and an officer. In each phase of my career a great Chief Petty Officer appeared at just the right time, guiding me, pushing me when necessary, leading me and, when it was appropriate, letting me think I was leading him. There have been many chiefs in my life, all-important, many personal friends, all professionals. And I know, as every sailor knows, that the word leadership and the title Chief Petty Officer go together. You cannot say one without thinking of the other. In war and in peace, they teach, they provide technical expertise and experience, they know how to get the job done and they know how to make all the right things happen. They know that combat readiness is based on taking care of people, on keeping their ship and her requirement ready at all times. But all of that is just a preamble to leadership in war. No chief, no sailor, wants to fight in wars. We want to deter them. But when our nation calls, when the fight is no longer optional, no longer avoidable, but now is required, when "now" is the order of the day, that is when all that Chief Petty Officer leadership—honor, courage and commitment—really pays off. For deep down, each and every Chief Petty Officer knows that we are warriors and that he or she is a leader of warriors as well. In the smoke and fury and, yes, the confusion of battle at sea, it is then that the Chief Petty Officer proves again and again that everything else was simply preparation for the moment of truth. The moment when all that work pays off. When young sailors do what is required, they do it almost instinctively, and they look to the chief for the example of all that is great in our Navy."[3]

Command Master Chief McCalip:

Mike Boorda was the best. People who knew him as an enlisted sailor knew he was squared away, guys who served with him when he was skipper of *Farragut,* people who knew him as chief of naval personnel: he always stopped to have a word with sailors, no matter how busy he was. He was one of us, and if he felt that way about chiefs, well, it's a darn good bet that that's the way it really is—or the way that it really should be.

Master Chief Beldo:

Still, I believe that, in order for the Navy to run the way it does, you need the difference between the managers and the technical experts. We chiefs are the technical experts, but I still need somebody to figure out the numbers and all that stuff, because I have to deal with the technical issues, and with the people. I say, "Sir, you just take care of the money, and get me the parts; you give me the right parts and I'll fix things." I need someone who has been trained to say, "Okay, now's the time to push the button and go to war." And then I need to be the one to say "Okay, sir—roger that—we are going to push the button, but for the button to work, A, B, C, D, E, and F have to be in order." And that's my job, as a senior enlisted person, to be sure that when the button finally gets pushed, something happens.

Senior Chief Gentry:

Young officers need to know what Admiral Mike knew: that there is a respect factor here, and respect is something that has to be earned. If you go out there, and try to force your rank on everybody, and pretend to know things that you really don't understand, there are going to be problems. I once had an LTJG, and I had to tell him, "Hey, I realize that you are an officer, but it's my job to develop these people and carry out this mission, and I'm not going to let you do something stupid. And I do mean stupid, because a lot of times, if you ever decide that you don't want to listen to a senior enlisted guy, then all we have to do is to stop talking to you, and pretty soon you are going to have to fall on your sword. And both of us will look bad to the people that really know how things ought to go, because it will look like we failed to teach you, but you'll learn a valuable lesson." We're out here in a dangerous environment, and I just tell them, "You may be an officer, but you can't buy experience with a piece of paper, or in four years of school."

Master Chief Beldo:

The first thing that I try to get straight is that I understand where I fall on the food chain, and I know where they fall on the food chain, and I would never disrespect their position in the Navy. However, there is an experience level that they have not attained yet, and it's my responsibility to teach them. If they hang on tight and listen to the CPO, he or she will never ever steer them in the wrong direction, or let them hang out there to dry. A good chief will always make sure that you know what you are talking about when you go greet your boss, but you have to listen. But sometimes, they lose focus, but the reality of the situation is that I do know more about this job than they do. And so I tell them, "If you would just listen, you might learn something, and you will in turn become a good commanding officer, and respect your chief petty officers."

Capt. Martin Erdossy, currently commanding officer of the USS *George Washington*, is himself a former enlisted sailor. He sees and appreciates the role of the chief petty officer from many perspectives; from that of an adolescent influenced by CPOs in his community, from the perspective of a young airman, and from the perspective of a test pilot, active aviator, and commanding officer of a nuclear-powered carrier on war patrol off Afghanistan.

Captain Erdossy:

Chief petty officers have played critical roles in my own professional life. I grew up in central Pennsylvania and worked as a mechanic in my dad's garage. I remember a master chief gunner's mate who retired to my hometown. As I worked on his car, I listened to his stories about being all over the world and, well, that got me interested in this way of life and this business. I'd sit at home on Sunday afternoons, watching *Victory at Sea,* but he got me thinking about all of this, about his real-life experience. And then I became attached to a wonderful young lady, whom I later married, and her father had been a Navy chief as well. I had a low draft number back then, so I knew the military was in my future, and he urged me to enlist. I came into the Navy and ever since then, I think back on the fact that a chief petty officer, my father-in-law, really was the single most important person to convince me that this was the way to go. And when I was a young enlisted guy, I was an aviation machinist mate, working on the flight line down in Pensacola. I was working for an aviation machinist's mate who had spent most of his twenty years off the coast of Vietnam; he was one of those special sailors that had crossed decks several times in Hawaii to stay out there where the action was, doing what he loved so much, just working the flight deck. He was the most squared-away guy I've ever seen. He knew about honor, courage, and commitment, and he taught it in a way that I know changed me. He made me realize that I could take advantage of the opportunities the Navy offered, and that was obviously a good choice because I am sitting here today. It was people like him who taught me about accountability and responsibility and all those wonderful qualities that CPOs embody. And that chief was able to accelerate my growth by sharing his sea stories with me. I think that's an important part of the way a chief does business—it's not exactly textbook or chalkboard, it's sharing those sea stories.

Chief Henry:

Sure, we tell them sea stories. Just sit around the mess here sometimes and listen to all the stories that come bubbling out. I tell the junior officers to listen carefully! I still respect their rank, and I don't care if they are on the first day out of the Academy, or the first day out of ROTC. I say to them, "Hey, I can see that the Academy prepared you very well, but you have to pay attention, because the book didn't tell you everything, and the chiefs are going to help you to understand how the system works, and how they fit into the system."

Master Chief Barrett:

Training officers is different than training enlisted. Chiefs have a lot of history; we're the memory of the Navy. There's a lot of tradition, lots of honors and ceremonies, things that we do that the junior officers don't really know yet. They don't understand the whole routine, how the Navy works. Chiefs usually have a pretty good clue how things are going to go or not go. Junior officers who listen to their chiefs and follow the program do well; the ones who fight it have a hard time. Chiefs understand the guys who are actually doing the job, the guys turning the wrenches that are making the ship go. And that makes or breaks those division officers, those enlisted guys that are actually doing the job. Nine times out of ten, they don't have experience dealing with the younger sailors— whether they have problems or where they are going wrong, when they need discipline or when they don't. There is a big learning curve there for them, and they usually understand that right away. I've never had a problem with a junior officer. They usually won't go to their officer community to ask for any assistance or help, and when they do, they usually are told, "Hey, ask your chief. Stick with your chief—he's been there and he's done that, and it will work out fine."

Captain Erdossy:

We've got thirty midshipmen aboard right now for their summer cruise. Most are from ROTC programs; many are first-classmen, ready to graduate, but some are brand-new. I took those thirty young midshipmen, and rather than put them in the wardroom, which is where they probably expected to be, I berthed them in the chiefs quarters and made sure that they had running mates in the chiefs mess. Young officers are young adults too, and while they may be a bit more educated than your standard enlisted recruit, they still need to develop. They need to mature—I don't know if that's the right word, and I don't mean this in any condescending fashion—but they are inexperienced, and the chiefs can provide that for them. They can give them insight, they can give them the words, hopefully in a better way than our dads did to us when they were trying to tell us how to be better young citizens. Chiefs have always looked out for the young officer, and chiefs know that sometime down the road, that officer might be looking out for them. It's a mutual respect that is so important in the development of that young officer. Making sure they know how to do things right, making sure they know what to focus on. I think the chief petty officer is the person to do that.

Master Chief Machinist's Mate (AW/SW)
Bruce McDugald, USS George Washington:
I tell junior officers that the biggest thing is to observe and use common sense and watch what is going on. Almost every chief I've ever worked with is going to go by the book and do the right thing, and I tell him or her to observe that and to take that advice of the chief petty officer. That's one of the things in our Creed: to train and to assist that junior officer, to get them on board. But it's up to them to listen, because I've seen too many times when the young officer didn't want to take advice, and wound up falling on his sword. And some chiefs might let a junior officer do that; it's like, "Hey, if you don't want to listen when I offer advice, well , you're on your own."

Capt. Mark D. Guadagnini, deputy commander of Air Wing Seventeen, is a graduate of the Naval Academy (USNA 1980). While his perspective may differ from Captain Erdossy's, he nevertheless agrees with Erdossy.

Captain Guadagnini:
I've had a number of favorable experiences with chiefs over the years. There are three who stand out most vividly. During Desert Storm, I

was on the USS *Theodore Roosevelt,* and the air crews were flying combat missions around the clock. The officers—the division officers and the department heads—could no longer accomplish all the functions that the officers normally performed because they were so busy. And yet the squadrons didn't falter, they did not miss a beat, indeed, they thrived. And they thrived because of the dedication of the chiefs, who stepped up their participation. The chiefs stepped up their leadership, and it's the chiefs' technical expertise, especially in the areas of maintenance, that is crucial for a squadron. Their technical expertise carried the day; solving some very difficult problems and managing people to get assets combat-ready and maintain them combat-ready. So that was a very telling one for me.

The next one was during my department head tour. Ivan Woods was our command master chief. And, I am proud to say that he became a personal friend, and he has remained a personal friend now for fourteen years. When I was going to start my department head tour, my first major department was as the maintenance officer. He and I sat down together, before I started the job, and he offered me some very sage advice, especially in dealing with the troops. He also reminded me that chiefs could work for you and make this job incredibly successful if you let them. But if you don't let them, you might be successful, but it's going to be a painful experience for you and it's going to be a painful experience for the squadron. I chose to take Master Chief Wood's advice. And our squadron that year won the Battle E for effectiveness; we won every award there was. We even won the Captain's Cup for being the best athletic squad on the base. I believe we won those awards because the squadron was successful, but really, the bottom line was that the personal and professional relationships and the command climate that existed in that squadron were a huge credit to Ivan Woods. It all had to do with the way he ran the chiefs mess and the chiefs in it.

And then my third extremely positive experience was when I worked in the Bureau of Naval Personnel right after my department head tour, and was fortunate to deal with MCPON John Hagan two or three times a week. And seeing what the MCPON does and his relationship to all of the enlisted personnel in the Navy, and his relationship to the senior Navy leadership, really opened my eyes on what chiefs can do. You see, on a long deployment such as we're making now on the *George Washington*, that's where the experienced chiefs really come into play.

I have been relaying that same story to my chief petty officers and telling them they do have a critical role, and information flow is key. Especially from the air crew point of view, there will be many times when, due to the tasking, we just won't have the chance to get down and talk to the guys the way we should and let them know what's going on. So the chiefs take that role, and their communication skills are absolutely key. Another thing that the chiefs do extremely well, and which is very important in combat—and this will be my fourth time in combat—is that they take the plans, whatever those plans might be, and translate them into action. And the final piece of communication that they do very well is translate the importance of what each guy turning a wrench or each guy typing a message is doing. They know intimately every single function which we have here, and they translate the importance of that, and are able to pump the guys up and let them know the success of everybody on the mess decks is critical to our combat success. And that's not a link that can be made without the chief petty officers.

Master Chief Waldrup:

A lot of the officers I deal with are fighter guys, as is Captain Guadagnini. And they are a different breed than most other officers, because they want to be at the same level as you at times, and that's the hardest thing for them, I find. I tell them the one thing you don't want to do is to put yourself at my troops' level, and that there is a definite difference between you and them, and that the petty officers and chiefs need to be used so that the communication flows both up and down the chain. You don't want to be the guy going to that junior enlisted person and saying, "Well, this is the decision." You need to be sure that every level in the chain is covered. Now, there's nothing wrong with the officer being there when it's being said, or even saying it, but you want to be sure that the chief is there when you are doing it, so that you can be sure that he is there when things are being carried out. It's very important to communicate with the chief, just to get to know him, and that's one thing that we are sort of lacking these days. Out on the flight deck, it's critical that the pilots trust the maintenance crew, and that the maintenance crew have absolute trust in what the pilots tell them.

Captain Guadagnini:

If Captain Erdossy asked me to address the midshipmen now on board, I'd remind them that the most important thing to do is to listen. The chiefs may not always frame their ideas in the most eloquent fashion, but they are going to give you the common-sense perspective almost all the time. And they are going to have good ideas, and they are going to have the good ideas the junior officers need to be successful. Now, the junior officers, as they pass things up the chain, might put them into, well, more proper language, if you will—but the chiefs are going to have good ideas, and junior officers need to listen to those ideas that bubble up.

Master Chief Barton:

Right. Education is a glorious thing, and it's a great and noble cause to have that education, but junior officers, when they walk into their division, should not take it for granted that their chief petty officer, their first-class petty officer, and any other sailors in their division are dummies. Many of us have a college education. I have many in my department right now, and they're not dummies; today's sailor is very well educated. Young officers should listen to their chief petty officers and their first-class petty officers and not think that they are God's gift to the U.S. Navy, because their careers, their success, and their failures, hinge on the people who work for them. No matter who told them, or what they think, their career is dependent on the success or failures of the sailors who work for them, through me. Most new officers develop a very quick understanding, especially the new guys from the Academy or just out of college. They understand what side the bread is buttered on. Especially if the master chief petty officer is very respectful of their position. I don't think it has anything to do with my being so much older than they are, but they understand that I have a lot to offer and that I can guide them, help make their career successful.

Capt. Dennis G. Watson, executive officer,
USS *George Washington:*

I think the more you understand the person you are working with— what their frame of reference is, what their goals are, what they are trying to do—the better off you'll be. That's all based on where they've come from, and how they have been trained, and what has been important before in the history of their career. So, if you can understand the person you are working with better, there is a better chance coming to common goals and being able to get there. And I think for a brand-new junior officer showing up on a ship, well, he or she really doesn't understand all of that, and in fact, probably can't be expected to understand that. A chief petty officer is probably the same age as his or her father, and that officer/subordinate relationship is really a pretty complicated thing for a junior officer to work through. But the sooner they can develop that, the better their tour of duty will be.

Seven

Mustangs

At some point in a Navy career, high-potential enlisted personnel such as Captain Erdossy and Admiral Boorda are faced with a critical choice. They may continue through the chief petty officer ranks and strive for senior or master chief status, or they can attempt to "fleet up" to warrant or commissioned officer ranks. The Limited Duty and Chief Warrant Officer Programs provide the Navy with a vital and invaluable form of leadership—officer technical specialists with the expertise and authority to direct the most difficult and exacting technical operations in any skill area. The most popular program develops limited duty officers (LDOs) who continue in their specialized skill areas, but assume much broader responsibility than the average chief petty officer.

Chief Ahmed:

To tell the truth, I have considered fleeting up. In fact, it goes back to training. Where I was initiated there was an old master chief who had been in the Navy for thirty-two years, and he said, "Once you are a chief, you are a chief forever. You are an enlisted man, you are a chief petty officer, and that's what you ought to stay." And I believed that till I came to the *George Washington*. Here, people said to me, "Hey, that was just old poppycock. If you have the potential, if you think you have what it takes, put in an application." So I considered that, and I did put in an application. It is in the rudimentary stages right now. But once again, if you have the potential to go further—to go to the wardroom—I'd say apply for it.

LDO status provides a commissioning path for outstanding E-6s through E-8s and CWOs to perform in management positions that require strong technical backgrounds, but which are outside the normal development pattern of an unrestricted line officer, restricted line officer, or staff corps officer. Of all the services, the Navy provides the greatest opportunity for an enlisted member (generally a first-class petty officer or above) to become a Navy captain (equivalent to full colonel in the other services) and to have an opportunity to serve in command at sea or ashore, depending on the designator, individual qualifications, and billet requirements. However, not every outstanding chief petty officer feels that it's the right decision.

Chief Swain:

I'm not tooting my own horn here, but I've had a lot of good fitness reports and evaluations, and I've had plenty of pressure from department heads, commanding officers, and executive officers to fleet up. Particularly in the smaller commands, where you really stand out and become, say, Sailor of the Year—then they really push that. But, honestly, I cannot think of a better rate in the Navy, a better job than to be the chief. I'm right out there every day. If you go LDO or warrant, you can't help but get separated a little bit from your people. And maybe it's just me, but I feel that where I am right now, I can best serve by being there, to take care of my people every day. Right in the niche I'm in.

Chief Grodski:

I considered it for about four years. In fact, I considered it the whole time I was a first-class, and the first year I put on chief. But that's not what I want to do now when I get up in the morning. And I think I would lose the contact I have with the blueshirts. As frustrating as it is sometimes, just by virtue of putting on that officer's collar device as an LDO or a warrant, you're going to lose people. And I don't want that. And I don't want to give up the camaraderie. I don't think wardroom has anything like what we have down here, in terms of camaraderie.

Command Master Chief (SS) John Kidwell,
Naval Training Center, Great Lakes:

I don't want to sound negative, but sometimes I look at it this way: A chief is usually a guy who wants to take care of his people. I look at LDOs and warrants—not all of them, but some of them—as guys who are, maybe, just a little more interested in taking care of themselves. When a chief steps on a ship, he has a job, when an officer steps aboard, they have to find him or her a job. Some of the people who were the toughest on me, the ones I respected the most when I was coming up, were the master chiefs, not the officers. And I wanted then, and I want now, to be as much like them as I can.

Both Chief Swain and Chief Grodski were well qualified when they considered, but rejected, the possibility of accepting a commission. And a surprising number of chief petty officers feel the same as CMC Kidwell. But others feel differently. The minimum requirements for a service member who is a U.S. citizen, with a high-school diploma or GED, and who seeks a limited duty commission in the Navy are as follows:[1]

Must meet or exceed current physical standards
Must be recommended by commanding officer
Must have an exemplary disciplinary record
Must have at least eight, but not more than sixteen, years
    of active naval service, although there are no age restrictions
Must have at least one year's service in present rating

Perhaps surprisingly, the requirements for promotion to warrant officer (a position junior to a limited duty commissioned officer) are somewhat more stringent. For example, the commissioned warrant officer grade is open only to chief petty officers, unlike LDO, where a highly qualified or motivated petty officer first-class is encouraged to apply. This is generally considered to be a path for very motivated chief petty officers who will possess the same authority as any other commissioned officer, but generally who have slightly lower levels of academic achievement than those who strive for LDO commissions. Warrant and chief warrant officers are well qualified by extensive technical training, experience, and leadership in a specific occupational field, and are considered a major asset to any command, where they serve primarily as division officers and officers in charge.

For chief petty officers, the requirements for warrant officer are similar to those for limited duty officers, with the following exceptions:

Must have at least twelve but not more than twenty-four
    years of active service
Must be serving as a chief, senior chief, or master chief petty officer

It is interesting and useful to compare the average characteristics of newly appointed limited duty officers and warrant officers. These are the figures for Fiscal Year 2001, the last year for which definitive statistics are available:

	LDO	CWO
Age	33	38
Total years of active service	13	17
Average rank	E-7	E-7
Average years of total education completed	14–15	14–15
Warfare-qualified	Yes	Yes
Average personal awards (NCM/NAM/FLOC)	4	5
Former unit SOQ/SOY	Yes	Yes
Average total number of duty stations	4	6

	LDO	CWO
Prior Recruiting/RTC/ Instructor tours:	Yes	20%
Average number of sea/overseas tours completed:	2	3
Average total number of correspondence courses not related to advancement	7	7
Average number of training schools completed	7	12
Average sustained performance trait	EP	EP

When interviewed, most former chief petty officers who have chosen to "go up through the hawse pipe" list several reasons for their decision, including more challenging assignments and greater responsibility, greater authority and accountability, and a sense of personal pride in having achieved something that many desire, but relatively few obtain. Many also speak of improved quality of life for themselves and their families, and the ability to be seen as "an officer and a gentleman," after overcoming earlier deficiencies in their formal education. The LDO and Warrant Programs continue to be two of the very few routes to an officer's commission available to those without a college degree.

Lt. Wanda S. Peacock (ACC), USS George Washington *(CVN-73):*
I decided to go the limited duty route for two reasons. First, I joined the Navy at thirty-one, and when I joined I had two goals in mind, and one was to become an officer, and I wanted to get my master's degree. Second, my father is a retired chief yeoman with over twenty-three years of service, and, knowing about the Navy, I felt I could do more for a larger group of folks as an officer than as a chief. Now, if I had that decision to make over again, would I do it? I really don't know—because I think now that I would have made senior chief, and probably

master chief. Seeing the different fields that master chiefs can lead these days, well, I might have been able to do something at AIRLANT or AIRPAC, and still have helped a large number of folks.

Ensign Elton Potts (PRC), USS George Washington:

My main consideration was my family. There's no doubt that the retirement benefits are better, and I've always been taught about upward mobility, to go as far as you can. My first goal was to make chief, and I did that as a PRC, and then I put my LDO package in. But I was a chief already when I was selected for limited duty officer. Now, when you make chief, everybody stops to say hello to you—they notice you when you make chief. I was an aviation survival equipment specialist—a parachute rigger in the vernacular, I guess—and riggers are a small community. You are listened to more as a chief; there is more authority in the chief. People automatically believe in you, like the household term "ask the chief." Sure, you might give the same answer you would have given when you were a first-class petty officer, but it sounds better coming out of the chief's mouth. So I really enjoyed being a chief, I surely did.

Lieutenant Peacock:

Well, when I fleeted up to ensign, I realized that the buck stops here, so it's a little scary. Where do you go for all the answers? I fell back on my chiefs' experience in networking. I'd pick up the phone and call a fellow division officer, and I'd say, "This is what I have, what would you do?" So I relied on the chief experience I had when I became an ensign if I had a doubt as to what to do.

When others see your ensign bars, they don't know how you got there. So if they see the bar and think that you are an Academy type, then you are very young, you've not experienced the world, you're probably very immature, and you're not going to get a great deal of respect. In that sense, being an ensign is a lot like being an E-1 or an E-2. But once they find out that you are a mustang, now you have a lot more respect, because they know that you have been a chief, and that you have a lot of experience.

Ensign Potts:

Well, for me, going from the chief's anchor to the "butter bar" wasn't a major change in the respect I got. I had eleven years' enlisted service, and about two of those were as a chief petty officer. So they can tell from this stack of ribbons on my chest that I must have been at least a first-class petty officer and, judging by the ribbons, how old I must be. Most chiefs will ask you, flat out, if you have ever been a chief. But, to tell you the truth, I think I got a little more respect as a chief than I do as an ensign.

Lieutenant Peacock:

Well, it does get better as you go up the officer chain, too. But I miss that camaraderie of the goatlocker, definitely. I don't think people in the wardroom are as close as they are in the chiefs mess. I don't think they take the time to get to know the other person as easily as chiefs do. It usually is a little more formal, it's just a bit different.

Ensign Potts:

Today I was talking to a guy who was getting commissioned. One of the things that I miss is being able to walk into the CPO mess and say whatever I want to say. It's a little stuffier where I am now—not quite the same demeanor in the wardroom as in the chiefs mess, sometimes. It's more formal, but the table I sit at is all limited duty officers, it seems. So we're the loud ones down there. They have to put up with us. But we do get along well together; a lot of the junior officers will sit over with the LDOs. They like to listen to our sea stories. We try to stay away from talking about work all the time, but we tend to talk more about things with the junior officers. We talk about things they need to think about regarding their careers and so on, because they are just starting out, and they are a lot like our junior enlisted in that way. We try to give them some idea of how the Navy really works.

Lieutenant Peacock:

I've only been in two wardrooms, and I haven't sensed any segregation or separateness between the mustangs and those who arrived through other sources. They may rely on you a bit more, though, because they know that when you say you're going to do something, you will get the job done.

Sometimes you need to remind the junior officers that they have to work through their chief. The chief needs to be right there with them, they are basically in charge, you work through the chief to the troops. You can't manage the division if you cut the chief out of the loop—I guarantee you won't be able to do that as an officer. Those troops are going to that chief for everything, and the sooner the officer learns to rely on the chief, the better off we will be. That's what we are here for—we're the backbone of the Navy. And that's so very true. Oops! Did I just say *we*? [laughing]

Ensign Potts:

Well, there's definitely a transition period, and in some ways I'm still trying to get used to it. I've just been commissioned for less than a year. And in a way, you are on the outside now, looking in, because the chiefs are taking care of business, as they should. Sometimes I have to ask what's going on. Now, it's not like they are trying to keep things from me, but they handle things at their level very well, and it doesn't have to rise to my level. Eight months ago I was doing the exactly the same thing, so I understand. But they pass on what the division officer needs to know.

Lieutenant Peacock:

As far as the transition goes, the hardest part for me, for a while, was recognizing the name "Ensign" when being called! And being on the bottom of the totem pole again was compounded a bit, I think, by being a female. I'm in a year group where there's a lot of retirement, and a lot of the folks moving in were not particularly comfortable working with a female ensign, until they find out that you are an limited duty officer, and you've been a chief for several years. We were back to that whole thing: "Oh, she's female, and an ensign, and what could she know about anything?" But that's the advantage of having been a chief petty officer. It gives you credibility, and that was part of my inbrief when I arrived here. I have seventeen years in air traffic control, four years of which were as a chief. I sat in that seat, I understand what you are going through, and if you have a problem, let me know.

Off duty, there really wasn't much immediate impact on my family. Others have a lot more dislocation—moving from enlisted to officer housing or whatever. But my family was very proud of me, of course. My dad, who's a retired chief, was supportive of me when I made the change. But in terms of immediate family impact, not much. I wasn't in base housing, I was living in town, so that wasn't a factor for me.

Ensign Potts:

I actually am still living in enlisted housing, but I'm the senior person in there now, so they look to me to fix everything. But not much else really changed, except that my wife now gets saluted when she drives through the gate, and she really enjoys that. But, then, she liked being a chief's wife, too; it doesn't matter very much if it's the chiefs' wives or the officers' wives, especially when the ship is at sea; the wives are always a close-knit bunch.

Lieutenant Peacock:

If someone asked me which way to go, whether to stay enlisted and try for senior or master chief, or go LDO, I would try to show the advantages of both. But I'd be clear that only he or she could make that decision. I had a female chief who transferred here a while ago. Last year she put in an LDO package, this year she didn't. The week we pulled back in, she got a call that she was picked up for LDO—she's now at North Island—and she had to make the decision. She had just put on chief a while ago, and we had been friends since we were second-class petty officers together, but I really couldn't do anything but say, "Well, you have to go through the checklist of pros and cons and determine what's really best for you." Each person may see things differently.

Ensign Potts:

In the end, the person has to know what they want to do. I can give them the benefits of both sides, what they can expect as a junior chief, say, and as an officer, how it's going to be. But the decision lies with the member, and only they can make the decision for themselves. But as for me, yes, I would do it again. I was limited as to how fast I could advance because in the small rating community I came from, they were only rating one PR master chief a year, and I wanted to move a little faster. There are only about ninety chiefs, and about forty-five senior chiefs in the PR ranks. Here, as an officer, the opportunities are much greater.

Unspoken, but very real, are the benefits of improved pay and retirement programs that prevail in the officer corps. A first-class petty officer who fleets up to ensign at the ten-year career point, will receive at least $750 more in average compensation each month, and housing and living allowances will also increase. A chief petty officer, making the same transition at the twelve-year career point, can expect to see at least $500 more in her paycheck. And master chief petty officers who are directly commissioned at the CWO-3 level and remain on active duty for a full thirty years may expect nearly $100,000 in increased compensation over the remainder of their career.

Understandably, tensions can arise between junior officers who have "been there, done that" as chief petty officers, and incumbents remaining in the mess. While most relationships are smooth and easy-running, there are times when the inevitable question of positional authority versus professional competence, or even pride in position, comes into play.

Chief Helderman:

It's usually easier with a guy who has at least been a chief for a while, if he fleets up to warrant or LDO. You don't have to teach him the day-to-day routine of being in the Navy, as you would have to with most junior officers. But sometimes you have to get a message across to those who don't quite understand where the limits are. There are a couple of different ways to do that. One is, you tell him, "If you want to be the chief, I'll go sit in the mess, and you be the chief again." Because he can't go in the mess. Another way is, you kind of sidestep him, and try to pull him along a bit. When a chief starts sidestepping a division officer, somebody is going to open their eyes. Is the chief going to get a little sore from that? Possibly, but if it brings the division officer closer to the officer community, then it has been a success.

Master Chief Machinist's Mate McDugald:

Well, as Chief Helderman says, it all depends on the person. I've had some who were an absolute pleasure to work with who were previous enlisted—our commanding officer here on the *George Washington* was an enlisted guy once—and I've had some who didn't want to listen to you because they were a former chief, and they figure that you only know what they knew, so it depends on the personality. I had a couple, though, who were really great, and, a couple warrants who were a bit more difficult to get along with. When that happens, sooner or later, one of you is going to get disengaged, and then there will be trouble.

Master Chief Barrett:

I really do think it is harder to work with an LDO or warrant, sometimes, than with someone who came by another route. Ninety percent of our warrants and LDOs still want to be the chief. The chain of command gets kind of muddled at the top there, because they want to give direction, they want to give out job assignments, they want to do a lot of things that the chief should be doing. It's more of a problem on large-deck ships; aircraft carriers, like this one, have plenty of LDOs and warrants. They are all good people, they are all professional, but then again, most of the chiefs are pretty good, too. But it can get muddled up a little unless the chief and his officer have come to an understanding of who is going to do what.

Senior Chief Perry:

Sure they can be more demanding, but overall it's better to have an LDO for a boss, it really is. Because a limited duty officer better understands where you are coming from when you try to talk, say, radioman talk. And they understand what you are saying to them. Sometimes, if they are new, you have to step down and say, "Well, sir, let's back up a minute, this is how the system works." But when you say "system" to an LDO, he understands right off the bat, so he is considerably ahead of the game right there. But every now and again, it can be worse, much worse, too.

I once had an ensign who had been an RM1. He went LDO. We were on the USS *America,* and he was the radio officer. When I first made chief, my job was to run the message center, so I got together with the first-class petty officers and I said, "This is how I want it set up." So I set it up like that. I'd go down to my rack at night, come back up the next day, and it would be changed around. And I would jump on the first-classes and say, "Hey, I thought I told you guys to set it up a certain way," and they came back and said, "Chief, the ensign changed it." So I said, "Okay, well, change it back." And then he changed it back. And all day long, nothing was said. I got up the next day, came in to work—and it is changed back. So I said to myself, Enough of this; I'm not going to keep doing this every day. And I walked into the ensign's office and said, "Sir, apparently you and I have a communication problem here. I'm trying to set up the message center in there, so traffic flows easier." He reached up and grabbed hold of his shoulders and his butter bar, and said, "I wear the gold around here." So I looked at him and I said, "Well, sir, I guess I don't have a job." And he said, "That's right—you don't have a job." I said then, "Well, if you need me, sir, I'll be down in the chiefs' mess," and I walked out.

I stayed down in the chiefs' mess for about two days and didn't go up to radio. I called in, talked to the first-classes, and they said, "Chief, he is hosing it, he is really hosing up bad." I said, "He told me I didn't have a job, so good luck, and talk to the ensign if you need anything." Well, I sat down in mess one morning drinking a cup of coffee, and a first-class came down and said, "Chief, the ensign wants to see you right now, he needs to see you." So I walked topside, went into radio and said, "Yes, sir?" He said, "I need the 3M report, the department head needs it, and they needed it yesterday, where is it? Where did you put it?" I said, "Give me two minutes, sir." I walked back to my office, turned on my computer, unlocked it, and turned out the 3M report in about three minutes, just as any chief radioman would do. I walked back in, put it on his desk, and said, "There." Everything was back on my computer, I had things set up, just as any communications supervisor would, and that was exactly what I was trying to do in the message center, too. He said to me, "Well, while you're here, we've got this missing, and that's missing, and this is hosed up and . . ." And I said, "Do I have the job back, sir?" He said, "You have the job back, oh yeah, you have the job back." I said, "Well, sir, that's all I ever wanted." And by the time we parted company, he was a pretty good communications officer. But sometimes it's a little rocky.

You see, my job was to make this guy a lieutenant j.g. It's as simple as that—no ifs, ands, or buts about it. And he kind of stepped back then and let the chief run things. But he doesn't need to get in there, and he didn't want to point the finger and say, "You do this and you do that." He wanted to get in there and actually do it. And as a radio officer, as an officer, you shouldn't have to do that. That's what you've got chiefs for. "Chief, I need this, I need that." All you have to do is ask, that's what chiefs are there for.

Unfortunately, not every chief petty officer who fleets up is happy with the change of station. Retired Master Chief Machinist's Mate (SS) Greg Peterman operates *The Goatlocker,* a very popular Internet site frequented by active-duty and retired chief petty officers. One former chief petty officer, who accepted appointment as a warrant officer, now looks back on his decision, and has granted me permission to quote from a message he posted on the site. He has asked—for reasons which will become obvious—that his name not be used in this context.

I screwed up back in 1998 and traded in my anchors for what I thought would be a good deal and put on warrant. Now that several years have gone by and I have been totally screwed over by my last CO, I'm faced with the end of my career cut short by taking warrant in the first place. I have serious regrets about leaving the mess and I want to share this with all the CPOs out there who may have any inclination toward becoming an officer. Here's my warning, take it for what it's worth.

First of all, remember that if you take a commission as a warrant, you must be competitive to be promoted, unlike LDOs who just need to be breathing to be promoted. Why is this important? Because you only get one shot at promotion. When you come "into zone" after being commissioned for three years, the bureau will tell you that the promotion opportunities are roughly 95 percent for

W-3 and 90 percent for W-4. What the bureau won't tell you is that some designators will be promoted at 100 percent and others will be promoted at 75 percent, it all depends on which designators are undermanned, but overall the average will be around what they've advertised. So you may think you've got a good chance at promotion, but it may not be so.

If you don't get promoted while "in zone," your chances of being promoted "above zone" drop to almost zero. Again, the bureau will advertise that it's around 25 percent above zone, but once you miss the one and only chance for promotion "in zone," you might as well start updating your resume.

When I took this commission, I had delusions that I'd be able to make a greater contribution to the Navy. Boy, was I wrong. I landed in one of the "1 of 5" wardrooms out there that are completely dysfunctional. They warned us at "knife and fork" school that there are wardrooms out there that will virtually destroy your career before it even gets off the ground, and they were right. I started out okay, but I eventually told the truth (meaning I didn't toe the CO's political line), and the CO took against me and messed up my fitness report. Nothing really bad, dropped a few grades, but that's all it took to ruin any chances I had for promotion.

One of the most admirable qualities of any good CPO mess is the esprit de corps and teamwork. In the wardroom it's typically every man for himself. The backstabbing that went on defied description. And as a warrant, you are already an outsider to start, the rest of the college and Academy boys won't think twice about squashing you to make themselves look good in front of the old man. I was miserable most of the time, there was no joy in being an officer, sure I got to drive the ship, got OOD under way and SWO qualified, but we also had CPOs doing the same thing and they got much more respect from the CO as a result.

My parting words to you fine chiefs is that if you are happy being a chief, then stay in the mess. If you have political aspirations and think you can handle the bullshit of being an officer, then to you I say good luck. Just remember that I was a chief once, very happy and content in the mess, and now I am a miserable warrant being forced to retire because I didn't get promoted. Remember the old slogan "Move up—not out—stay Navy"? Well, in the officer world it's "Move out—not up—leave Navy." Good luck and stay in the mess; that way you won't have to write a message like this someday![2]

Master Chief Quartermaster (SW) Martha Kastler,
Naval Training Center, Great Lakes:

In the mess, we're a team, we're a family. We do things together because we want to. In the wardroom, it's all mandatory—spouse and officer go to functions because they have to. And I don't want to be in that situation.

Command Master Chief McCalip:

Vice Adm. Henry Chiles asked me one time what it would take for me to decide to become an officer. At the time, I was a chief. And at that point, I absolutely thought I would never become a senior chief, and certainly never be a master chief. I had a great sailor job, and had a huge impact on sailors. But to be honest, I was right on that edge—it's kind of like when you talk to MCPON Bob Walker, who was right there on the edge of going warrant officer, because that was the only advancement available back then. And right before he had to decide, they developed the senior chief and master chief rates, and he decided that he would try that route. And he wound up as our third Master Chief Petty Officer of the Navy. So, right at my decision point, I made senior chief.

When I made senior chief, I knew then that I would become chief of the boat on a nuclear submarine, and I knew that someday I would be a CMC, and I knew that the doors were opening for senior enlisted every day. And, realistically, I knew that there were lots of LDOs out there, and that they tend to fall in the officer rank structure somewhere, well, kind of at the bottom of the wardroom. Now, don't get me wrong—they bring a very important and valuable level of experience to the wardroom, and that's something the wardroom really needs, from young officers to even department heads sometimes. But what I said to Admiral Chiles was this: "We do need some top chiefs to become LDOs and CWOs. But we need our absolute best CPOs to stay in the enlisted ranks to become CMCs and COBs. They need to be focused on giving back to the enlisted community, relaying the lessons learned, the tradition, the heritage; building sailors. That's what we need the best in our chiefs mess to do.

So, it came to the point where he was staring me in the eye, and I took a chance and said what was really in my heart. I said, "Sir, we can let our second-best go be LDOs and CWOs, but we have got to encourage our best to be CMCs or we are never going to grow. We are never going to really close that gap between the wardroom and the chiefs mess, and become a better team." I'm not sure if that scared him, or if he liked that answer very much, but he shook my hand, and said, "Well, if that's how you feel, fine, now where do you want to be COB?" I responded, "Any fast attack submarine that is going to sea." A couple of months later, I was the COB of the USS *Boise* (SSN-764).

ITCS (SW) Chuck Perry and ITCM (AW/SW) Ben Barrett, USS *George Washington* (CVN-73)

MACM (SW) Gregory Ciaccio

MAC (AW/SW) Will Scheer

The author aboard USS *George Washington* (CVN-73), somewhere between Norfolk, Virginia, and Crete, Greece

BMCM (AW/SW) Bob Heinrichs, USS *George Washington*

CMDCM Mike Sanchez, Navy Helicopter Squadron Fifteen

HMCS (AW/SW) Larry Gilbert

DCC (SW) Terry Wylie

ABHCS Mike Genry, USS *George Washington*

AOCM (AW/SW) Carl Barton, USS *George Washington*

SKCM (AW/SW) Antonio Decana, USS *George Washington*

NCCS (AW/SW/SCW) Dolores Buie, USS *George Washington*

ASCS (AW/SW) Tracy Padmore, USS *George Washington*

ATC (AW) Julie Grodski and ATC (AW/SW) Eric Oitzman

ETC (AW/SW) Doug Helderman

Chief Journalist (SW) Luis Luque

ICC (AW/SW) Kevin Henry

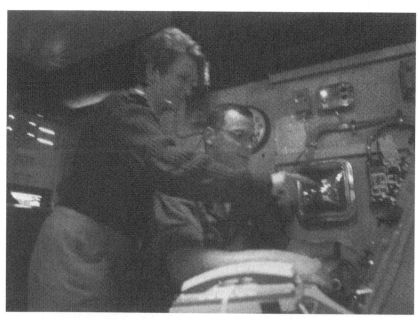

ACC (AW/SW) Leslee McPherson

FCC (AW/SW) S. "Mario" Ahmed

HMC (AW/SW) Tiburcio Estampador

RPC (AW/SW) Donna Norman

ATCS (AW/SW) Mark Raab

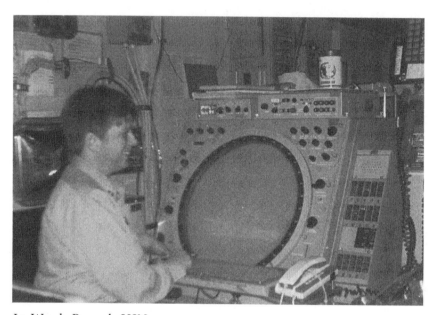

Lt. Wanda Peacock, USN

MMCM (AW/SW) Bruce McDugald

ITC (AW/SW) Mary Williams and SMC (AW/SW) Mike Swain

AZCM (AW/SW) April Beldo

CDMCM (AW/SW/SCW) Scott Benning, Carrier Air Wing Seventeen, and
CDMCM Mike McCalip (AW/SS/SW/PJ), USS *George Washington*

Capt. Dennis G. Watson, USN, executive officer, USS *George Washington,*
the author, Capt. Martin Erdrossy, USN, and CMC Mike McCalip

Scott Benning, the author, and Mike McCalip in Chania, Crete, Greece

Commonwealth War Graves Commission Cemetery, Chania, Crete, Greece

The author with MCPON Terry Scott, Washington, D.C.

Eight

Then and Now

In many ways, today's Navy is not much different from the Navy of twelve, twenty, or two hundred years ago. Sailors still go to sea; families are left behind on the pier; ships still go into harm's way. While new mottoes may replace old ("Forward from the sea" sounds modern and current, but what else did Halsey and Nimitz do but control the littorals and project the nation's strengths across the beachheads at Tarawa, Iwo Jima, and Okinawa?), the Navy sails on. Change, great and small, has always been a constant in sailors' lives.

As one example, the Navy has recently placed increased emphasis on physical fitness. Tight standards are published and enforced; the era of two-for-one happy hours has ended at most service clubs; smoking is restricted to very limited areas aboard ships and stations. Indeed, at some commands, such as Recruit Training Command, Great Lakes, smoking is prohibited anywhere on base, even within privately owned vehicles. Other changes are even more apparent. Since the mid-1990s male and female sailors serve side by side on all surface vessels. There has been a marked increase in authority and respect granted to enlisted members. Long gone are the days of "Officers and their ladies, sailors and their wives," or "Sailors and dogs, keep off the grass."

With change has come resistance and controversy. Many prophets of doom warned of rocks and shoals ahead, grumbling in the 1970s that "Admiral Zumwalt is ruining the Navy," or nodding sadly in the 1990s that "Admiral Boorda will ruin everything we've built." Many predicted that women would never succeed afloat, and held that their presence on combat ships would ruin morale. And some august chief petty officers, mostly retired, grumbled that elimination of the sophomoric pranks, hazing, and humiliation that were hallmarks of initiation would terminally weaken the ranks of chief petty officers, evidently believing that somehow, the ability to drink to senselessness was part of the essence of "chiefness." And yet the Navy sails on.

Many feel that the key to successful change has been the attention paid to the level of job satisfaction felt by sailors. In an all-volunteer military, successful recruiting is only part of the manning strategy; sailors, many of whom have been extensively and expensively trained, must choose to remain on active duty. Retention levels have varied over the years, but when viewed in the harsh light of cost-effectiveness, low retention levels in critical skills were, and continue to be, a drain on scant resources. Beginning in 1970 Admiral Zumwalt forced commanders and senior petty officers to confront the reasons for the demeaning and often humiliating requirements mindlessly laid upon sailors. He challenged the fleet's perception that obedience and good order had to be enforced from above, and argued that internally driven motivation was a much more powerful force for order and discipline upon ships.

Some stability returned by the end of the 1970s, although retention levels still were a matter of concern. A decade later, the Navy had embraced "Pride and Professionalism," and long-established traditions, including the bell-bottom uniforms, were reintroduced. Senior leaders realized that additional steps to develop the Navy's cadre of senior enlisted leaders were warranted, and in 1981 the Senior Enlisted Academy was established at Newport, Rhode Island. There, senior and master chief petty officers were exposed to modern leadership concepts, and the revitalized cadre of senior enlisted returned to the fleet to vigorously enforce traditional uniform and grooming standards, as well as to reintroduce concepts of naval heritage that had lain dormant during the Vietnam era. Quality-of-life programs at sea and ashore were instituted and funded, signaling again the Navy's interest in the well-being of its sailors. Pay and compensation, long a sore point and a major disincentive toward reenlistment, were adjusted, with improved housing benefits and sea pay improvements. Sailors began to "homeport" in a single geographical area, eliminating the expensive, disruptive, and often unnecessary moves from coast to coast. Ship and squadron deployment schedules were rationalized, giving most members a chance to spend more time with families. Reenlistment rates soared from fewer than 5 percent of first-termers during the darkest days of the Vietnam War to 58.7 percent in Fiscal Year 2002. The Navy was ready for the challenges of Desert Shield, Dessert Storm, and activities in support of U.S. commitments in Somalia, Bosnia, Afghanistan, Iraq, and elsewhere. "The superb performance of our people and our systems in Operations Desert Shield and Dessert Storm validates the decisions made by our predecessors," reported Adm. Frank Kelso in an article in the *Naval Institute Proceedings.* "Today, there is no better military organization in the world than the United States Navy."

Every chief petty officer recognizes that today's Navy differs from the Navy of the past—even the recent past, when many of these chiefs were "on the deckplates" themselves. Some see the change as good, others as not so good, but all recognize that change, inevitable as it is, has had an impact on their lives. One of the most striking changes is in the educational level of new recruits.

Master Chief Waldrup:

The biggest difference, I feel, is that sailors are a lot smarter now, a lot better educated. But once some time goes by, the stuff they learned in boot camp fades away, and the standards and discipline go away a lot faster. I know that when I came in, if I was talking to the first-class, I was in trouble. I was working for second- and third-class petty officers, so there's been a significant change in authority levels over the years. Now, you may be working for a first-class, and he or she may be your first point of contact, and your chief is second point of contact, and that's the first real level of authority you have these days. But for those new guys coming in, I really do think they have about the same mentality as I had when I came in, but you lose them quickly, and their performance starts to degrade. Sure, there are many you get who are outstanding, respectful, intelligent, with good initiative—all those good qualities—but then there are the others, too. I don't know if it's the computer games and whatever that they are into now—they seem to have plenty of time for that—but you don't find them hitting the books for their exams and qualifications as they used to.

Chief Scheer:

When I joined in 1987, well, we might not have been quite as mentally prepared as today's sailors. But I'm not all that sure that is a bad thing, anyway. Back then, I think, there was good order and discipline, and a whole lot more respect to our senior people—not just to chiefs, but to all petty officers. I'm amazed, standing at mast each week, to hear what these sailors have said to their petty officers. Things that would have been unheard-of back when I joined the Navy. And I think the work ethic has changed, too. You don't see hard workers quite the way you used to; these kids come in and they've got all the answers to everything.

Senior Chief Gilbert:

Sure, the type of kids that we are getting in the Navy are smarter than we were. They are less gullible than we were. And I think the frustration in the mess is—and we often sit around and talk about this—that these kids today really are different than we were. For one thing, they just don't listen. And when things don't happen the way they should, then they get frustrated. In our day, a petty officer would walk up to you and say, "Sailor, I need you to do so and so." And we would do it. These kids today question, "But why do I have to do it?" Back in our day, it was "Because I said so." Nowadays we try and communicate more and talk to them. But there's no doubt about it—not that we were dumb back when I came in—these kids are lots smarter in some ways than we were.

In addition to the increased level of education and intellectual capabilities of sailors noted by almost every chief petty officer interviewed for this book, significant and worrisome changes have taken place in attitudes toward authority, customs, traditions, and even the Navy itself.

Master Chief Waldrup:

I honestly think that one of the big problems we have today is the way we advertise the Navy. When I came in, the ads used to say, "The Navy wants you." And that's about all they said. "We want you, we need you." But today we promise them college, and money for school, and whatever, and I don't necessarily think we should be using that as the selling point to get people in the service. I think that we ought to be selling service to the country, that sort of thing, rather than making promises of what will happen afterward. This isn't a scholarship program, it's not a travel program, it's not a way to get away from mom and dad. It's the Navy.

Senior Chief Gentry:

There's no doubt in my mind that attitudes have definitely changed. Now, I suspect that when my first chief saw me coming across the brow, he shook his head too and said, "My God, what is the Navy coming to?" And sometimes I say that about today's sailor, myself. But I think that one thing you don't find nearly as much today is the respect for rank, as well as the better work ethic. We were doers by necessity, and now they aren't doers nearly as much. They want and need to be challenged, and even though they are much better academically than we were, that lack of respect is there, and we were a lot more hands-on about things than they are.

Chief Martin:

A lot has changed since I was a junior sailor. If my chief was around at all, then things were going wrong. Now we always have to be around, whether something is wrong or everything is all right. If we are not seen, then we are not working, at least in the minds of some people. I think that now we have to be much more visible and proactive within a division or department to make things run more smoothly.

Command Master Chief Hickman:

There have been extreme changes. There is not nearly as much pride in oneself. It's a different generation, whether we call it Generation X, Y, Z, or whatever, but it all goes back to pride. There is more of a tendency to be concerned about looking cool, acting cool, instead of doing what's right. And a lot of that is upbringing. The generation of parents that came after my own parents brought up their children differently. Now, I may be extreme: I am the son of a Navy chief myself, so I was brought up with core values, long before we classified them as core values. The generation after my parents did not instill those values to the extent that the earlier families did. Some may have, but the majority of them did not.

Master Chief Barton:

I think that our sailors nowadays, while willing to do the job and wanting to do the job, want the satisfaction of "right now." "I want what I want, and I want it now." They are tremendously impatient. They are willing to do the job, and want to do the job, but they cannot see down the road. So we have to work with them a lot and say, "Before you can walk, you have to crawl to get where you need to." And we were easier to guide, I think; I remember when I came in, if my chief said something, you did it. But that may have been because I lived under more dictatorship back home on the farm than a lot of these kids did. Now, we have good education and training programs on the flight deck, don't get me wrong. It's just that the sailors are impatient, and if there's one thing you can't be up on the roof, it's impatient, because people get killed that way. Often enough, we have to stop and tell them, "This is where you are heading, this is where you want to go, this is what you have to do to get there."

I find, myself, that we are handholding the sailor a heck of a lot more nowadays than when I came in. I had to go find out what it took to make grade, I had to find out what correspondence courses I had to do to make rate.

If there is one characteristic immediately visible when crossing the brow of a modern warship, it is the diversity of the crew. You'll find young and old, black and white, Anglo and Hispanic, and newly naturalized citizens from dozens of countries. Ten percent of recruits lack high-school diplomas, yet the number of enlisted personnel with college degrees, or sometimes even graduate degrees, has never been higher.

Senior Chief Information Technician (AW/SW)
Adriana Lewis, Naval Training Center, Great Lakes:
> I came in with a college degree. And there are lots more people that are coming in with degrees, and we keep working on things, and we wind up with master's degrees. But, really, a lot of people, I think, do that for their own personal satisfaction and accomplishment, and not necessarily as a route to advancement.

There is danger in assuming homogeneity among chief petty officers as well. The same demographics, smoothed somewhat to account for the age of the participants, operate at this level, too. But there are some common threads that most exhibit when interviewed about their reaction to today's military.

Senior Chief Buie:
> The way that chiefs respond, I think, depends on the individual. For me, I have managed to balance it out, I have adjusted and adapted. And it's not hard, really. It's hard if you go against the grain though, if you don't adjust to the environment around you. I tell everyone, you can be a product of your environment, or you can choose to excel. It's tough just being in any job, and maybe the military is a bit harder, to tell the truth. But it doesn't make any difference who you are, a service member, a chief petty officer, whatever, you have to adjust to this new Navy. That's what I call it and that's what it is. Is it a bad Navy? No. It's like

anything else, wherever it is, that's where you are. There is always constant change. If you choose to change along with it, it will not be hard. You have to adjust as you go along. If you are dealing with young sailors, you have to know the lingo, you have to know the slang and you have to talk to them continuously. If you have children their age, that makes a difference.

But if you keep that dinosaur mentality—and I say that because we've got some dinosaurs in every mess—if you say, "I'm not going to change, the Navy will change, I will remain the same," then you will not do well, and it's time for you to go home. The only thing you are hurting is the service member and yourself. Because you can't deal with them, just because their parents failed them, or they were raised in a different environment or whatever, you can't hold that against them. You have to be willing to change and adapt to help them out.

Senior Chief Gilbert:

When sailors come to me, or I walk into a new job just as I have done here, I'll sit down, first of all, and tell them what my expectations are and then ask what their expectations are—their expectations of me, and of the Navy. For me, communication is the key. If they have issues, then they have to let me know what's going on, and I'll follow up. Following up, I think, is the key. Showing the kids that I care, that's a huge thing from what I hear from their side of it. And when I see a leader who really cares about his troops, these kids will bend over backward to do anything for him.

Chief Swain:

It just takes a different leadership today, I think. I know when I was a young sailor, when I came in, and with my counterparts, there wasn't a whole lot of asking why. You were told what to do, and you did it. To be honest with you, my first couple of chiefs, I was terrified of them, I really was. I hoped I didn't see them all day, because it was a bad thing if I did. But now, these kids are smart coming in; if you give them an order, they want to know why, and you really have to take time to tell them. It takes a little time, but I'm not disappointed. I thought I was there for a while, but now that I look back on it, well, what I have in my division are some really, really smart kids, and once I developed my leadership style to adapt to them, I've had no problems.

The Navy does not exist in a vacuum. Two significant recent events—the attack on USS *Cole* in October 2000, while refueling at Aden, Yemen, and, even more, the events of September 11, 2001—have changed the way the Navy operates. Gone are the leisurely cruises around the Mediterranean, gone too are the frequent port calls that allowed a young person to "join the Navy and see the world." Operational tempos are vastly increased. USS *Theodore Roosevelt* recently set the all-time Navy record for continuous days at sea. In support of Operation Enduring Freedom, under extremely unpleasant conditions in the north Arabian Sea, *Theodore Roosevelt* spent 159 straight days at sea without a port call. And some chief petty officers are concerned that these new realities haven't fully sunk in to the average sailor.[1]

Senior Chief Gentry:

You know, as strange as it may seem, we have young sailors on this ship who haven't really figured out that this is a war patrol. Now, after the admiral talked the other night about the challenges we are going to face in the Arabian Sea, I had more young people come up to me and say, "That was a real awakening for me, I never really understood," but now they are realizing that, hey, no kidding, this is the real thing. Some are still oblivious, but then again, there are always a few such. They go to work every day, they do the same thing, and they are in their own little world. Maybe that is one of those differences between us older guys and the younger guys; maybe they were more sheltered or something; until something bad happens to them or someone they know, or something bad happens right here on this ship, they seem to think, "Okay, we're in a war, but that's got nothing to do with me, we're away from it," and that's not true at all. For us older guys, we know what the mission is, and we tell them every day, because we want them to have a sense of what's really going on.

Master Chief Barton:

I check on board every sailor in my division, and I personally interview them all. I usually take four or five redshirts at a time, and I sit down and tell them what the job is that they are going to do, and I make sure that they know that what they are going to do is a very dangerous job, but it's the most important job on board this ship, and don't let anybody else tell you different. This ship is designed to deliver ordnance on target. That's the only reason why we exist in the U.S. Navy. I tell them—and I'm as blunt as I can be—that people are going to get hurt, and people are going to die doing this job. And the only way they can avoid being killed or hurt is to follow the rules and regulations that are set down in front of them. And I say that these rules and regulations are written in blood, and what that means is that something has happened in the past where either someone was killed or hurt, building bombs, or building missiles, or whatever. And we do it this way because of that. And they get that understanding about the high degree of danger that faces every ordnanceman, male or female, seaman or master chief.

Master Chief Beldo:

I believe when we say this is a war patrol, they hear it, they believe it, but they don't understand what that entails. They don't really know what that means. If I say we are going to war, they know what that means, because they've been watching the news. They were around on September 11, 2001, and they know what has happened between September 11 and today. And they can say, "Okay, we are going to war"—but I don't think they really understand what that means. I almost feel—and again, we're talking young people, they relate to TV, to the media—that for them it's not real life. It hasn't hit home yet. It's the "I know something might happen, but it's not going to happen to me" type of thing.

And when we do daily tasking, and some people take it for granted and take it as a joke, you have to stop them and explain to them that this is not playtime, this is real. And you might think, for instance, that the drills we go through daily might be preparing them. But they kid around with it, and joke about it. Even things like man overboard drills. But the reality of the situation is, well, nobody thought a boat would pull up alongside of USS *Cole* and kill seventeen people, either. I think what we do is, we don't sugarcoat it and we don't try and make it something it's not. We're straight up and honest, and that gets their attention really fast. I tell them, "If you came in the military to go to college, if you came in the military to get your degree, I'm sorry to have to be the one to tell you, but that's not what the Navy is here for. Sure, you may get your degree and good luck to you. But the reality of it is, we're here to go to war if we need to go to war. And somebody will get killed. And that's the harsh reality of it, and that's why you join the Navy. If you didn't join for that reason, well, let me be the first one to tell you that's why you're out here. Those bombs are real, kids."

Nine

Quality and Leadership

Chief petty officers worry a lot. One constant worry at sea and ashore is the fear that increased operational tempo and the stress of long and frequent deployments, coupled with the need to make the right decision instantly, will somehow degrade the Navy's war-fighting abilities. It is an extremely fast-paced, dynamic environment, and there is no room for error. New weapons systems, new tactical concepts, and new leadership ideas all continue to confront members of most wardrooms and chief petty officers messes.

To better manage constant change, the Navy has wholeheartedly embraced a formal system of quality management, loosely styled after the precepts of W. Edwards Deming, who, among other accomplishments, led the quality improvement process that returned Japan to industrial prominence in the decades following World War II.

Beginning under Adm. Frank Kelso, and with the energetic buy-in of Master Chief Petty Officer Duane Bushey, the Navy moved aggressively toward a concept of Total Quality Leadership (TQL), with gradual but steady implementation aboard all ships and stations throughout the 1990s. Kelso and Bushey knew, as management theorist Alvin Toffler had earlier predicated, that it was not change itself that was disturbing the Navy, but the ever accelerating rate of change. The Navy needed to effectively manage gender integration, a return to a concept of physical fitness for all hands, and other important managerial and human relations issues as the century came to an end. New weapons systems, new shipboard platforms, and new mission tasking compounded the problem. The success of many of these initiatives was dependent on the enthusiastic buy-in of the CPO community. In June 1991 CNO issued two Navy-wide policy directives, NAVOP 011/91 and NAVOP 018/91, which directly established the commitment, tone, and timeline for Navy-wide implementation of TQL. Kelso and his advisers were convinced of the desirability of continual process improvement espoused by Deming. The admiral was particularly struck by the congruity of Deming's famous fourteen points of quality assurance with the mission and ideals of the Navy, and soon generated a Navy version of the cardinal principles, couched in terms of reference that sailors could understand and relate to.

In Kelso's view, "a basic tenet of TQL is that quality cannot be inspected in. The Navy has a habit of inspecting everything from a sailor's haircut to how ships handle nuclear weapons. If you look at inspection reports over the years, you'll find that some of the same deficiencies surface over and over again. The reason for that is our focus on results rather than process—we correct the problem and then move on to something else rather than examining the process to see if it is the source of the deficiency. As we implement TQL and improve our processes we'll be able to rely less on instructions."

Kelso also felt that "the operational Navy is a classic case of inspecting for quality at the end of a process. This is expensive, ineffective and time consuming. Navy commands go through an exhaustive regime of inspections during their at-home training cycle. The purpose of the inspections is to ensure the unit (people and equipment) can perform the mission. The inspectors become the command's customer, and the unit does all it can to delight the inspector, sometimes at the expense of its real customer—the operational commander. If a unit fails an inspection, bad things usually happen. Seniors hold people accountable and the unit comes under even closer scrutiny. To avert failure, local commanders often schedule pre-inspections, which are as difficult and time consuming as the formal inspections. Our sailors are working twice as hard, but they are working harder for all the wrong reasons. They are working 'not to fail' when they should be working to make the system better. The approach of working 'not to fail,' is dead wrong! It must be fixed."[1]

Powerful words from a CNO—words that reflect a significant change in philosophy of how commanding officers should now lead their people, manage their processes, and attack the problems they encounter in their commands. Long-service chief petty officers could identify with Kelso's sentiments.

Chief Storekeeper Arnie K. Dellinger, USN (Ret. [1996]):
   About the only thing that I don't miss after twenty-one years in the Navy are those damn inspections. Personnel, "heads 'n beds," material, operational readiness inspections, you name it. We spent more time— way more time—getting ready for inspections, dry-running inspections, hiding things that we knew wouldn't pass inspections, and talking about what happened at the inspections than we ever did maintaining or operating the ship. Half the time when we were on operations, we had "riders" aboard, from the type command, PacFleet, or whoever, and everything you'd do, you would do looking over your shoulder at some guy with a clipboard, who usually knew about one-tenth as much as your average seaman apprentice about what was going on.

One common thread noted in all implementation models is that TQL is leader-driven. And anyone who has spent any time around the Navy knows that any program—especially one that relies on proactive leadership—must fully engage and be accepted by the ship or station's chief petty officers. Over a period of several years, and continuing to the present, chief petty officers and others began to use a new vocabulary, learn new metrics, and view things differently than their predecessors may have done. No longer was the excuse "that's the way we've always done it" acceptable, nor was the concept of "if it ain't broke, don't fix it" accepted as conventional wisdom. Posters with the Navy's versions of Deming's fourteen points began to appear in repair spaces, operational offices, and, often enough, in CPO messes.

Chief Personnelman (AW) Freddy G. Padgett,
USS Normandy (CG-60):

There's no doubt about it, TQL changed a lot of the ways that we did business, when it first came in. Sailors used to ask why we had to jump through all these quality hoops, but after a while, I think it caught on pretty well. When I was coming up, all the officers and chiefs were going through TQL and that had a big impact, I think.

CNO FOURTEEN POINTS

1. Understand the mission and principles of the Navy. Have a clear grasp of how your command supports the Navy's mission and how the principles apply to your day-to-day actions.

It is an accepted truth in operational research that organizational structure greatly influences results. Military organizations are command-driven and mission-focused. Many chief petty officers are concerned that the "smokestack effect," where each warfare community tends to its own interests, with little overlap, harms their overall effectiveness.

Command Master Chief Hickman:

If it were up to me, I'd make every CPO attend the Senior Enlisted Academy. Every single one. And I would train as close to those standards as I could get. I realize that nine weeks in lovely Rhode Island might be too much—it wouldn't be cost effective. But every chief needs that training. I went through Senior Enlisted Academy in 1993, as a brand new senior chief, and the first thought that passed through my mind, when I got done, was "You know, if they had given me this as a chief, I would have been a better chief. Going through and dealing with the other peers was an eye-opener. I was in a group with twelve guys, all from different ratings; they purposely separate people in the different ratings so that you can learn from your peers. We had a command master chief in my class back then, a guy named Roger Dumont, and just learning from him was great. "This is how I handled this; this is the way to make that happen." Whether I agreed with the way he handled it or not, it was a way to do it. I would put that in my toolbox.

I think that one thing Navy leadership could do is take chiefs, between duty stations or whatever, and send them someplace for four weeks and just give them the wisdom and the tools to make them better chiefs. Teach them things that they can't learn at their own command—teach them things from peers—take people from every different rating in the Navy, and every warfare community, and see how they do things. We all bring different things to the table. Some people don't like the way I do things. That's okay. Some people think I am the greatest thing since sliced bread. That's okay, too. I just think that if I were CNO, that's what I'd do.

2. Quality is the essence of TQL. Insist on quality performance and material. Do the job correctly the first time.

It's hard to do the job right the first time if parts are not available or platforms are used well past their design life. Material shortfalls continue to plague the Navy. Unfortunately and tragically, increased operational tempo and reduction in the number of available platforms often causes deterioration in war-fighting capabilities.

Master Chief Kastler:

If you really want to improve quality, then I'd use whatever funds we have available to fix our shipboard equipment. That's the only way we can stay the greatest Navy in the world. On the *Ticonderoga*-class cruisers, well, this ship type is nearly twenty years old. And it's not just on the Ticos—all of our ships, subs, and aircraft need replacement, or at least serious upgrades. Some of these helos, you get on them, and you get squirted by oil, from some leak, somewhere. We have helicopters, right now, out there in the fleet, that flew in Vietnam. And that's a long time ago.

Chief Dellinger:

I don't know what it's like now, but up until 1996, when I got out, we were scrounging around for parts all the time. If you had seventy airplanes on a carrier, maybe, if you were lucky, you could get enough parts to get fifty of 'em off the deck. And I'm not talking about being out in the South Gedunk Sea somewhere; I'm talking about sitting off Kuwait in the middle of Desert Storm, laying live ordnance across the beach. How you are supposed to do the mission "by the book" when half of your parts and tools are missing is beyond me.

3. Know your job. Analyze and understand every facet of your responsibilities and those of your people.

Most Navy man and women, when pressed, will tell you that the Navy's technical training is a cut above that of the other armed services. Navy technicians have been known to look down their noses at the "box changers" of the other services; repair to the component level is the norm on Navy warships. "There ain't no Radio Shack at sea" is a frequent observation by technicians; the implication is that, as Master Chief Ciaccio pointed out in chapter 1, when things fail, self-sufficiency is expected. The fire department is a long way off.

Chief Radarman John D. Kline, USN (Ret. [1981]):

The greatest lesson I learned as a chief, or as a sailor, for that matter, is "If it's to be, it's up to me." I came into the Navy right before Vietnam, when most of our ships were World War II issue. The old chiefs who taught me the radarman rating knew that equipment inside out. Half of the fixes were "white wire," things that fixed previous problems, but were never written down in the manuals, anywhere. We had guys, chiefs and senior petty officers, who could stick their noses into a piece of equipment, never look at a meter or look at the schematic, and tell you what was wrong. That's job knowledge, right there.

Chief Boilerman Willie J. Metsenger, USN (Ret. [1988]):

I always thought of myself as, first and foremost, a boilerman. It didn't make any difference if I was lighting off a 1,200-pound plant, or sitting at the desk, or standing watch as the assistant—first and foremost, I tried to think like that guy with the oily rag stuck in his back pocket. Because the minute you stop thinking like that—the minute you get more concerned with the watch bill, or what parts you need, or what good shore billet you can get next—then you're done. It will show right through you, and you'll lose 'em—and you'll never get that respect back.

4. Words alone don't solve problems. Look first at the process and the system for faults and solutions, not the people. Improve the process, train the people.

Chief Helderman:

It sometimes makes you wonder, it really does. If you only knew the number of systems that are brought on board ship at midnight—tossed across the brow when nobody is looking. And you wake up in the morning, and there it is. And nobody has got any documentation on it, you have not gotten any training on it, and you don't get the extra bodies to fix it, either. Somebody shows up with another computer, plugs it in, and runs out the door. I know the Navy is trying to standardize at least between the carriers, with all these new systems, the networks, and all the different applications that run on them. Growing faster than the movement of technology out there is hard to do, but somebody needs to take the pulse of technology so they can at least match it up with the Navy.

5. Quality training is the key to success. People must be fully trained to do their jobs. You are never too senior to learn. To do your best is not good enough unless you are properly trained to do the job.

Senior Chief Raab:

To me, that means strengthening the leadership. For our community, the chiefs, we need to focus on leadership a lot more. We're losing a lot of time in comparison to previous years. We're going to have people who don't have the leadership skills that we expect, if we don't invest the time right now to grow these new chiefs. Most of the problems that we have come right back to a failure in leadership. If we have a young sailor getting in trouble on the job, you can usually trace that problem back to leadership somewhere. Same thing goes for equipment casualties, accidents, or whatever. So I firmly believe that if we fix our leadership issues, we can fix anything.

6. Use analytical methods to understand and improve your jobs. Graphs and charts, properly used, are invaluable tools in this effort.

Command Master Chief McCalip:

I can show you data on just about every facet of this crew that you'd want to see. My predecessors did a great job in setting up the system here, and it was easy for me to follow up. Want to know the average age on the flight deck? The number of berths and where they are located? Want to know how many lefthanded quartermasters we have on their first tour? I can probably find that for you, too.

Master Chief Nelson:

The data collection part of TQL is very important, because you want to know how well you are performing, and you can compare that to how well you did last year, or how well you need to do in the future. So those tools were and are very important to the Navy. To me it's been most beneficial in that area. It's really true—you can't inspect-in quality, but you have got to be able to observe, and measure and make corrections from those measurements.

Senior Chief Garcia:

We used TQL to run the bachelor quarters in Okinawa, and we used the charting and graphing tools to identify problem areas and set them up for correction. We could track satisfaction or dissatisfaction data, and we made things happen to improve the process. I'm a real proponent of that, because it keeps people from just trying things out, without getting any idea of what works and what doesn't. If you just tamper with the process, without good recordkeeping, you don't really know, and can't prove, what worked and what didn't. It's all intuition at that point.

7. We are a team. We must work together across departments and commands. We must listen, even to the most junior people. All are charged with making the workplace and quality of life better. All suggestions for improvement must be explained and action taken or rejected by the leadership. We must provide those who suggest improvements and ideas with feedback as to what is being done with the suggestion. The leadership will not necessarily adopt all ideas, but the leadership must provide the feedback on every suggestion.

Master Chief Barton:

This is a really tough situation right now. We talk about teamwork, but I'm not sure that everyone really buys in to what it all means. Right now, force protection is vital. I'm in the weapons field, and yet I have a number of new sailors who are sent to me from boot camp, from the schools, reassigned from other divisions on the ship, wherever, who do not meet the minimum criteria for being able to handle a weapon. And I'm stuck with those sailors, and I can't move them to another division. So it means my sailors have to stand double and triple watches some-times on a duty day. I mean, it's fairly simple and straightforward. If a sailor has been convicted of an assault or DUIs or something like that before he or she comes in the Navy, that sailor cannot hold a weapon. It's a federal law, as far as assault, any type of assault, spousal abuse, or any of those types of things.

I would say what we need to do is screen our sailors a whole lot bet-ter in boot camp, and in each command, to direct those sailors to the proper department, and not send them to a weapons department or a job that involves handling weapons. I mean, I build bombs—that's what we do all day. And I get sailors who come in, and we find out when we start screening them that they are nonresidents or non–U.S. citizens, and I can't use them. And I can't move them out to another department for one reason or another. A little teamwork here would be greatly appreciated.

8. Create an atmosphere of trust and open communication where everyone shares a sense of pride in their work. We must drive fear out of the work place. Create an atmosphere in which people tell you what is wrong in order that it can be fixed. If we don't recognize the problems, we will never improve. We'll reward people who have the courage to tell us what they see that needs improvement so we can get better.

Chief McPherson:

Well, everybody talks a good fight, but sometimes I'm not so sure. I complain about this every time there is a meeting, but it never seems to change. There are so many little things we can do that would make a sailor's life better. For example, when we pull in off deployment, these kids don't get to leave this ship, because this is their home. The Army goes out on maneuvers, and when they come back they get to live in the barracks, they're not living in a tent still. The Air Force goes overseas, they stay there, they come back, they go home, or they're living in a barracks. We go on deployment, we come back, that kid is sleeping in the same rack he just slept in for the last six months; he doesn't get a barracks or housing out on base; he has to stay right here. He can't afford to live out in town, it would have to come out of his pocket because he is an E-2 or E-3. At the end of the day, when we are in port, I say, "Okay, we are done with our work, everybody can go home." And you see everybody all excited: "Yay, I'm going to change clothes and hit the beach." And then you've got that one group that walks away dejected—some of them don't even have a ride if they want to go out the gate. And that just kills me.

9. Inspect smarter. Inspections should be methods of learning and improvement rather than threatening events. As we learn to do the job correctly the first and every time, the number of inspections will decrease.

Senior Chief Equipment Operator
Roscoe G. Witherspoon, USN (Ret. [1982]):

Everybody hates inspections. I hated 'em as an E-1, and I hated 'em as a senior chief. Best inspection I ever saw, though, was out at Port Hueneme. We were getting ready to deploy, and regiment was conducting the inspection. We had a tape of music that every battalion used for inspections, and the guys from regiment pretty well learned to pace themselves to the music. Somebody cut and edited the tape, sped it up, and I swear, those guys were running to get through the seven-eighty-two gear inspection. I was just an EO3 in Alpha Company back then, but we were rolling on the deck, just rolling, laughing so hard.

10. Demand quality, not quotas. If we get quality, all other goals and quotas will follow.

Master Chief Nelson:

Well, you talk about quotas. Now, we don't have quotas here at Recruit Training Command, but we do everything in our power to keep the attrition rates low. And sometimes, I think, we send guys on to the fleet who maybe don't need to be out there, and it just winds up costing the Navy more money in the long run. So maybe a little spent on the front end would save lots on the back end.

Senior Chief Perry:

There are quotas everywhere you go, even when you go to the housing office. Somebody decides that we need to improve housing for all levels. But the real core of the problem is that we don't have enough housing to go around, and what we do have is terrible. You go onto any Navy base now, and you get a young kid coming in, maybe E-3, with a wife and kid, and he asks for base housing. And he's told, "Well, you can't have it, you are an E-3." And that's wrong, all wrong. Because who do you have living there? First-class and chiefs, and those are the guys that are making enough money to live out on the economy. But they take that base housing, and here we've got that seaman, and the third- and second-class petty officers, and they are the ones who really need it.

It's a crying shame when you've got someone in the military—and it's not just the Navy, it's any of the military out there—and they have to go get food stamps to feed their family. Something is wrong with this system. And I think it is housing. You get a young kid trying to go out and live on the economy. And they can only afford just so much, so where do they live? Now you are creating more problems, because they are coming into work, and they've got problems outside that carry over. He is worrying about his wife out there, he is worrying about something happening to her or to the kids in the neighborhoods we force them to live in. And on a six-month deployment like this one, he's a nervous wreck. But if you put him in base housing, you take away all that stress and a lot of that worry, and he can concentrate on what he is doing. Save money on housing—pay for it somewhere else, that's my feeling.

11. Education and self-improvement are just as important as training. We must always get better. Everyone must be involved in training and self-education.

Chief Wylie:

We talk about how everybody coming in is lots better educated than they ever were, but I would still change the way we recruit. I used to be a recruiter, and I put a lot of good guys into the Navy. One of the things that we were taught to do was sell the Navy, and I don't think that works. You have to be honest with people, and I used to tell them, "Look, the Navy is not the cloud with the silver lining. It's not the answer to all your questions. It's not going to solve all your problems. The Navy takes people, not based on your experience, but on your aptitude, your ability to learn. So therefore I am going to do something for you that nobody else will. I am going to tell you just exactly the way it is." I used to tell them about P-days in boot camp. I used to tell them that boot camp is eight weeks long, but really, you are going to be there for ten to twelve weeks, maybe longer.

I used to get letters from my guys all the time saying, "When I got here, I was the only one that knew about P-days, I was the only one that knew about mess cranking, and it really helped." If you trust a guy enough, you tell him, "Look, your first year in the Navy—maybe your entire first enlistment, who knows?—is all about learning, it's all about experiencing the lowest level we have. But it does get better. At the end of that four-year period you have a tremendous amount to show for it." A lot of guys will buy that, but we go around and invite potential recruits, "Tell me what you want, and I'll fill the bill," and then we say, "Oh yeah, the Navy can provide that, and here's how, now sign this paper." Well, you are dealing with a seventeen-year-old kid; what the hell do they know about what they want? They haven't got a clue. And whatever it is, it changes every five minutes. Then he gets to boot camp, where he's not even sure he wants to be to begin with, and then we are surprised when he doesn't make it through. And when he gets here, he is disillusioned, because we told him he could be a SEAL or a jet pilot or whatever line of bull we threw at him, and he's down on the mess decks, or in the laundry, or whatever. I think that we can do a lot better. I think we could do a tremendous job if we just tried.

12. All improvements, big and small alike, are important.

Chief Williams:

Little things mean a lot. There was a discussion once about bringing civilians on board, when the ship was in port, just to cook, clean, that kind of thing. Just so we could give that seaman apprentice, or airman, or whatever a break. Assuming that the tempo of operations, which is very fast these days, doesn't change, that's what I'd do. Just simple things like that; we're not looking for floating palaces or cruise ships, just simple things that would reduce the stress by eliminating a lot of the nonessential stuff we make sailors do.

Senior Chief Lewis:

As far as the gear goes, you see ships at sea in a critical situation all the time. Not just habitability items, but mission-critical things, all the time. As a radioman, I experienced times when half my transmitters and transceivers were down, and I couldn't get message traffic off the ship for hours. And I just can't do business like that.

13. [The CPO's] job as a supervisor is to guide and assist sailors, of all ranks and ratings. As leaders, we must insure they have the tools and training they need to do their jobs correctly. It's the leader's responsibility to ensure his people are properly trained for the job before they are placed in a position of standing a watch, starting a pump, lighting off a radar, loading a gun, loading a missile, etc.

Chief Helderman:

It's all about training. The training commands, sometimes, are so narrow-minded in what information they are providing to students that when the fleet changes, the schoolhouse doesn't keep up. I would like the schoolhouse to take a step up. It's great now what the Navy is doing with commercial off-the-shelf technology. When something new first comes in, they usually put it on the next battle group to go out, which is typically how these major installs go. The next install should go in the schoolhouse. They should train the instructors, to ensure that the next group of technicians coming to the fleet has the ability to maintain that equipment. Frankly, our job is to fix things, and if we can't fix it, now we've got to call people on the beach for help, and that costs a lot of money. I think it would pay for itself in time. If you could do that it would help quality, no doubt about it, if we could just put more fleet or seasoned technicians on the podiums, and not just the next guy rolling in to teach these guys—sometimes we have instructors teaching things they've never seen before. If you don't have experience on that equipment, how can you expect to teach anyone about it?

But I think if we could take that training and turn it around, so that when a technician walks out of the schoolhouse, he walks on board the ship and sees that system for the first time, then first, he's going to recognize it. And second, other than the fact that he is scared to death of that multi-million-dollar system, he's got the ability, day one, to potentially do something with that system, to help out without having to sit there and watch for two or three months and relearn the different configurations, and the changes that have happened since the schoolhouse got its system. You can't fix it if you can't understand it—it's that simple.

14. All hands from seaman to admiral must learn and use TQL.

Chief Electronics Technician (AW/SW) Brandt Boardman,
Naval Training Center, Great Lakes:

In TQL, one of the concepts that encountered a lot of resistance was that idea about the inverted pyramid, that some seaman apprentice would be telling an experienced first-class petty officer or chief how to run his or her shop. And, quite frankly, there was a lot of resistance to that, especially at sea.

Senior Chief Garcia:

Six years ago I was a big proponent of TQL. But, as it got implemented, a lot of people began to say, "Hey, why do we have to listen to the opinions of a seaman over, say, a first-class petty officer?" And there were lots of things in TQL that can't be applied to shipboard life—steer left or steer right, but there's no time for a PAT meeting or a big discussion. You just have to do what you have to do.

Master Chief Nelson:

Not all TQL was implemented, and not all has gone away, either. We still use some of it. We still have those process action teams. But to have a seaman with three months at sea telling you how to set up a department, well, that's awfully hard to make work in the structural Navy. And everyone recognized that, I think.

Ten

Throughout the war years, chief petty officers were the senior enlisted personnel afloat or ashore. While it was traditional in the submarine service to identify the most senior chief as "chief of the boat," all chiefs served in pay grade E-7 throughout World War II and the Korean War. After Korea, at the urging of the army, Congress authorized pay grades E-8 and E-9 for all services in June 1958. Within the Navy, which had not energetically supported the new pay grades, potential nominees were screened by time in grade and time in service. CPOs with ten years of service and four years in grade were permitted to test for senior chief, and outstanding chief petty officers with at least thirteen years of service and six years as CPOs were permitted to test for promotion to master chief. Two cadres were promoted, the first in November 1958, and a second group in May 1959. From that point onward, the current hierarchical structure of promotion from chief petty officer to senior chief and onward to master chief petty officer became operative.[1]

One problem that immediately faced the Navy was the definition of roles and responsibilities for the new "super-chiefs." Indeed, for a considerable period of time, the major distinction among rates was the pay increment only. Particularly on the khaki working uniform, the different grades were identified only by one or two very small stars above the traditional fouled anchor; a situation that, even today, causes consternation to recruits and others when first determining the proper form of address to a newly introduced chief petty officer. While there are no recorded instances of senior personnel reporting to their juniors, there was little, if any, attempt to immediately identify billets requiring or suggesting assignment of senior personnel. Indeed, it was not until the mid-1960s that the present custom of addressing E-8 and E-9 personnel as "Senior Chief" or "Master Chief" came into general usage. Master Chief Del Black, the first Master Chief Petty Officer of the Navy, once noted, "You'd run into some strange situations out in the fleet. There'd be confusion about seniority. In an aviation squadron, for example, you might have a line chief and maintenance chief. Now, the maintenance chief was a Master Chief Petty Officer, but the line chief is only a Senior Chief, yet he was running the squadron."[2] Black, recognizing the problem, formed a Navy-wide network of senior enlisted advisers—soon renamed command master chiefs—selected by fleet, type, and district commanders. By 1969 this network was representing sailors worldwide, and these senior enlisted advisers met with sailors to resolve local and cross-command problems, while referring those which appeared to have broader implications directly to the MCPON's office. While several officers complained privately that there seemed to be a separate chain of command developing for enlisted issues, this ad-hoc process worked well for several years, and is credited with alleviating many of the drug, race, and morale issues that plagued the late Vietnam and post-Vietnam eras.

In 1971 Adm. Bud Zumwalt, at the urging of MCPON Whittet, issued a "Z-gram" formalizing the program, which identified the "best and brightest" as master chief petty officers of the command (MCPOC). Twenty-three outstanding master chief petty officers were identified and assigned to major commands ashore and afloat. To add to the credibility of these individuals, the Bureau of Personnel changed the specialty mark within their rating badge, and permitted the use of a single large gold star in lieu of their identification as radiomen, torpedomen, or the like. The two small silver stars above the eagle on the chevron were also replaced with small gold stars. These command master chiefs would meet frequently to develop policy recommendations regarding enlisted issues. These concerns and recommendations would be routed to the CNO via the MCPON, making the senior enlisted, in effect, an advisory board to the senior policy makers of the Navy. Later, Admiral Zumwalt extended the practice to include the senior enlisted representatives of smaller commands, allowing all sailors to be at least one voice away from direct input to their highest superiors.

To further streamline the process, Master Chief Petty Officer of the Navy Bob Walker revised the organization to a fleet, force, and command structure in 1977. That structure, which has proven to be effective and efficient, has remained in place to the present time, with only minor revisions to reflect change in mission and doctrine.

MCPON Walker also saw the need for quick and efficient communication among the now growing command master chief community. A series of newsletters, first entitled *The Word* and later *The Direct Line,* addressed issues that concerned the fleet. MCPON Walker and others soon realized that a chain of communication stretching from his office in Washington to and through the fleet, force, and command master chiefs to the CPO on the deckplates, was an important step in strengthening the visible links among the evolving "senior management" of the enlisted community.

A most significant revision to policy took place in the summer of 1978. After a great deal of study and debate among the command master chief community, MCPON Tom Crow persuaded the chief of naval operations to formalize the roles and responsibilities of chief, senior chief, and master chief petty officers. Chief petty officers would be expected to become the top technical authorities and experts within a particular rating, providing the direct supervision, instruction, and training of the lower rated personnel within their skill area. Senior chiefs would be expected to be the senior technical supervisors within a rating and occupational field, and would provide the total command with technical expertise. Finally, the master chief petty officer would provide administrative and managerial leadership on issues involving enlisted personnel, and was expected to contribute in matters of policy formation and implementation across the full spectrum of rates. In practical terms, a chief radioman might be responsible for the ship's transmitter room; a senior chief might be responsible for the entire message center; and a master chief might take responsibility for development and implementation of the ship's communication plan, as well as, perhaps, acting as the leading petty officer for the entire operations department.

MCPON Crow foresaw the disruptions that these innovations might cause, and worked to implement the roles carefully. "Changes which impact the chain of command are ones which provide job satisfaction for the affected personnel and strengthen the organization in such a way as to improve the credibility of both the senior and master chiefs, and the junior officers in the Navy," he wrote. To further solidify the credibility of these new incumbents, Crow proposed and championed the development of a Senior Enlisted Academy at Newport, Rhode Island. "We, the senior enlisted personnel have continuously asked to be given more responsibilities commensurate with our paygrade and expertise and to be held accountable for our actions," he said. "And future expansion of responsibilities for Senior and Master Chief Petty Officers will be determined by how we react and perform to meet these new challenges." Under the leadership of MCPON Crow, the Senior Enlisted Academy opened in September 1981 and, since that date, has provided upper-level leadership for the Navy's top enlisted.

The guidelines concerning the Command Master Chief Program were further clarified in February 1986, when all E-9 personnel were made eligible for the program, and provisions were established for follow-on assignments after completion of a CMC tour. MCPON Placket led the development of a formal course of instruction for command master chiefs, which was implemented during the term of office of his successor, MCPON Dwayne Bushey.

By late 2000 it was once again desirable to formalize procedures regarding these key enlisted leadership roles. In a December directive, the Navy stated:

1. Fleet, Force, CNO Directed Command and Command Master Chiefs uphold the highest standards of professionalism and stimulate better communication at all levels of command throughout the Department of the Navy. They strengthen the chain of command by working within it to foster a better understanding of the needs and viewpoints of enlisted members and their families. [They] are the senior enlisted leaders, who report directly to their respective Commanders/Commanding Officers. They participate in formulating and implementing policies concerning morale, welfare, job satisfaction, discipline, utilization, and training of Navy enlisted personnel. By reporting directly to their Commanders, [they] keep their chain of command aware and informed of sensitive and current issues.

A. To qualify for selection as a CMC, the individual must possess and maintain the following qualities:

1. Have demonstrated superior leadership abilities and broad management skills.
2. Possess effective communication abilities (oral and written) and proven administrative capabilities.
3. Have demonstrated effective personnel counseling.
4. Have a sharp military appearance, demeanor, and military bearing and meet all health and physical readiness standards.
5. Have an outstanding performance record.
6. Be a highly motivated role model for all hands to emulate.
7. Have demonstrated active involvement in command Quality of Life initiatives and programs.
8. Have strong overall potential to be successful as a CMC.
9. Have no trait mark below 3.0 in any area on fitness reports for the last 5 years. Member must maintain this standard while assigned as a CMC.
10. Be able to deal effectively with all levels of the chain of command.

B. Commander/Commanding Officer recommendations must certify that the candidate is fit to assume duties as a CMC, paying particular attention to the following factors:

1. Physical fitness standards. Member must meet Navy standards and have an active disciplined personal physical fitness program.

2. Medical. Any documented condition that could preclude assignment as, or impair performance of a prospective CMC.

3. Alcohol. Personnel with a documented history of alcohol abuse are considered unsuitable for assignment as a CMC. If successfully treated, with no alcohol involvement for 3 years, member may be considered for a waiver to participate in the CMC program.

4. Human relations/personal behavior. Personnel with a documented history of human relations problems will be considered unsuitable for assignment as a CMC. Similarly, documented (service or medical record, Enlisted Master File, or Navy Central Registry) personal conduct issues (indebtedness, alcohol, substantiated or unresolved family advocacy, etc.) in the past 3 years will be considered disqualifying.

C. Attendance at the Navy Senior Enlisted Academy (SEA) is required prior to reporting as a Primary Duty CMC or COB. Master Chiefs having prior assignments to a Primary Duty CMC or COB billet, but who have not previously attended the SEA, will be assigned to attend the SEA prior to their next assignment in a Primary Duty CMC or COB billet.[3]

Anyone with experience in the Vietnam-era Navy or earlier who now embarks aboard a naval warship immediately discerns a major transition from historical subservience to cooperative responsibility shared between wardroom and chiefs mess. This is most apparent in the markedly increased responsibility accorded to today's command master chief petty officers.

Command Master Chief McCalip:
The distance we have come over the last thirty or thirty-five years is astounding, it really is. I had the chance to talk to MCPON Del Black many times before he passed away recently. And it's almost scary when you think about it, but it's refreshing too, because back in MCPON Black's time, there was just this huge gulf—a class gulf, actually—between enlisted and officers. And that class, that wardroom in many

cases treated that young sailor badly and disrespectfully. We still have a couple of senior and master chiefs, right here aboard *George Washington,* who were around in the pre-MCPON days. Ask them what it was like, they know. Sure, the Navy got the job done, but today—well, it all goes back to communication and education, and smarter, younger sailors. It was the MCPONs, and the fleet and force master chiefs and the command master chiefs, who got us to where we are today.

Command Master Chief Benning:

For almost all my time in the Navy, I knew that someday I wanted to be a command master chief. I wanted to have a hand in making critical decisions. I had originally been a storekeeper, and made it to master chief in about fifteen years. I was always on the blackshoe side, in small boys, and that's one reason why I applied to became a command master chief. I don't think you can have a full appreciation of everything that goes on in the Navy if you just stay in one community for your entire career. I had always wanted to be in the aviation community, but unless you become a command master chief, there's pretty much no way to get in there as an SK. I'd become very familiar with the surface community over the years, and I knew I'd very much enjoy the aviation community.

Command Master Chief Hickman:

I think the changes over the years have been a good evolution. My goal is to handle everything I can at my level or lower, allowing my CO and XO to focus on their junior officers and train them how to be war fighters and to do our mission. In a squadron, enlisted guys don't do the mission—I don't do the mission, my maintenance guys do not do the mission—but they get the planes ready to do the mission. It's those young aviators who get in the cockpit who are flying into harm's way. So we want them focused on that. It's a good thing. Now the negative part of that is that most of us came into the program because we honestly wanted to help people. That came very easily for me, since I'm a hospital corpsman. I wanted to help people, and I wanted to do all these neat, great things. Well, in reality, with all of these new jobs that we are taking on that the XO used to do, it's taking time away from that. I spend way too much time, in my mind, dealing with bad sailors—that 5 percent or 10 percent of nonconformists is taking up 90 percent or 95 percent of my time. I can't focus on helping that good kid who one day is going to be the MCPON, or CNO, himself. I just don't get to spend time with that young man or woman. So I delegate a lot of that time, down to my chiefs mess, giving them the tools to help sailors focus.

Command Master Chief Benning:

Over the past ten years or so, I've seen a strengthening of the role, certainly. It's very important that people see the triad—the senior leadership of CO, XO, and CMC—all on the same page. They spend a tremendous amount of time talking to each other, and it creates a calm among the crew, knowing that everyone is going in the same direction. It's the same with the air wing with the deputy CAG and the CAG, and also the relationship between the ship CMC and the wing CMC, and I think the smart leaders understand the strength of that.

As the role of the command master chief has expanded, many have questioned the boundaries between junior officers and senior enlisted. Indeed, the U.S. Coast Guard—which because of its much smaller size is often viewed as a leadership laboratory for the other services—has empowered "executive petty officers" for many years. These senior enlisted serve as officers-in-charge and craft masters, and serve in a number of billets that, in the Navy, would be reserved for commissioned officers.

Command Master Chief Kidwell:

If things happen the way that Admiral Clark seems to want them to happen during his time as CNO, then I think you will see some major changes in the relationships between wardroom and chiefs mess. If you have, as you have now, a chiefs mess where more than half the guys have college and graduate degrees, as well as fifteen or twenty years' work experience, and you compare that to a wardroom where you have new college graduates with limited experience, well, the chief is undoubtedly more qualified than the engineering officer, or the weapons officer, or whatever. But the way the military rank structure is set up, that doesn't make much difference. I sort of like the way things are set up right now, by the way. I don't think that the Coast Guard model, where there are executive petty officers, is a direct comparison, apples-to-apples, to the Navy. The Coast guard does great work, don't get me wrong, but they are structured like a police force, which is their job, and we're the deployed military force.

Command Master Chief McCalip:
The lines of delineation about what makes a good chief and what makes a good officer are getting cloudier every day, I think. I spent quite a lot of time talking with MCPON Herdt about that delineator. To a certain extent it is still education. But that is much less dramatic that it was in the past. Rather than the college guys leading the rest of the crew, now it's the teamwork between the wardroom and the chiefs mess that makes a ship successful. Look around the chiefs mess here on the *George Washington*. College degrees everywhere in the mess— unheard of twenty, thirty years ago. And that was happening even when I was CMC of USS *Stout,* which was seven or eight years ago now. When you looked around in *Stout,* and you started looking for postgraduate education, you'd look at my chiefs mess, and you'd look across the wardroom, and it was about equal. It's even more visible today. You are going to be on the same destroyer, you're going to look at one side of the compartment, and you're going to see a chiefs mess with a whole bunch of folks with master's degrees. You're going to look on the other side and have a CO with a master's degree, an XO maybe with a master's degree, and maybe two of the five or six department heads, and you look across at the chiefs mess and there is going to be ten of them. Now, a lot of that has to do with age; most chiefs are about the same age as, say, department heads or executive officers on

larger ships. They've had more time to complete a graduate degree than, say, a twenty-three-year-old division officer. But the day of "all muscle, no brains" for chief petty officers is long gone, if it was ever here at all.

One thing that strengthens the role of command master chief is the strong relationships between commands at all levels. On large-deck ships at sea, with many commands embarked, the unit command master chiefs are usually part of the same CPO mess.

Command Master Chief Hickman:
When we sit down together in the ship's CMC office for meetings, we all realize that we are all NEC9580s. Every one of us were selected to be master chiefs, we were all selected to be CMCs, so we are all equal. We are very fortunate—and you might not find that on every carrier, even with two brand-new CMCs who just got here, one of them the day before we left Norfolk—in that we are all friends. We all get along very well. We all bring something different to the plate. While we're all command master chiefs, we come from all over the Navy, two hospital corpsmen, a boatswain's mate, a couple Airedales, a storekeeper, electronics technician, everything. And we each bring something different to the table, we work off each other.

There's no doubt that the incumbents know that what they do is important, and that they are among the fortunate few who practice real policy decision making at an enlisted level. But there is no question that it is a stressful and taxing job.

Command Master Chief (SW) Bennie Pierce, USS Normandy *(CG-60):*
It's an interesting and a critical job, since I'm taking some of America's youngest to war, and I'm responsible to the captain for bringing everybody back, and I take that job seriously. For me, the hours and all that, I don't worry about that, because for me taking care of the sailors is what it is all about, and getting these guys back home, that's the impor-

tant thing. And I can't emphasize it enough: I tell everyone, the things I do, I'm not doing them to be a jerk or anything, I take this seriously, and I want to get you back home.

Command Master Chief (AW) Mike Sanchez,
Navy Helicopter Squadron 15:

Man, I love this job. I've been in the helicopter community since I joined the Navy, and I'm now responsible for 180 of the best darn sailors anywhere. As the command master chief, I'm the senior enlisted adviser and director of standards for the commanding officer. I look after the welfare of the enlisted troops. That can be anything from being sure that they get the berthing they need on the ship, to dealing with e-mail from wives and families, to being sure they know their jobs, whatever. I spend a lot of time talking with the guys and seeing how they are feeling and how they are doing and what I can do to make things better. We're probably the busiest people on the carrier, most days. If there's any kind of flight operations, the helos are up. We count all sorties, so it varies depending on what the mission is, but you don't see the helos on deck much. We do basic antisubmarine work, launch with SEAL teams on board, carry parts and mail to other ships; even on nonflight days, we're flying. And don't forget, our aircraft take about twenty hours of maintenance work for every three hours of flight time, so we stay pretty busy.

Command Master Chief Kidwell:

Sometimes being the chief of the boat—CMC, for the surface guys—is overwhelming, but it's lots of fun. I spend a lot of time fixing small problems before they turn into big problems. Sure, I have my share of big ones, too. But the important thing is to let every single sailor know that his or her work counts, whether he is a mess cook, or standing watch up in operations or in radio; to let everyone know that he's a part of a team, and that his work is important, and counts. Sometimes the captain puts out suggestions, which get interpreted as orders, which then get interpreted as policy; by the time it gets to the deckplates, everyone says, "Man, this is pretty stupid." Yet you were in the same meeting, and sometimes you can say, "This was what was really meant," and still recognize the chain of command. You can get things back to what the original intent was, and get on with the mission.

Command Master Chief Benning:

My first billet as a command master chief was pretty overwhelming. My first job was as CMC of a fighter squadron, and I thought that was pretty neat, being CMC of a Tomcat squadron, to be part of the Jolly Rogers. But when I had a chance to become command master chief of a complete air wing, and went from a command relationship with three hundred people to responsibility for eighteen hundred, including other CMCs—that was pretty overwhelming.

Command Master Chief Hickman:

As CMC Benning says, being a squadron CMC is a busy job. There are about one hundred seventy folks in my squadron right now, and you have to balance the health and welfare of the sailors below you with accomplishing the mission. It really makes for some busy days.

Command Master Chief McCalip:

This job is unbelievable. When I think back to twenty-four years ago, when I first came in, I never imagined I'd end up in this position. On an average day—if there is an average day—I usually start off in the chiefs mess, talking to whoever is there about what's going on. Then I usually get up to the bridge, walk around, and take a good look at the ship. Every morning I talk to the captain and the executive officer, making sure that we are on track for the day, and that we are in sync. I hit my office, and do something I never dreamed would ever happen, and that's check e-mail; I never imagined we'd have the instant connectivity, to shore commands, to home, to everybody, that we have today. As an example, I just passed a message to the air wing CMC concerning the death of a sailor's grandmother. Today, I'll run off and teach a session of senior "school of the ship." It's a three-day course for the first-class petty officers and above; I'll talk to them about command philosophy, and what I think our young sailors should be doing—successes and failures and the direction that they need to go.

Even with the acceptance of the enhanced role for command master chiefs at the highest levels, it would be naive to feel that every officer, or every wardroom, has made an emotional, as well as intellectual, buy-in to the changes in role and responsibility.

Command Master Chief McCalip:

There's still some resistance that comes from the wardroom, although much less than there was in previous years. I have personally run into that, not today, but maybe seven or eight years ago, you'd run into COs and XOs who grew up in a system where the CMC wasn't expected to be much of a player. This is an evolving program over the last twenty or thirty years, so of course there were tensions as things fell into place. Today our CMCs come in, they are educated—they are board-selected, educated through the Senior Enlisted Academy, most of them have college education, and graduate degrees are not uncommon. They are high energy players, and they have all the things that the CO and the XO want.

Command Master Chief Kidwell:

On a submarine, we always say that the chiefs run the boat, the officers fight the boat. And I think that for a long while, the officers were moving into the chief's realm: they worried about Johnny's wife, or his kids in school or whatever. And that has traditionally been the chief's responsibility. We need to keep building up the wardroom as war fighters, and a lot of XOs, I think, understand that. We need to develop the XOs as tomorrow's commanding officers, the guys who operate the war platform, and to the extent that we relieve them of that day-to-day responsibility for good order and discipline among the crew, I think we are doing well. A good COB is firm, fair, consistent, treats everyone straight up. He says, in effect, "If you do this, I'll support you, and if you don't, then I'll make it hurt."

Command Master Chief Benning:

I think that the wardroom realizes that there is a natural progression now, once you enter the Command Master Chief Program. It's not unlike what happens with officers; they progress from division to department to command, or whatever, and we do something similar. One of the best benefits of having first been a squadron CMC, and now having the wing, is that a lot of the squadron guys can rely on me for advice. And here on a carrier, much more than on a small ship, you can have ten or more CMCs who can interact and work problems together. On a carrier there is an amazing number of people that have the professional expertise to help, whether it be legal, EEO, medical, whatever.

Command Master Chief McCalip:

Some people have accused the enlisted community of wanting to make the CMC a mini-XO. I'm not sure that I agree that that is happening, or that we would want it to happen. When I look at how we work in a command today, the XO and the CMC both report directly to the commanding officer. You have that triad there, they all work together. Now, what the CMC has brought to the plate is a stronger connection to the enlisted community, as someone who has come up from E-1. He is now the senior enlisted leader on board a ship and he understands the challenge of being a sailor, both professionally and personally. What the CMC brings to the CO and XO is somebody who takes care of those personnel issues, and everything from watch bills and cleanliness of the ship, to logistics issues, like liberty planning and uniform readiness. All of the things that are the routine of being a sailor. It allows the CO and XO to focus on fighting the ship.

Eleven

The Master Chief Petty Officer
of the Navy

Every command master chief and chief of the boat knows that, as satisfying as their time in office might be, there's much more available before they hear "Shipmate Departing" at their retirement ceremony. In the most recent realignment of the senior enlisted ranks, three levels of senior leadership were identified, even though all remain in the same Navy Enlistment Classification (NEC) and at the same pay grade. CNO-directed command master chiefs (CNOCM), at major commands, force master chiefs (FORCM), and fleet master chiefs (FLTCM) are the stepping stones to the ultimate role in enlisted leadership—the office of Master Chief Petty Officer of the Navy (MCPON). Since 1967 only ten individuals have held this, the highest office to which an enlisted sailor can aspire.

When the Office of the Master Chief Petty Officer of the Navy was created in 1967, the U.S. Navy took a giant step forward in untapping the leadership capabilities of its enlisted force. In the act of adding an extra gold star to a master chief's crow, the senior levels of command were, in effect, saying to the enlisted community, we respect and value your opinion, we need your input, and we will listen and act. No one could have known 25 years ago that the office would grow into the position of influence and credibility it enjoys today. No officer, regardless of his position in the chain of command or Washington bureau, demands more respect, gains quicker access, or is listened to more intently than the Master Chief Petty Officer of the Navy. Like so many other good ideas that take years to ripen, the MCPON did not work overnight miracles. But, as those of us who have spent our careers as officers know well, there is no one more patient or more persistent than a chief with a mission. He might yell and cuss, bang on tables or stomp a few toes, but eventually, he will get what he wants, if you give him the time and resources. (Adm. Elmo R. Zumwalt, U.S. Navy [Ret.], chief of naval operations, 1970–74)

No matter what we think is the reality of a situation, there is probably another reality on the deck plates, and our people need and deserve leaders who know what that reality is. The Master Chief Petty Officer of the Navy is chartered to observe and act, not to supersede the regular chain of command, but to strengthen it and make it work better. His or hers are the experienced eyes that can see the reality of the deck plates. Indeed, he is the pulse-taker of the command. (Adm. C. A. H. Trost, USN, former chief of naval operations, on the occasion of the MCPON change of office, 9 September 1988)

It was inevitable that the office of Master Chief Petty Officer of the Navy (once called, for a very short period, the senior enlisted adviser) would eventually be created. There were many factors working in favor of the creation of such a post. The Marine Corps had established a billet for a sergeant major of the Marine Corps in 1957, and the Army had followed suit in July 1966. Congress saw value in creating a position for a senior enlisted member who could act as a representative of a large, previously untapped contingency. In 1967, reluctantly bowing to both congressional and internal pressure, the Navy established the office as part of the personal staff of the chief of naval operations.[1]

The ten men who have served as MCPON shared a desire to help sailors improve their lot. They have all expressed an immense satisfaction in their ability to "cut through the red tape" in responding to requests from the fleet for assistance. And every one of them has been a shining example to the sailors whom they were chosen to lead.

Master Chief Gunner's Mate Delbert D. Black (1967–71) freely admitted that his great advantage was going first. He could set the standard without being judged by it. His leadership style was a combination of presence and authority. With young sailors, he was attentive and courteous, always aware of the example he set. In the chiefs mess, he pushed for leadership. He earned respect without demanding it, and with that respect came credibility for the office itself. On his way to the Navy's top enlisted billet, Black had survived the Japanese attack on Pearl Harbor aboard the battleship *Maryland,* earning eight combat ribbons in World War II and numerous other decorations. He served a tour in recruiting, and later served with the Ceremonial Guard in Washington. The forty-five-year-old master chief was not afraid of challenge. He had joined the Navy when he was eighteen to get off the family farm near Orr, Oklahoma, and he brought his work ethic with him. Through twenty-one years at sea, from seaman recruit to master chief, he built a reputation as a sailor's sailor. "I was determined to be the best sailor I could be so I wouldn't ever have to go back to that farm again," he laughed.

Del Black developed his own leadership style and philosophy. The role of chief petty officer, and, indeed, the role of petty officers in general, had evolved substantially since he first went to sea before World War II. In his earliest years in the service, it was not unusual for leading seamen to run a division, or even a department. "Most of the time, that leading seaman had served throughout the Depression, and had eight to ten years' service, and yet still was a seaman. Rate came very slowly in those prewar days. He might still be a seaman, but he knew everything. If you had a problem, you didn't talk to the chief or the first-class. You talked to the leading seaman." During the wartime emergency, things changed quickly, and petty officers assumed greater levels of leadership.

By war's end, though, abuses and defective leadership styles crept in that detracted from the efficiency and morale of some commands. As readers of *The Caine Mutiny* can attest, commanding officers sometimes ruled with an iron fist, often making decisions for sailors that *Navy Regulations* said they could make for themselves. As a petty officer and a chief, Black became a leader who tried to protect his men against such abuses, using the chain of command to make his objections known. He also learned that taking the time to listen and help sailors solve their problems was key to being a successful leader.

When MCPON Black assumed office in January 1967, not every senior officer agreed with the concept of a single spokesman for enlisted concerns. Indeed, during his time in office, MCPON Black met with CNO Adm. David McDonald only once. McDonald's successor, Adm. Tom Moorer, however, quickly realized the value of the office, and the particular skill and personality that Del Black brought to the position. They traveled together extensively, and it was during this period that the concept of fleet, force, and then district senior enlisted advisers was developed.

During the most active part of the Vietnam War, at a time when morale and discipline were at all-time lows, MCPON Black frequently visited chiefs messes to explain that everything that was going on could not be blamed on the Navy. Admiral Moorer felt that Congress shared much of the responsibility. It was a very difficult time to develop the positive attitude sailors needed to improve readiness. Poor morale was just one of the symptoms of the larger problem that was affecting the Navy and the other services in the mid- to late 1960s. The Vietnam War was sending thousands of young Americans home in body bags, college campuses were erupting in protest of the war, racial rioting was dividing the country on civil rights, and a strange, new youth culture was creating a wide generation gap.

The divisions and shifts in American society found their counterparts within the military services. For the Navy these problems were reflected in high attrition rates among first-term enlistees, low retention rates among career personnel, and high absenteeism and desertion rates. MCPON Black helped implement changes that reduced these high attrition rates, and he credits these innovations as being among his most important contributions.

Del Black's relief, Master Chief Aircraft Maintenanceman John (Jack) D. Whittet (1971–75) was charming, easy-going, and relaxed among officers and enlisted alike. He served in a very tumultuous period, marked by drastic changes implemented by then CNO Elmo "Bud" Zumwalt. Jack Whittet became a good friend of the CNO; together they symbolized the officer-enlisted teamwork that was essential for the changes that Zumwalt sought. According to Admiral Zumwalt, Whittet was liked by everyone he met. "They might not have agreed with what he was saying, but they still liked the guy."

Whittet, who died in a tragic diving accident in 1989, had been in the Navy for twenty-eight years when he became MCPON. Just seventeen when he left his home in Providence, Rhode Island, he enlisted in 1943. After almost a year of training as an aviation machinist, Whittet went to Guam with Torpedo Squadron 38. He won his combat air crewman wings, and flew thirty-one missions from the carriers *Lexington* and *Anzio*. During the Korean War he was aboard *Bon Homme Richard* with Carrier Air Group 102, which flew combat air strikes against the North Koreans. He served in various aviation billets for the next fifteen years, and advanced to aviation master chief (AFCM) in 1967. He was stationed at Argentia, Newfoundland, when recommended by his commander for the job of MCPON, and then transferred to Norfolk to serve as the senior enlisted adviser to the commander, Naval Air Force, U.S. Atlantic Fleet.

On 31 March 1971 Vice Adm. Dick H. Guinn, chief of naval personnel, appointed Whittet the second Master Chief Petty Officer of the Navy. MCPON Whittet's term of office spanned the most volatile and dynamic period in naval history. Widely known as "Admiral Zumwalt's MCPON," he greatly influenced many of the significant policy changes affecting sailors. One such radical innovation changed the enlisted uniform from "crackerjacks" to a double-breasted suit, a change not universally appreciated and one that was reversed a decade later. He managed the transition from a draft-motivated to an all-volunteer force, and walked a fine line between those who advocated, and those who resisted, change in the Navy's cultural focus. He worked tirelessly to reduce racial strife at sea and ashore, and helped implement the Navy's zero-tolerance policies toward drug use. His time in office was marked by increased operational tempo, particularly in Southeast Asia and the Seventh Fleet areas of operations, and he is credited with strengthening the concept of fleet, force, and command master chiefs initiated by his predecessor.

In many ways, Master Chief Operations Specialist Robert J. Walker (1975–79) was an echo of an earlier, more disciplined military era. Clean-cut and close-shaven, he soon realized that he could not change the liberal grooming standards of the day, yet he fought for standardization and uniformity in their interpretation. He was relentless in his messages to the chiefs: stand up and act like chief petty officers. Joining the Navy in 1948, Bob Walker advanced quickly, making radarman first-class in four years, an extraordinary achievement for the period. Deployed aboard USS *McKean* during the Japanese occupation, Walker endured the harsh and often arbitrary discipline of the times. It was on his first cruise that Walker had his first opportunity to show his leadership abilities. "The leading radarman, a seaman, went home on leave, and I was selected to be the leading radarman," he said. "I had the job for thirty days, and I found out that I could get along pretty doggone good without him. I could handle it. That was my first indication of what being a leader was like. After that I wanted to continue to have the responsibility. It was a helluva letdown when he came back off leave."

Eight years after joining the Navy, Walker was a chief petty officer, at that time the highest step for enlisted. Two years later, the Navy joined the other services in creating pay grades E-8 and E-9. In 1961 he was selected for E-8 and two years later for E-9. At age thirty-four, he attracted a lot of attention as a young master chief with only three hash marks. In the late 1960s Walker was director of training at radarman "A" School, when the announcement for the position of a senior enlisted adviser for the Navy was sent to the fleet. His command recommended him, but his young age and relatively short service precluded his selection. He continued in fleet leadership roles, and in 1972, now an operations specialist (OS), he transferred to the carrier *John F. Kennedy*, where he served as leading chief of the Operations Department and later as master chief petty officer of the command (MCPOC). In November 1974 he was nominated and approved as force master chief for Naval Air Force, Atlantic. While serving in that billet, he was tapped for the Navy's top enlisted job in 1975.

Walker was faced with serious concerns upon taking office. Grooming standards had been generally neglected over a period of several years, and it fell to Walker to vigorously enforce traditional grooming guidelines for both male and female enlisted personnel. In addition, physical fitness standards, often overlooked previously, were reconstituted and vigorously enforced.

MCPON Walker energetically supported off-duty educational programs, realizing that in an all-volunteer force the ability to continue one's education was a prime motivator for recruiting and retention. In one small, but enormously significant, directive he urged the Navy to drop the traditional forms of reference for enlisted personnel (addressed by last name only) and substituted rating titles such as Seaman Smith or Petty Officer Jones. He energetically supported the introduction of Surface Warfare qualifications for enlisted personnel, which soon expanded to include Aviation, Seabee, and other specialty warfare qualifications. It was during his term of office that sea pay, as well as imminent danger and other specialty payments, were raised, vastly improving morale of sailors and their families.

Master Chief Aircraft Maintenanceman Thomas S. Crow (1979–82) was on the ground floor of the "Pride and Professionalism" era. A native of McArthur, Ohio, he looked forward to the day when he could join the Navy. In January 1953, after graduating from high school, he attended boot camp and began training as an aviation structural mechanic. For the next twenty-one years he served as a mechanic, switching periodically between types of aircraft, platforms, and environments. Though advancement to E-6 had come relatively quickly, he hit a stone wall at the E-7 level. "I was probably one of the Navy's most senior first-classes," he said. "Chief just never seemed to open up. It became a real test of will to keep going back to take the test." The wall finally crumbled in 1971, and by 1974, as a senior chief, Crow was looking for a new challenge. He found it in the issue of race relations.

"We were having some very serious problems with race relations in the Navy," he said. "Equal opportunity was an issue. We were having problems dealing with different races and cultures. I prided myself on being a person who takes people as they are. A good person is a good person and I really don't care what race or culture they come from. I felt the impact of what I thought were some very racist, sexist kinds of things going on during that time. The Navy was looking for people to work in the area of human resources, so I volunteered." He trained as a race relations education specialist and was chosen to attend the Defense Race Relations Institute, Patrick AFB, Florida. He was then assigned to COMNAVAIRPAC where he served as a trainer for race relations and a member of the quality control inspection team for overseas WESTPAC units and carriers. After completing equal opportunity program specialist training at Cheltenham, Maryland, he became a program manager for AIRPAC, implementing Phase II of the equal opportunity/race relations program aboard carriers in the Pacific. Meanwhile, Crow was enhancing his own opportunities by attending National University in San Diego, California, where he earned an associate's degree in business administration. Shifting in 1977 to the Navy drug/alcohol counselor program, he was assigned to the AIRPAC Human Resource Management Support office. He was selected as AIRPAC force master chief in December 1977. He continued his off-duty education, earning his bachelor's degree in business administration.

On 29 June 1979 CNO Adm. Thomas B. Hayward announced that he had chosen Force Master Chief Crow to be the Navy's fourth MCPON, and Crow relieved MCPON Walker three months later. In his first meeting with Admiral Hayward, Crow said he was made to feel very comfortable. "We talked about 'Pride and Professionalism' and discussed how we intended to do the job we felt needed to be done. Based on my experiences of force master chief and from watching Bob Walker, I felt that I needed to be out in the fleet. I asked how much access I would have to the CNO, and he answered, as much as I needed." In their discussion on leadership, Crow was pleased to discover similar philosophies. "Admiral Hayward's idea of leadership was that the CPO mess should be the focal point of the community. Because of their seniority and experience, he placed a lot of weight on the CPO. We both believed that leaders needed to be honest with their people. They needed to be the teachers, trainers, and role models. And they needed to speak up when necessary."

MCPON Crow continued the fight for responsible compensation for enlisted personnel, including increase in allowances for quarters and family support. It was during his term of office that the public became aware that many junior enlisted personnel had become eligible for welfare payments, a circumstance Crow and others thought shameful and scandalous. He worked tirelessly on issues concerning habitability of ships and stations, and on issues that directly affected the quality of life of sailors at sea and ashore. He had particular interest in seeing that sailors registered to vote and exercised their franchise, realizing that the voting bloc of active enlisted personnel would have impact on those who controlled military budgets. He was particularly interested in continuing the development of senior enlisted personnel, particularly chief petty officers and above, and it was during his term of office that the Senior Enlisted Academy opened at Newport, Rhode Island.

Master Chief Avionics Technician (Air Crew) Billy C. Sanders (1982–85) was a quiet man, intent on doing the right thing for sailors and for the Navy. He made his own way without the benefit of a close relationship with his CNO. A strong advocate of the democratic process, he encouraged sailors to use their vote to force Congress to listen to servicemen. He enthusiastically endorsed the decision to outlaw beards and the return to a more traditional standard of grooming. An Alabama native, Sanders originally joined the Air Force, but after three years returned home to college. Within six months of joining the Navy in 1958, he sewed on the crow of an aviation electronics technician first-class. Six years later he was a chief, three years later a senior chief, and three years after that he was a master chief avionics technician. "Joining the Navy was the best decision I ever made," Sanders said.

Throughout his career Sanders made good, solid leadership and career decisions, based on common sense and what he felt was right. In June 1979, twenty-one years after joining the Navy, he was serving as command master chief for NAS Pensacola and Training Air Wing Six. A year later he took over as command master chief at Naval Air Facility Lajes, Azores. Shortly before his tour ended at Lajes, Sanders hosted a visit from the Master Chief Petty Officer of the Navy. Crow was nearing the end of his tenure, and nominations were already coming in for his relief. He took Sanders aside and recommended that he put in for his job. Sanders told him that he had already been through that once before and did not see any point in doing it again. But the commanding officer at Lajes submitted a nomination package for Sanders anyway. Meanwhile, in February 1982 Sanders was transferred to the Naval Education and Training Program Development Center at Pensacola, Florida, to serve as the special projects division officer. Soon after, Chief of Naval Operations Adm. James D. Watkins announced that he had chosen Master Chief Billy Sanders as the next Master Chief Petty Officer of the Navy.

In making the announcement, the CNO described the candidates as "the best the Navy has to offer," and said that his decision was a "very difficult one." He also noted the increasingly responsible position of senior petty officers in the Navy, citing the newly instituted chief petty officer indoctrination course, the Senior Enlisted Academy, and the new third-class petty officer indoctrination as examples. "We are seeing the final moves toward cementing the chief's hat to its rightful place on the Navy leadership pedestal," the CNO said.

Sanders agreed with the CNO that the Navy was on better footing than it had been in a long time, but he also knew there was still much work to be done. "I stepped in at a good time," he said. "Admiral Hayward and the people who worked for him, including MCPON Crow, had brought us back to a point where there was pride in serving in the Navy. We were still having problems with discipline and leadership, but in my mind, we had just let that get out of hand in previous years. It's difficult to change something in a short period of time."

MCPON Sanders assumed office on 1 October 1982. He continued the emphasis on sailors exercising their right to vote, and he spoke frequently before congressional committees, alongside his colleagues from the other armed services. His term was generally a time of stability on the human relations front, although during those years the Navy reversed its decision regarding the traditional "sailor suit" and reintroduced the "crackerjack" uniform for all personnel E-6 and below. Beards—which had been introduced yet again—were again banned, and Sanders urged all senior enlisted personnel not only to enforce the letter of the law regarding uniform regulations and weight and grooming standards, but to reflect the spirit of the rules as well. He continued the emphasis on senior enlisted leadership and championed a return of the chief petty officer community to its traditional role as trainers of junior enlisted personnel and junior officers alike.

Master Chief Radioman (Surface Warfare) William H. Plackett (1985–88) was the first to be groomed for the office as a fleet master chief. He took over with a solid network of contacts, having served first as force master chief for commander, Training Command, Atlantic, and then as fleet master chief of the Atlantic Fleet. With his wife, he helped to strengthen the Navy family image through work with family service centers, ombudsmen, and command master chiefs. He had been educated by the Navy through the Associate Degree Completion Program (ADCOP), and he pushed other sailors to set high educational goals. He was a strong advocate of the Leadership Management Education Training (LMET) program and guided it toward the more compressed Naval Leadership (NAVLEAD) system, which he implemented during his term of office.

Born in Paxton, Illinois, Bill Plackett had been influenced by area sailors returning from World War II. He joined the Navy in 1956, seeking challenge and educational opportunities. After graduation from boot camp, he began training as a radioman at "A" School in Norfolk, Virginia, and was assigned to Bahrain, in the Gulf of Arabia. There, he met Radioman First-Class Travis Short. "The thing that impressed me about Short was that he never stopped trying academically to improve himself," Plackett said. "He started out just about like I did, a non–high-school graduate from a small town. He continued to improve himself, making chief, and later retiring as a lieutenant commander. He had a very positive impact on me." After eleven years' service, Bill Plackett was selected as a chief petty officer. After a tour aboard *Forrestal* he served as an instructor at radioman "B" School at Bainbridge, Maryland. Completing his associate's degree in 1972, he was awarded an academic scholarship to the University of West Florida in Pensacola, and one year later graduated magna cum laude with a bachelor of science degree in vocational education. Following a second tour on *Forrestal* and his selection as master chief, he assumed duties as director of the Communications School, Fleet Training Center, Norfolk, Virginia. In 1979 he was named command master chief for commander, Training Command, U.S. Atlantic Headquarters, and subsequently became the first force master chief of the Atlantic Fleet Training Command in July 1981.

Selected as fleet master chief, U.S. Atlantic Fleet, in July 1982, Plackett began travelling with MCPON Sanders during his last month in office. As a fleet and force master chief, Plackett had lots of experience listening and talking to sailors in large or small groups. During a visit to Memphis, Tennessee, where Sanders was the guest speaker at the Navy Memphis Khaki Ball, Plackett fielded a question from a young sailor who wanted to know why he had stayed in the Navy so long. "Well, there are a lot of reasons," answered the incoming MCPON, "but it's mainly because no matter where I am or what I do in the Navy, I'm always having fun. We had some problems but we were willing to admit it and say, 'Let's take them on and fix them the best way we can.'"

MCPON Plackett set out eight goals for his term of office:

1. Enhance the "One Navy" concept through improved cooperation and communications across all warfare lines.
2. Maintain currency in attitudes and issues in the fleet and the naval shore establishment. Identify problem areas affecting welfare and morale of the Navy and work within the chain of command to correct them.
3. Continue to promote individual pride and unit esprit de corps through improved professionalism throughout the Navy.
4. Promote improved military professionalism through entire enlisted community of the U.S. Navy.
5. Improve dissemination of information on personnel-related matters down to the deckplates.
6. Place the command master chief program on solid footing.
7. Enforce the Navy's drug/alcohol program.
8. Stimulate interest in the Navy-wide "Get Out and Vote" program.

During his term of office, Plackett vigorously supported leadership training for all levels in the service. He also dealt with the major social change that, for the first time, permitted women to go to sea in previously closed ratings and led to the gender-integrated Navy of today.

Shortly before retirement, MCPON Plackett reflected on his position. "The challenge as Master Chief Petty Officer of the Navy is to face each new situation, deal with it with dignity, and overcome the problem," he said. "My goal as MCPON was to do these three years and finish knowing that I have not made any Chief Petty Officer ashamed of being a chief. It goes back to ethics and being able and having the courage to stand up to the CNO, or any flag officer or captain, because you hold those individuals in high esteem, and say to them that they are wrong. It's a very lonely feeling, but that's what this position is for," he said.

Master Chief Avionics Technician (Air Warfare) Duane R. Bushey (1988–92) was pulled from the fleet as a command master chief with a reputation for making things happen. Known as a hard worker, he was constantly driven by self-made deadlines and the haunting feeling that he could or should be doing more for the fleet sailor. He was frequently compared to the first MCPON, Del Black. A native of Maryland's Eastern Shore, he never planned on making the Navy a career, but was driven to see what might be on the other side of the oceans. Joining at Salisbury, Bushey scored high enough on the entrance exam to be guaranteed any "A" School he wanted in the Navy.

Later, when asked by a young petty officer to state who in his naval career had made the biggest impact on him, Bushey said it was the "chiefs' community as a whole."

My company commander in boot camp was an engineman chief named Lamb. The meanest son of a gun I ever met. But he taught me something that I never forgot. One day we were waiting to get our dress blues issued. I was standing by my locker and he walked by. I came to attention, and he looked at me and asked why I was just standing around. I told him I was waiting to get my blues issued. He made me do fifty pushups. When I was through, he walked off but fifteen minutes later, he came back and I was standing in the same place. He asked me again why I was just standing around, and I gave him the same answer. He made me do fifty more pushups. Well, we did this about three or four times and finally, he stopped me and said, "You sure aren't very smart, Bushey. Haven't you figured out why you are doing these pushups?" And I said, "No, sir." He said, "Well, I'm going to give you a hint. In the U.S. Navy, you never just stand around waiting for something to happen. You make things happen. There is always something to do."

Bushey said that lesson stayed with him throughout his career. "If I was standing somewhere not doing something, I felt that I was going to have to do fifty pushups," he said. "I didn't want to do that, so I always found something to do."

Comparing today's leadership with chiefs like Lamb, Bushey believes that he was right for the times. "It was a different style of leadership back then, but it was effective because young sailors like me feared and respected authority. We didn't ask questions as sailors do today. I'm not saying the way we do it today is wrong. It's just different. Everybody who grew up in society today is different." When he made third-class in 1963, he married and reenlisted under the STAR program for an advanced electronics "B" School. After graduation, he reported aboard USS *Kearsarge* at San Diego.

In 1965 Bushey was advanced to second-class and in 1967 to first-class. While on board *Kearsarge*, he earned designation as air crewman and plane captain in the C-1A aircraft. Bushey and his shipmates were awarded the Meritorious Unit Commendation for their performance in support of Seventh Fleet operations off the coast of Vietnam. He served in several aviation-related billets and in 1973 was named the CINCPACFLT Shore Sailor of the Year.

Leaving the West Coast in 1973 for Norfolk, Virginia, Bushey was assigned to Aircraft Ferry Squadron Thirty-One, where he qualified as an overwater navigator in several aircraft, a flight engineer for the P-3 Orion, and a bombardier and navigator for the A-6 Intruder. He accumulated 4,283 flight hours and 844,506 "stork" miles as an enlisted navigator. In November 1974 he was advanced to chief petty officer and became senior chief in 1977. As the command senior chief, he sampled his first taste of the leadership role that would eventually take him to Washington, by attending the Army Sergeants Major Academy at Fort Bliss. Returning to aviation billets, he served as a command master chief, and then as command master chief for commander, Tactical Support Wing One, in Norfolk. While there he was named as Tidewater Virginia's Military Citizen of the Year for 1982.

In 1985, as his tour at COMTACSUPWING One drew to a close, Bushey submitted his retirement papers and set a date, but Capt. Paul W. Parcells, commanding officer of the precommissioning unit for *Theodore Roosevelt* in Norfolk, convinced him to do one more tour as his command master chief. For two years Bushey worked hard, convinced that he was in his twilight tour. His goals were to make the new carrier "the best ship in the Navy, take it on a Med cruise, and then retire." Throughout his career, he had used spare time to talk to other sailors, asking about the jobs they did and their commands. "I was always curious," he said. "If I was in between flights somewhere, and I saw a bunch of sailors standing around, I'd go talk to them. I was also a door opener, curious to know what was on the other side. There's hardly an air station in the U.S. Navy that I haven't been on." On *Theodore Roosevelt,* he opened a lot of doors and talked to a lot of sailors. Using closed-circuit television, he talked to the crew during a weekly question-and-answer session. A strong believer in community involvement, he encouraged his sailors to volunteer their services during off-duty hours. In 1988 he and his family were recognized as Tidewater's Family of the Year. On 17 June 1988 Adm. Carlisle A. H. Trost announced that he had selected Bushey to be the seventh Master Chief Petty Officer of the Navy.

During his time in office, MCPON Bushey began the process that resulted in the development of the "Journey into the CPO Mess," and fought successfully to control many of the excesses that had plagued the initiation process. He worked closely with the leaders of the other services to ensure an orderly and humane introduction of the concept of high-year tenure, whereby long-service personnel who had been unable to advance in rating were encouraged and assisted in their transition back to civilian life. He urged the development of additional remediation programs for sailors with basic educational deficiencies, and it was through his and others' efforts that, at the time of the Persian Gulf War, the Navy was adequately staffed and exceptionally well motivated to carry out the nation's policy under arduous and dangerous conditions.

Twelve

If you're looking for an interesting sailor, you'd do well to chat awhile with Master Chief John Hagan. Born in 1946 in the United Kingdom, John Hagan grew up in Asheville, North Carolina. After high school, he enlisted in the Navy in December 1964 and attended basic training at Recruit Training Center, San Diego, and electronics technician "A" School at Naval Training Center, Treasure Island, California, before assignment to the Naval Air Test Center Patuxent River, Maryland.

MCPON Hagan:

> Well, you might say that I was an underachiever in my younger days. I was working at a large department store and my manager, Clifford Boone, had recently left the Navy after one enlistment. He told a few sea stories from time to time, and once he brought several trays of 35-mm slides and showed a few of us scenes from his around-the-world cruise on

the USS *Enterprise*. He had been an AO3, and his pride in that rating and how hard they worked and how important they were to the mighty carrier was clear. Well, shortly afterward, I walked past a recruiting poster outside the post office. I remember it clearly; it showed a sailor in dress blues on the bridge wing, jumper flap blowing in the wind. And so I walked into that recruiter's office and took a test. The recruiter told me I had gotten the "highest score ever attained in his office," and the next day I left for Recruit Training in San Diego. But it's funny—a while later I got a letter from my mom saying that my cousin had taken the test for the Navy at that same recruiting office, and the recruiters told him that he had the "highest score ever attained in that office." Now, isn't that interesting?

It may seem strange to today's sailors, but at "A" School I hardly ever saw a chief in the year I spent training to be an electronic technician. And, you know, I don't really remember any instructors either; it was a very impersonal place with almost no military training to augment the classroom electronics instruction. In fact, back then, if you were a seaman or junior petty officer, and you were having a conversation with a chief, things were not going well for you at all.

Like many young sailors, though, Hagan came into contact with a few Navy men who influenced his career and his life.

MCPON Hagan:

At Patuxent River, I met a chief petty officer through the chapel who turned out to be a lifelong role model, father figure, mentor, and friend, although I was never in the same command with him and we seldom talked about career matters. Martin Gallion went on to become a phenomenally professional and caring command master chief, who is remembered by all who served with him as truly exceptional and unique. He retired after thirty years' service, and even today my wife and I maintain contact with him as frequently as we can.

Later at NAS Whidbey Island I became the LPO and site supervisor of the Long-Range ATC Radar Site. I was a very junior ET1, with seven sailors and a couple of civilians working for me. One of the civilians was a retired World War II CPO who had served the entire war in

the battleship *New York* as an electrician and then changed rates to aviation electrician before finally retiring a few years later at Whidbey
Island. Rather than resent being subordinate to the military site supervisor, Walter Yake was my biggest supporter. When I instituted some
military protocols, such as Quarters, GMT, and such, Walt was the first
one to fall in. He gave me advice in very discreet and nonthreatening
ways, and he gave me some affirmation that what I was doing was positive. He was a devoutly spiritual Mormon and a loving family man, and
he was a proud retired chief petty officer whose CPO pride was shown
in more ways than just bumper stickers or CPO club activities.
Recently I attended his ninetieth birthday party. Those are just two of
several of whom I remember with fondness and affection.

Hagan's next assignment was aboard USS *Lester* (DE-1022), homeported in Naples, Italy. During a subsequent tour of sea duty as a maintenance
technician at Underwater Demolition Team 21 in Little Creek, Virginia, he
was advanced to chief petty officer and qualified as a naval parachutist.
While assigned to a shore tour at Naval and Marine Corps Reserve Center in
Louisville, Kentucky, he was advanced to senior chief petty officer. While
there, he earned his bachelor's degree in business administration from
McKeendree College, graduating in September 1980.

MCPON Hagan:

I got my first experience as a leading chief petty officer in Louisville,
where, after my promotion to senior chief petty officer, I took over the
job of leading chief (and executive officer, since the CO was our only
officer). I relieved a very capable chief, and I found the challenges of
leading both daunting and invigorating. I then reported to USS
Richmond K. Turner (CG-20) as a very young and junior SCPO and
was the interim command senior chief on an occasional basis. I held
the job until the first command master chief ever assigned to the
Richmond K. Turner reported aboard. You've got to remember that it
was a tough time for our Navy; drug and race problems still challenged
us daily, especially aboard ship. And it was there that I realized that a
squared-away command master chief could do so much good if he

were proactive and so much harm if he were just satisfied to claim a parking space on the pier, follow the CO around during zone inspections, and perform a few recurring ceremonial duties. So I decided then that I'd try to go the command master chief route, to see what I could do for sailors and for their families.

While aboard *Richmond K. Turner,* Hagan qualified as an enlisted surface warfare specialist and was advanced to master chief petty officer. Shortly after reporting to his next assignment at the Naval Air Technical Training Center at Memphis, Tennessee, he was selected as the force master chief for naval technical training.

MCPON Hagan:

As the force master chief for naval technical training, I worked very hard to raise the standards in our "A" Schools for both instructors and staff members. More important, I made sure that those standards were enforced. At the time, there were many serious problems in the training commands. The technical courses of instruction were satisfactory, but just as I remembered from my own "A" School days, physical fitness, general military training, personal improvement, financial responsibility, and so forth were largely ignored. We addressed the problems and implemented the Integrated Training Command (ITC), which took responsibility for all aspects of the sailor's life during their "A" School experience. We then did similar things at Recruit Training Command. We built the first confidence course there, and even though we need more than a single course, given the throughput at RTC, at least we had made a start. Many of us felt, both then and now, that we could make Recruit Training Command much more effective with just small investments but serious leadership. And I'm truly pleased to see so many of the things we recommended back then finally implemented today.

While in that billet, I also placed myself on the IG team and took over the inspection of about a dozen areas, which had never been given any serious scrutiny. Specifically, I inspected the health and physical readiness programs at every command. We felt that the training commands where young sailors reported first after boot camp were really a continuation of the "Quarterdeck of the Navy," and we wanted them to see and experience the Navy at its best. My second flag officer in that job, RADM Dave Harlow, required all commanding officers and executive officers throughout his command to participate in a special Physical Readiness Test and report the results directly to him. This was unprecedented flag-level interest in the subject, and the training commands were soon getting the message.

In April 1988 Master Chief Hagan reported as command master chief for the precommissioning unit for USS *Philippine Sea* (CG-58) at Norfolk. After commissioning, USS *Philippine Sea* reported to her homeport in Mayport, Florida, and was subsequently deployed in support of Operation Desert Shield and Desert Storm.

MCPON Hagan:

Desert Shield and Desert Storm were trying times for the Navy. We talk even today of increased operational tempo—well, there's nothing like a full-scale war to stress the manpower and ships of the Navy to the limit. Increase ops tempo seems to be greeted with the same cross-section of response that it always has been. Most sailors suck it up and do their duty with little comment, while others complain loudly but do their duty nonetheless. Navy leadership works extremely hard to prevent extending sea tours so most sailors knew that the madness would end at some predictable date. But even while they complained, there was always an undercurrent of pride in knowing that they were sacrificing a little more than was in the plan. Similarly, the impact of increased op tempo on family life seems to vary with the individual. Generally, strong families get stronger, but that is not always the case. Perhaps the most difficult challenge I had on *Philippine Sea* was helping sailors deal with the negative impact on their families and loved ones of so much time away from home.

During this tour of duty, Master Chief Hagan qualified as officer of the deck (under way). Later, after serving as command master chief of Helicopter Anti-Submarine Squadron (Light) 48 at Mayport, Florida, he was selected as the eighth Master Chief Petty Officer of the Navy in August 1992. His five-

and-a-half-year tenure makes him the longest serving Master Chief Petty Officer of the Navy to date.

MCPON Hagan:

I think we did some good things during the time I was in office. But still you are only one person with only seven days in a week and all the normal limitations. I knew I couldn't do everything we wanted to do, but I was determined that I was going to try to do as much as possible and, not knowing what was possible, I worked hard to find out. Some of the greatest challenges turned out to be these:

Downsizing was just beginning, and it was ugly. My first day as MCPON was the first day of a monthlong Involuntary Separation Board for E-7 to E-9. It was gut-wrenching to lose many good senior petty officers. The board was a twelve-hours-a-day, six-days-a-week function.

Enlisted Warfare Qualifications were poorly and inconsistently administered. I came to the MCPON position determined to end the abuses. I found Enlisted Surface Warfare qualifications being "awarded" at stations five hundred miles from the nearest body of water. I found an Enlisted Aviation Warfare qualification program at, of all places, the Bureau of Personnel. How they managed that I can't tell you—it's hard to find an aircraft inside BUPERS. The program was not true to its intentions, and the pins certainly were not the rich source of pride they should have been. It wasn't easy, but we developed new and meaningful guidelines, with teeth, and we restricted the program to sailors serving full tours of sea duty in the warfare community. I'm very proud of what we accomplished to make Warfare Qualifications the meaningful program that it is today.

Homosexual policy became an issue with the recent election of President Clinton. This totally unnecessary and terribly distracting issue came to the fore for several years.

Physical fitness and weight standards for senior enlisted leaders were a problem. I instituted mandatory physical training at all fleet and force master chief meetings. It wasn't pretty in the beginning, but I can recall several PT sessions later in my MCPON tour with some impressive cadence-calling group runs, with every member of the panel participating.

The Command Master Chief Program had very loose guiding instructions, and even these were largely ignored. There was no selection process, and some of the most qualified and motivated candidates were not eligible because of artificial restraints in the rating communities. I wrote the CMC instruction, personally walked it through every chop, and got the CNO (Admiral Boorda) involved. He was very supportive and rolled all the opposition, and we set up a sensible selection process, training requirements, and standards for service.

CPO initiation was still out of control, despite some pretty strenuous efforts on the part of my predecessors. They, like me, wanted to clean up the tradition without killing it. I worked this one hard. I defined CPO initiation as a "Season of Pride." I made physical training, led by sponsors, mandatory, and we instituted heritage reading as a requirement for every CPO selectee.

Voluntary education for sea duty sailors was another issue. Inexplicably, when I came to the MCPON job, there were good off-duty education opportunities for everyone except sailors in ships. We had a very small and ineffective Program for Afloat College Education for ships at sea, and that was about it. And so my goal was to see off-watch education opportunities available to all on sea duty. Opportunity was the key word; I was not interested then, and still don't support mandating off-duty education (degrees, etc.) or tying it to promotions.

Career sea pay for the single sailor was a key concern. Getting Basic Allowance for Quarters (BAQ) for sailors at sea and housing allowances for sailors ashore, as well as resolving other pay inequities, was one of the major tasks of my term in office.

One area that will always be close to John Hagan's heart is the lore and traditions of the sea services.

MCPON Hagan:

One day, speaking at an all-hands briefing, I was startled to realize that most sailors knew little, if anything, of what our forefathers and predecessors went through to get us where we are today. And not just the

Navy; this nation would be vastly different without the sacrifices of the men and women who served their country in wars from the Revolution to Desert Storm. And I realized that day that their stories and their legacy could help inspire all of us to better understand and live our core values of Honor, Courage, and Commitment. I thought it sad that sailors could serve on ships named *Guadalcanal, Philippine Sea, Midway,* or *Normandy,* and not know the sacrifices that their predecessors made at those spots. So when I got back to Washington after that trip, I had my staff work closely with the Naval Historical Center and the Naval Institute to develop and implement the Naval Heritage Reading List. I'm proud that that is still an integral part of the journey into the mess for newly promoted chief petty officers. Because, you see, we have an opportunity, during that six-week period, to do things that no other service has ever tried. We have the undivided attention of the best members of our commands, and it's really incumbent on us to use that time as effectively as we can to reinforce some of the lessons that our forefathers learned while serving their country. Tradition, lore, and history: those are vital parts of the "second boot camp" that we are able to provide to our newest chief petty officers.

Retiring as the eighth MCPON in 1998, Hagan has received personal awards including the Meritorious Service Medal, Navy Commendation Medal, and Navy Achievement Medal (with gold star), as well as unit and campaign awards. He serves on the board of directors for the Surface Navy Association and the Navy Memorial, as well as Navy Mutual Aid Association, and is an active member of the Fleet Reserve Association. He maintains close ties to the Navy as a consultant to a major defense contractor, providing valuable insight and input to the design of the next generation of surface combatant ships. His thoughts about the role of the chief petty officer and today's sailors are both challenging and encouraging.

MCPON Hagan:
I'd tell every young chief petty officer that I expect that the chief of the near future will continue to care about the full spectrum of command

issues. Chief petty officers occupy a unique position in the "middle management" niche, and the CPO has the potential to influence junior enlisted sailors, junior officers, department heads, and even the CO and XO. When the chiefs are confident, optimistic, and exhibit obvious pride in the command, it radiates throughout the ship. When they are not, it has an equally widespread impact. My hope is that ten years from now the CPOs will be even more aware of this phenomenon and act accordingly. And I hope too that the CPO of the near future will be not only a military role model and a technical authority but also a lifestyle role model. When the chief finds the discipline to eat right and maintain his or her weight and the time to PT regularly, then no one else in the command has any excuse for not trying. That's what leading from the front is all about.

But mostly, I'd tell every chief and every sailor to enjoy and appreciate your Navy life in real time and in the present tense. Don't wait until you have completed a tour of hard duty to realize that pride and satisfaction. And stay connected to your heritage. Reflect sometimes on the privilege of following in the footsteps of sailors who served in an even more arduous time and sacrificed even more. Too often we focus on the hardship of the rough tour (understandable and to a degree unavoidable) to the exclusion of an occasional pondering of the privilege of even being a part of such important and meaningful work.

It's interesting that most of the ten master chief petty officers of the Navy grew up far from the sea. Master Chief Jim Herdt, the ninth Master Chief Petty Officer of the Navy, is certainly no exception.

MCPON Herdt:

Somehow, growing up in Wyoming, I knew I'd find myself in the Navy someday. My dad was a World War II battleship sailor on the USS *Mississippi* (BB-41), and although he never talked much about the war, he had a glass-bottomed serving tray with a lithograph of the ship and the battle stars and ribbons she earned during the war. I grew up looking at that, so at the height of the Vietnam War, I said, well, I've had enough of school for a while, and maybe now the Navy is the place for me. After my selection as MCPON, my wife, Sharon had that lithograph professionally framed. I hung that picture opposite my desk when I was the Master Chief Petty Officer of the Navy, just to remind myself of those who have gone before us. And even after a career that spanned thirty-five years, twenty-seven of which were as a chief petty officer, I reflect on that plaque nearly every day as it hangs over my home office desk.

Jim Herdt, a native of Casper, Wyoming, first enlisted in 1966. After attending machinist's mate "A" School in Great Lakes, Illinois, and various nuclear power training schools, he served sea tours aboard the USS *Independence* (CV 62) and USS *Will Rogers* (SSBN 659G) and shore tours at Nuclear Power Training Unit, Windsor, Connecticut, and Radiological Repair Facility in New London, Connecticut.

MCPON Herdt:

I had two years of college when I finally went down to the recruiter's office, and after some discussion, determined that the best place for me would be in the nuclear submarine program. I became a nuclear-trained machinist's mate. And to be honest, I didn't particularly like the Navy at first. I had a hard time finding anyone whom I wanted to emulate. The leadership style back then was pretty rough. I was married, and neither my wife nor I thought much of Navy life at the time, at least the parts that we saw. Many of our impressions were formed before the Navy developed programs recognizing that sailors have families, too. I worked hard back then and quickly made petty officer first-class, and in fact was selected for chief, but after eight years I took a discharge and went back to school at Kansas State.

After leaving active duty in 1974, Master Chief Herdt enlisted in the Naval Reserve and served in various Selected Naval Reserve units while attending Kansas State University. Returning to active duty in 1976, he served as a Naval Reserve recruiter in Milwaukee, and in 1978 returned to active duty.

MCPON Herdt:

I enjoyed the freedom of being away from the military, but only for a short time. So, about six months later, I affiliated with the Navy Reserve, mostly for the money, but also so that I didn't throw away the time I had invested in the service. I had left active duty even though I'd been selected for chief petty officer, and, upon joining the Naval Reserve, I was advanced to CPO. But after experiencing the important business of making Fleet Ballistic Missile patrols, I felt there was just something missing from my civilian life. I worked in a number of routine jobs while attending college full time; I was a night clerk at a Ramada Inn, I remember. But what I was doing just didn't seem all that important to me.

I had a few good mentors when I was a young sailor, of course. And I think one of the most important elements of leadership is that people recognize certain attributes in their leaders, and say, jeez, I'd really like to emulate that. Unfortunately, in those early years, I really didn't experience much of that, in fact there were a whole lot of people whom I realized I didn't want to be like. But in 1974 I met Master Chief Barry Bearse at the Radiological Repair Facility at New London, and he was just an outstanding role model. He was slim, trim, wore his uniform with pride, spoke well, understood people, and, well, if he had been in my career earlier, I'd probably never have left the Navy. He pushed me to finish my courses for chief, and pushed me to take the test. I did and was selected, but I chose instead to leave the Navy and try my hand in the civilian world. When I finally made chief in Kansas, he sent me a complete set of uniforms, because he knew there wouldn't be a uniform shop close by. He even made sure that I had the right hash marks and crow already sewn on the left sleeve. Years later, after my selection as MCPON, I made an effort to contact him, and he was dumbfounded that he had had such an impact on me and that I'd remember him after all this time. But that's a characteristic of great leaders, too: often they don't even understand the impact they are having on their juniors. If I had to characterize when I caught fire, it was when I first became a chief petty officer, because it was then that I realized that I was responsible for people, and not just machinery, and I realized that this was something that I really wanted to do, long term.

Master Chief Herdt served aboard USS *Texas* (CGN 39) and USS *Cincinnati* (SSN 693), and on the staff of the Nuclear Power School in Orlando, Florida, before his tour as chief of the boat aboard USS *Skipjack* (SSN 585). He has served as command master chief at Nuclear Field "A" School, Orlando, on board USS *Theodore Roosevelt* (CVN 71), and at Naval Training Center, Great Lakes, Illinois.

MCPON Herdt:

I didn't immediately return to the fleet when I came back to the Navy. I spent two years on active duty as a Naval Reserve recruiter, but really wanted to get back into the "regular" Navy. I thought that's where I could make the greatest contribution as a chief petty officer. I did a split tour aboard the USS *Texas,* followed by a tour on the USS *Cincinnati* as the "Bull Nuke," the senior enlisted member responsible for the nuclear propulsion plant. After that, I became an instructor and section advis-er—really, a counselor—at the nuclear power school at Orlando. And then, in one of the best events of my entire career, I was selected to be one of six exchange students at the Army's Sergeants Major Academy, and that was a place where I really caught fire. It was the first formal leadership class that I ever attended, and it was a life-changing event. I knew then that if I could just carry some of what I had learned back with me to the Navy, then I'd really make a contribution.

I wound up on the USS *Skipjack,* which was about thirty years old and scheduled for decommissioning in less than three years. I had reported aboard as the Bull Nuke, but the chief of the boat retired shortly thereafter, and the skipper asked me if I'd consider fleeting up to be the COB. I had already passed a COB board by then and was anxious to take on more leadership responsibility, so I jumped at the chance. Now, I'd spent most of my active Navy time on submarines, and nothing about them ever frightened me—I never was scared when we were at sea at all—but I was frightened by some of the things that I saw on the *Skipjack*. It had just come out of a very difficult overhaul period. In fact, I actually joined the boat down in Panama. There were oil leaks all over, things were not well maintained, things were in disarray, people were dispirited, and it was not a good feeling at all. So, taking my newly honed leadership skills to heart, during my welcome-aboard visit with the XO, when he asked me what I was thinking, I told him, "Sir, I'd like to be relieved." He about fell off his chair, and in a very few minutes we were both before the captain, who had reported aboard a few months before me, and I told him about the things that I had observed that made me uncomfortable. And the skipper, to his credit, said, well, if you take care of things back aft, I'll fix things up forward. And, with a handshake between the two of us, and a lot of hard work from what became a great crew, we got that old boat in great shape. By the time she was ready for decommissioning, she was one of the best ships on the river, up there at New London.

Master Chief Herdt is a graduate of both the U.S. Army Sergeants Major Academy and the Navy's Senior Enlisted Academy at Newport, Rhode Island. He has earned a master of business administration degree with a concentration in human resources management from Florida Institute of Technology. He qualified as an enlisted aviation and surface warfare specialist, and qualified to wear the enlisted submarine breast insignia. Herdt also certified as a master training specialist. He relieved John Hagan as Master Chief Petty Officer of the Navy in March 1998.

MCPON Herdt:

After leaving *Skipjack*, I got a call asking if I'd consider taking the job as command master chief at the nuclear "A" School in Orlando. My family had stayed in Orlando when I went back to sea from New London, allowing our son to stay in his high school, so that was an easy decision. And it wasn't long after that I was assigned the Navy enlistment classification (NEC) as a command master chief. Those were the days before there was a formal selection process for the CMC program. Nuclear field "A" School staff—and the nuclear school staffs in general—are composed of the absolute best people in their ratings in the Navy. They're the type of sailor who, if you can get one or two aboard ship, give you reason to consider yourself fortunate, and here I was, the leader of nearly one hundred fifty of them.

So, together with Master Chief Bill Gabler, who was serving in the personnel shop of Naval Reactors, we worked to bring nuclear power program CPOs into more active participation in the Navy's CPO mess. Up to that point, there was a bit of bias regarding nuclear-trained CPOs, and frankly, some of it was justly earned as some nuclear-trained CPOs tended to hold themselves apart from the rest of the Navy. And so, when I was selected for the job of Master Chief Petty Officer of the Navy, with a bit of concern for the immensity of the job, and a great deal of humility, I thought that I might be able to further these and other ideas I had gained for expanded respect for the enlisted force of our Navy from the marvelous platform that office provides.

Master Chief Herdt served at a crucial time, as the nation faced the challenges of asymmetrical threats, greatly increased operational tempo with a downsized force and aging fleet, and, for at least the first half of his tour of duty, a presidential administration that many believed did not understand the military.

MCPON Herdt:
The job of Master Chief Petty Officer of the Navy, as well as that of the four senior enlisted leaders in the other services, is truly overwhelming. I came to the job with perhaps the most varied career of any of us in that position. I had been a nuclear-qualified submariner and chief of the boat; I had some reserve time; I'd recruited; I'd served on a cruiser; and I'd been CMC of a big-deck ship, the *Theodore Roosevelt*. I'd been CMC of Naval Training Center Great Lakes and the force master chief for naval education and training. But there is nothing in an enlisted career that can ever prepare a sailor adequately for that job. If you look at any flag officer, nearly every one of them had a tour or two in Washington before moving on to an executive, decision-making position. But that

doesn't happen for MCPON selectees; we come from the fleet, and we get thrown into that hothouse inside the Beltway. The biggest challenge of all is just understanding how the system works, who in Washington can make things happen, and what's possible, and what is just wishful thinking.

One example was the number of requests for assistance received in the office from individual sailors. Although most sailors had legitimate issues, many had gone directly to the MCPON, essentially doing an end-run around their own enlisted chain of command—not giving their CMC or their force or fleet master chiefs a chance to help them. It seemed to me that the MCPON's office was spending a tremendous amount of time addressing issues that could and should have been resolved at a much lower level. I saw that we really needed to get this thing under better control. So we began to redirect a lot of this traffic, telling sailors we were concerned about their issue, but we were handing it back to their fleet or force master chief for action, with the requirement that we be kept in the loop as to what was going on. Everyone, from the sailor's CMC to the fleet master chief level, welcomed that change.

Now, once we did that, it freed up time to become more strategic in our thinking and actions. We recognized that the environment was changing, but that all of us, particularly the chiefs' community, hadn't changed as much as we needed to meet the new realities. We were in a battle for people back then. We'd been in an all-volunteer mode for years, yet our mindset was still that of a draft-motivated force. We had a conscription mentality, as I told Secretary Dansig when he first came on board. We were acting as though there were an endless line of folks beating on the door to get into the Navy, and that just wasn't so, and it hadn't been that way for years. But all of us—especially in the chiefs' community—seemed to forget that things changed when the voluntary military became established.

We were in competition for a highly talented work force. These were people who had many options in their lives, not only with the other services, but in the civilian sector, too. All of a sudden we were looking at recruits and young sailors in the late 1990s, many with college degrees, and yet we were still treating them as if they were the sailors of forty years ago. It was clear that these sailors valued education, so I proposed establishment of what became the Navy College Program because we realized that people who completed voluntary education programs stayed in the Navy longer, advanced faster, and made better sailors while they were there. We worked with colleges to set up degree paths that awarded credit for what the sailor knew already, or what he or she learned on the job, and while we didn't want to remove any of the academic rigor, we made sure that these schools could tailor their programs to the reality of life in the sea services. We didn't change the academic requirements, but we got rid of most of the bureaucratic red tape so those sailors could achieve a degree while serving on active duty.

We also worked on the thrift savings plan so that folks could make intelligent investment decisions early in their careers, rather than have to wait until they were senior personnel. We fought for, and got, large targeted pay increases, so that we could fairly compensate our senior people for the skills and knowledge they'd developed over the years. Looking back, I consider those some of the most important benefits changes we made over those four years.

Although some civilians of the Clinton administration were not as attuned to the needs of the military as other administrations, MCPON Herdt was blessed with a capable and energetic leader in Adm. Vern Clark, the chief of naval operations.

MCPON Herdt:

I think Admiral Clark is one of the most far-seeing and visionary leaders the Navy has ever had. He realized that we had to change, and that the changes we had to make in the way we view resources, our mission, and our platforms were significant and immediate. He communicated that sense of urgency to all of us, and it was clear that these changes not only would affect the chiefs mess, but, in a very real sense, required the chiefs' community to make them happen.

Now, chiefs can be conservative—they are the experts in their rating field, and often say, with a great deal of conviction, "Well, what we're doing now must be working, because it's gotten us this far, right?" And if things were the same as they were, say, thirty years ago, then maybe they make a good point. But things are not the same. Leadership when I came into the Navy was pretty easy; you said, "Go do this" and followed up to be sure it was done. But today's sailors want to know why and how, and what-if, and that's a great thing, it really is, because it gives us a lot of additional brainpower to focus on the process.

MCPON Herdt's personal awards include the Distinguished Service Medal, Meritorious Service Medal with two Gold Stars, the Navy Commendation Medal, the Navy Achievement Medal with Gold Star, and numerous campaign and unit awards. Herdt was among the first to recognize the ongoing challenges for the Navy and the chief petty officer community in particular:

MCPON Herdt:

In the past, our common method of teaching leadership to chief petty officers was to have them stand around and watch others lead until it was their turn to take over. The other services were way ahead of us in that regard. They realized before we did that formal leadership development is an important adjunct to on-the-job training as leaders. Today our Navy is revolutionizing the way we grow sailors. Rather than giving them all their training at the beginning of their career and hoping we get a good master chief at the end of the career, our Navy is pursuing a system of lifelong learning and growth for every sailor. Every sailor will be developed over their entire career whether they stay for four years or thirty. That development will begin the day they enter boot camp and end only when they take the uniform off. Every sailor will have a growth path along separate growth vectors: performance, personal growth, professional growth, leadership, and certifications/qualifications. What used to be done largely at training commands will fall now to leaders throughout our Navy who will manage the growth of our sailors. But none of this is going to work unless the chiefs mess makes it work. The day of the chief being mainly a straw boss is gone now. Sure, they'll always be the leaders in crises, as they've always been, but they will have to help others grow throughout their careers regardless of where they are and what their job is, and that involves more than mentoring. In a big way, the fleet has felt and often voiced that they were the users of the knowledge and skills that sailors gained in "A" School—well, today it has to be a lifelong learning mentality. And the chief petty officers mess will be a tremendously important part of that because they will be not only users of that talent, but developers of talent as well.

Now retired, and acting as a consultant in the human resources area of the Department of the Navy, MCPON Herdt offers these final thoughts about the Navy he served for thirty-five years:

MCPON Herdt:

I sometimes wish that I could start over again today, maybe at, oh, the second-class petty officer level, because the changes that are coming are immense. Changes that I saw over a thirty-five-year period, today's sailors will see occur every five to ten years. I relate the pace of change they are about to experience to them walking just below the ridgeline of a very steep hill, and when they get over the top and start down the other side, their walk is going to break into a run. There is change coming regarding responsibility—you can't just recruit better sailors and build better sailors without giving them more responsibility—and I think the chiefs mess is going to wind up with much more responsibility than they have at present. This is the best time in history to be a member of the world's greatest Navy.

Herdt passed the ceremonial cutlass, symbol of the office of the Master Chief Petty Officer of the Navy, to Master Chief Terry Scott in April 2002. It's a long way from Buffalo, Missouri, to the Navy Annex at the Pentagon. It's an even longer

trip from seaman recruit to Master Chief Petty Officer of the Navy. If you don't
believe that, just ask Scott, the tenth Master Chief Petty Officer of the Navy.

MCPON Scott:

I'm from the Midwest, and my family moved around a little bit when I
was growing up. I had saved some money for college, but I saw others
start school and then drop out, and I thought to myself, do I really
want to risk the money I've saved, particularly when I'm not sure that I
am ready to go on to college right after high school? So there I was in
December 1976, in Louisburg, Kansas, looking around and trying to
decide what to do with my life—or at least that part of my life that I
could see from the vantage point of a seventeen-year-old. Both my dad
and my grandfather were military veterans, and there was always a
sense of patriotism in my family—that's a characteristic of small mid-
western towns, too, I believe. I visited the Army recruiter, and things
were sounding pretty good to me, and so, being seventeen, I brought
home the enlistment papers and asked my mom to sign them.

Well, you know how moms are. She looked at the papers closely,
and then looked at me, and then looked at the papers again. She told
me that she'd sign, but only under two conditions. The first was that I
had to talk to every branch of the service before making a commitment, and the other was that I had to promise her that I'd never get a
tattoo. And, even after twenty-six years in the Navy, I'm proud to
report that I kept both of those promises to my mom.

Scott did, indeed, check with every recruiter in town, and, based on the
educational opportunities and technical programs available, decided on the
Navy.

MCPON Scott:

I've got to say that the atmosphere in that Navy recruiter's office was
tremendously positive—you could tell that those guys loved what they
were doing, loved the Navy, and really represented the best that the
Navy had to offer. Now, I had a "cousin of a cousin" or some distant

relative of that sort who was a Navy Missile Technician—an MT3 at the time, I believe. And once I heard what his job was like, well, that pretty much helped me make up my mind. I went back to that recruiter and said, "Sign me up as a missile technician; that's what I want to do."

Like most recruits, Terry Scott didn't quite have a full appreciation of what steps needed to be taken to reach his final Navy goal. The recruiter was quick to bring him up to speed.

MCPON Scott:

That guy just looked at me and laughed! "Whoa there, partner, there are a lot of steps you have to take before you get to wear an MT3's crow on your left arm," he said. "First comes boot camp, and after that sub school, and then, if your grades are good enough in your 'A' School, there are a couple of 'C' Schools you'll have to attend before you ship out as a missile technician." And right then I learned that in the Navy, you pretty much have to earn whatever you are after, and that learning and earning go hand in hand. It took almost two years, but I reported aboard my first "boomer," the USS *John Adams* (SSBN 620), in October 1978.

Every sailor looks back at his or her career and can find chief petty officers who have made a tremendous difference: as leaders, mentors and, often enough, friends. MCPON Terry Scott is no different.

MCPON Scott:

There are a number of outstanding chief petty officers who influenced me. Two names come immediately to mind, MTC Roy Cripps and MTC Jerry Price. And if I had to pick just one name, it would have to be Chief Price. Another fellow and I had just finished school, and we drove down to Charleston, South Carolina, to meet the boat. And on the way down, the day before reporting on board, we thought, "Jeez, we probably ought to get haircuts to looks squared away when we show up there on the pier." So we stopped and got haircuts, and good ones, too, but the next day we reported aboard to Chief Price, and he just looked at us and said, "I ain't gonna deal with you two shaggy creatures till you go get haircuts." And then he turned around to the papers on his desk, and we just stood there with our mouths open. Until we had the sense to back out of the office and head out to the barbershop, that is. And when we came back, well, that's when we got an introduction into what real Navy leadership is all about.

Chief Price was the kind of leader who just flat out exhibited confidence and competence. And he was the kind of guy who would take time to really teach young sailors our rating. Not only the tricks of the trade; he taught us the trade as well. There were things that he could have easily delegated to the LPO or even to a third-class, I guess, but he wanted to teach us, he wanted to have a hand in developing our technical skills as well as our military bearing. He came over to me one day and said, "Come here, Scott, I'm going to teach you how to do something that you're going to do for the rest of your Navy career," and he taught me lock wiring, and you know, I've never forgotten the little things that he showed me how to do. He wasn't mean, but he was tough and fair, and if you needed somebody to stand up for you, he was the guy. And if you needed someone to get you back on the right track, well, he was the guy for that, too. When I look at the newly defined core competencies for chief petty officers—-Leading, Communicating, Developing, and Supporting—well, if we wanted to put an illustration next to those, we could do a lot worse than a picture of Chief Jerry Price. And I've known literally dozens of chiefs just like him, too.

The important lessons of continuing training and education whenever possible were not lost on Scott. After several patrols on ballistic missile submarines, he completed instructor training in 1983, and attended the Senior Enlisted Academy in 1990. He served aboard the ballistic missile submarines USS *John Adams* (SSBN 620) and USS *James Madison* (SSBN 627) as missile division leading chief petty officer. He was "chief of the boat" aboard the fast attack submarine, USS *Jacksonville* (SSN 699), and served as command master chief of Strike Fighter Squadron 192 (VFA 192) based in Atsugi, Japan, and deploying aboard USS *Independence* (CV 62) and USS *Kitty Hawk* (CV 63). During his career he completed a total of fifteen deployments and patrols to the Arabian Gulf, western Pacific, North Atlantic, and Mediterranean. And along the way, he completed his bachelor of science degree from Southern Illinois University, in Carbondale.

MCPON Scott:

> I really do believe that the biggest challenge we face—and this is particularly true of the chief petty officers' community—is managing and dealing with the time pressures we face, particularly with the increased operating tempo that is a characteristic of our recent history. Not only with the time pressures, but with change. Just dealing with constant change—it's not change itself that can be so disturbing, but the ever increasing rate of change that can wear us down. Education, I think, is one of the keys to managing that change. Admiral Clark, our present CNO, likes to say, "If you're not growing, then you're dead." Well, I like to think of it as "when you stop growing, then you start dying." And I'm not ready for that yet at all. I think the real challenge for all of us is to continue to grow, to continue to learn, so that we can continue to effectively lead these young sailors—most of whom are much smarter, particularly about technical things, than we ever were. Every generation changes, our sailors change, and we have to stay one step ahead of the curve if we're going to be the kind of leaders that our Navy needs.

Scott himself was quick to embrace the challenges brought by advancement. In addition to his deployments in one of the most sea-intensive ratings in the Navy, when ashore he served as an instructor in advanced missile flight theory and checkout for the Poseidon and Trident missiles at the Fleet Ballistic Missile Submarine Training Center, Charleston, where he earned his designation as a master training specialist. He later served at the forward-deployed SSBN base in Holy Loch, Scotland, assigned to Commander Submarine Squadron 14 embarked in USS *Simon Lake* (AS 33) as the squadron missile technician. He also served as the senior enlisted nuclear weapons technical inspector and department leading chief petty officer for commander, Submarine Force, U.S. Atlantic Fleet. And, after his own initiation into the community of chief petty officers while at sea in 1986, he began to fully understand and appreciate the role of the Navy's enlisted leadership in keeping the Navy ever ready for today's (and tomorrow's) challenges.

MCPON Scott:

The chiefs mess has always been the strong stabilizing force, the one constant in changing times. We still fulfill that role, I think, but we need to facilitate those changes that must, of necessity, occur. We need to be stable, yet we need to focus on the future. Right now, we're recruiting the young sailors who will be the leading petty officers in a few years on the DDX platforms—and, even today, we don't really know what those ships will look like. We don't yet know what the manning levels will be, we don't know how we'll organize the billets—but we know that those changes are coming, and we'll face them with resources that are just now coming into the Navy. And who knows? When the CVX platform comes on line—the new generation of carriers that will replace the *Nimitz* class downstream—well, we may have just initiated a young chief petty officer who will be the MCPON when those ships come on stream. And, whoever he—or she!—is, we've got to be sure that we're giving him or her the tools and the training and experiences so that when the time comes, they will have had the opportunities they needed to be able to step up to the job.

Like many senior enlisted, Scott faced career decision points throughout his career. Many highly skilled technicians left the service after four or six years; others remained on active duty. Many applied for and accepted commissions as limited duty officers, or continued to serve as the technical experts within their rating communities. And some took the opportunity to server broader communities, applying for and accepting assignments as command master chief petty officers. Scott's first ashore command senior enlisted billet was as base command master chief at Naval Security Group

Activity, Winter Harbor. In November 2001 he was selected to serve as the CNO directed command master chief for Naval Forces Central Command and Fifth Fleet during Operation Enduring Freedom.

MCPON Scott:

If I had one message I'd like to send to sailors, it's that it is an honor—a real honor—to serve one's country. Sometimes we stop talking about that, and sometimes I think we focus too much on peripheral things. We're called a military service, we say "my dad or my uncle was in the service," and that's exactly what we are. Service to our country is what we are all about.

We're in a war right now, and no one can predict how long it will last, or what is going to happen next. Considering that, we have to remember that what we do provides our president and Congress with options, options that, perhaps, other nations might not have. Now, am I going to ask a sailor on the *Theodore Roosevelt* to spend 159 continuous nights at sea and like it? There are certainly going to be hard days, and days that aren't fun, but there will be days when we're filled with a sense of pride and personal accomplishment because of what we do. We do things that the ordinary American can't or will not do, and we do them well. And that's a little bit of what service to our country is all about. I'm not saying that we have to preach to sailors, to browbeat them, but sometimes I think that we have to remind ourselves what it is that we do and why we do it. And we here in Washington always have to remember that there are things that we can be doing—things that will help that sailor who is out there in harm's way to stabilize his or her life as much as circumstances will allow. Things like good solid educational opportunities, and a solid sea-to-shore rotation plan that helps share the load among all of us. We talk a lot about quality of life—and those initiatives are desperately important, don't get me wrong—but sometimes I think we need to stop and think about quality of service, too. And that includes the condition of our ships, and giving sailors the tools and materials needed to get the job done, and serving the nation the best way we can.

These are the ingredients that will help our sailors do their best, even under the most trying conditions:

First, they have to have a visceral understanding that the job they are doing is important. In today's environment, there aren't any "skate" jobs anymore, and I'm not sure there ever were. It doesn't matter if they are a food service assistant, or working in the laundry, or out on deck during an Unrep, or painting and preserving the ship—they have to understand that what they do is important, and we have to be ready to communicate to them, and show them how it fits into the division's mission, and the ship's, and the fleet's, and the nation's. Because what every sailor does affects the Navy's ability to fight, in one way or another.

Second, every sailor must know that someone cares. Can you imagine being out there, doing a job that you knew was important, but feeling that no one cared how well it was done, or even whether it was done or not? They need to know that someone cares and will provide them the tools, equipment, and training they need to be successful.

Third, no matter where they are, whether at sea, or under the sea, sailors need to know that their family is being taken care of. They need to know that they are living in safe housing, and that medical care is available when needed, and that their pay and allowances are adequate. We didn't join the Navy to become rich, but every sailor has the right to expect that his or her family will be well provided when that ship or squadron pulls out for points unknown.

It's clear when talking with MCPON Scott, as with his predecessors, that the role of the chief petty officer looms large in his concept of how the Navy ought to treat its sailors. That sense of tradition, of fellowship, of taking care of its own, is a vital part of the vision that he brings to office, as the tenth Master Chief Petty Officer of the Navy.

MCPON Scott:

It seems sometimes that everyone focuses on CPO initiation, and what we do or don't do on 16 September. But you know, I care more about what happens on 17 September. Because on 17 September, well, all the blue and gold streamers are taken down, and we sweep up the mess decks, and that young chief petty officer goes off to work for his first day in khakis. And I'm more concerned that we've given that new chief the knowledge and competencies to do the job, and to help guide this Navy of ours through the challenges they'll face. We have a tremendous opportunity during that six-week preparation period to be sure that that future chief has the tools to lead, and has a firm grasp on what the fellowship of the chief petty officer community is all about. Do we need to continue some of the things that happened to me, back when I made chief, out in the middle of the Atlantic Ocean in 1986? Probably not. Just because we may have done something in the past doesn't make it a tradition. When I go down to the Navy Home at Gulfport, lots of the fellows there tell me that they went through a testing and training period, and that their charge books meant something to them. We've taken the best of the past, and we're building on it, and we'll continue to build on it as we go forward. Leading, Communicating, Developing, and Supporting—if we can equip our new chiefs to do that, our Navy will continue to be in good hands.

MCPON Scott's personal awards include the Legion of Merit, Meritorious Service Medal, Navy Commendation Medal (five awards), Navy Achievement Medal (four awards) and various service and campaign awards.

Thirteen

In Harm's Way

Every Master Chief Petty Officer of the Navy has left his mark on the service. For some, quality of life at sea and ashore was paramount. For others, straightening and strengthening the lines of communication between sailors on the deckplates and the highest levels of Navy leadership took precedence. Perhaps no issue was closer to the heart of Master Chief John Hagan, the eighth MCPON, than honoring the long traditions of the sea services. Shortly before he left office, Master Chief Hagan wrote:

> Our Navy life is immersed in tradition. Tradition dictates the way we greet one another and cross the brow. It prescribes the way we relieve the watch, begin and end the day, and it guides much of the routine in between. Naval traditions are the best parts of our past that we preserve in ceremonial and many other ways, from the routine to the spectacular.

Recently I was privileged to address the assembled Brigade of Midshipmen at the U.S. Naval Academy. "How do we tell the difference between a good tradition and a bad tradition?" I was asked. "There are no bad traditions," I replied. By their very nature, naval traditions can only be good—that is why they are preserved and ultimately classified as traditions—for their goodness.[1]

Chief petty officers are the living memory of the Navy. Junior officers, anxiously pacing the bridge as their ship enters a foreign port, take comfort in the knowledge that their chief signalman will have the correct flags broken out, and that the moment the first lines hit the pier, colors will be shifted, and honors rendered in accordance with the customs of the sea. Visit any CPO mess, ashore or afloat, and the history of the Navy is proudly displayed: buffed, polished, and squared away for inspection. To civilians, "Old Navy" is simply a clothing retailer. Among chief petty officers, "Old Navy" is "our Navy."

Once, long ago, I sat in the radio shack of station NRR, Roosevelt Roads, Puerto Rico. We'd finished maintenance for the day, the deck was buffed to perfection, and Chief Jack McCoy was in a talkative mood. One of us, I forget now who, asked about the history of our rating. Had any radioman ever done anything famous? Are there any radiomen in the history books? Chief McCoy just sighed. "Aren't they teaching you guys anything up there at radioman 'A' School in Bainbridge, these days?" he asked. And then he began.

"See that old TBS transmitter over in the corner? The one that we keep for emergencies if all these big Collins rigs go out on us? That transmitter, or one just like it, was in service at Pearl Harbor. Do you know about RMC Tom Reeves, by chance?" Seeing the blank look in our eyes, he began the story.

Chief Tom Reeves was the kind of guy who made sure that his crew got off on liberty before he did. And so, one Sunday morning, he got up early, dressed, and headed off to the radio shack aboard USS *California*. They'd been working on the transmitters during the midwatch, and, with a little luck, his crew had gotten the last TBS up on line, and they'd still have time to catch the liberty launch to the fleet pier.

Born in Connecticut in 1895, Reeves had served as a reservist during World War I, but enthralled with the new marvel called radio, returned to active duty as a radioman in 1920. During his two decades of service, Reeves rose through the ranks to become chief radioman of a battleship, the pinnacle of service for a prewar sailor.

Half the Pacific Fleet was there at Pearl Harbor that morning, and USS *California* lay on Battleship Row, on the west side of Ford Island. Alongside were the battleships *Arizona, Maryland, Nevada, Oklahoma, Tennessee,* and *West Virginia.* Monday morning would bring a material inspection, and Chief Reeves was determined that his radio shack would be squared away. Many had considered the *California* (The Old Prune Barge, as the ship was known) as not being fully prepared for war, yet Tom and the other chiefs on board were prepared to prove them wrong.

As Chief Reeves made his way to the radio shack at 7:53 A.M., an initial wave of nearly two hundred enemy aircraft—dive-bombers, torpedo bombers, horizontal bombers, and strafing planes—descended upon Pearl Harbor. While chaos reigned all around, the guns of the *California* kept firing at the Japanese planes targeting its decks. Even after being struck on its side by a Japanese torpedo, and faced with intense flooding, the *California* kept its antiaircraft guns firing at the Japanese planes circling overhead.

Chief Reeves was on the second deck at the moment the first torpedo hit, and it was clear to him that the *California* was badly damaged. The *California* was taking hits from torpedoes and bombs and was on fire, and the mechanized hoists that distribute ammunition to the large antiaircraft guns were soon out of commission. But still the guns kept firing. With the passageway filling with smoke and fire, Reeves took charge and began to manhandle ammunition to the guns. Surrounded by death and destruction, he fearlessly kept the supply of ammunition flowing by passing ammunition by hand up to the gunners. Without any concern for himself, he continued to help keep the big guns firing until smoke inhalation and fire overcame him.

Chief Reeves died in that passageway, just two days before his forty-sixth birthday. Due in large part to his work in keeping the ammunition flowing, and the heroic actions of the other *California* sailors, the *California* guns kept firing at the Japanese planes, until the ship finally sank into the mud of the harbor. For his extraordinary courage and self-sacrifice in sustaining the flow of ammunition that helped the USS *California* keep fighting, Chief Thomas James Reeves was posthumously promoted to warrant radio electrician and awarded the Medal of Honor, the first chief petty officer to be so honored during World War II. The first, but, sadly, not the last.[2]

Not only sailors afloat were heroes that day. John Finn was a redshirt, an aviation ordnance man. Born in Los Angeles in 1909, he enlisted in the Navy in July 1926. He completed his basic training in San Diego, and was transferred to the ceremonial guard company. In December of that year, he completed General Aviation Utilities Training at Great Lakes. By April 1927 he was stationed at the Naval Air Station North Island, where he gained experience in the wing shop and the aircraft repair division. Shortly afterward, Finn was transferred to the Ordnance Division, where he worked on anti-aircraft gun emplacements. Deployments on board the USS *Lexington,* USS *Houston,* USS *Jason,* USS *Saratoga,* and USS *Cincinnati* followed, and in just nine years he was promoted to chief aviation ordnanceman. Over the next five years, Finn was stationed with patrol squadrons in Panama, San Diego, and Washington.

On 7 December 1941 Finn was at Kaneohe Bay Naval Air Station. He was in charge of thirty ordnancemen, none of whom had ever faced combat before. That morning, Chief Finn was in his quarters, planning a quiet day with his family. In the distance, he heard the sounds of aircraft and, shortly thereafter, machine-gun fire. Knowing that he had not ordered any firing that day, he sped to the hangars and ordnance shop, where he was shocked to see Japanese planes flying overhead strafing the airfields. Under fire, Finn ran to the armory and broke out machine guns and ammunition, which he passed out to sailors. He then set up his own .50-caliber machine gun on an instruction stand in a completely open area of the parking ramp.

With only the smoke from the fires raging around him to conceal him, Chief Finn returned fire at the Japanese pilots. Later noting that he was too angry to be scared by the destruction surrounding him, Finn stood his ground. Even though painfully wounded numerous times by bomb shrapnel, shot, and bleeding from many wounds, he continued to return fire. Reports indicate that he shot down a Japanese plane, although Chief Finn admits that it was probably the combined result from all the sailors fighting back.

As the Japanese planes began to withdraw from the area, sailors began to urge Chief Finn to get medical assistance for his many wounds. Knowing, however, that his experience and leadership were desperately needed during this period, he resisted. It was only after he was ordered to seek help that he consented to first aid. He suffered over twenty wounds, ranging from minor flesh wounds to shrapnel in his arm, elbow, and chest. Still, knowing that his experience as a chief was needed, he returned to his post where he supervised the rearming of the planes that had escaped devastation.

On 15 September 1942 Chief John William Finn was awarded the Medal of Honor for his heroism and dedication in performing his duty after being painfully wounded multiple times. In his remaining years of service in the Navy, he was promoted to ensign and then lieutenant in 1944, and retired shortly thereafter. As this is written, Chief Finn is the oldest living Medal of Honor Recipient, and lives in southern California.[3]

Everyone knows that engineers keep the Navy afloat. If you don't believe that, just ask any machinist mate, engineman, or machinery repairman. If you want something done aboard ship, just ask the snipes. And when things get tough—well, having a few good engineers around can be very helpful.

Oscar Peterson and Peter Tomich were both chief watertenders in the prewar Navy. The watertender rating later evolved into boilerman, and today we'd think of them as machinist's mates. Peterson, from Prentice, Wisconsin, enlisted as a fireman third-class in 1920 at the age of twenty-one. Tomich, born Petre Herceg-Tonic in Prolog, a town on the Austria-Hungary border, on 3 June 1893, immigrated to the United States in 1913. Like many first-generation Americans, even those from enemy nations, he enlisted in the army in 1917, and during his time in the Army, became a naturalized citizen. Immediately after his discharge from the Army, Tomich reenlisted in the U.S. Navy at the age of twenty-six.

Tomich was initially assigned on board the destroyer USS *Litchfield,* and served continuously during his career in the Navy, advancing up the enlisted ratings, until he made chief watertender on 4 June 1930. By December 1941 he was regarded as one of the most experienced watertenders in the Pacific Fleet, having served eleven years as a chief. On 7 December 1941 Chief Watertender Tomich was at his post in the fire room of the USS *Utah,* not far from the USS *California.* At 8:01 A.M. on that fateful morning, two torpedoes, seconds apart, pierced the side of the *Utah.* Water filled the giant chasm in the side of the ship and began to flood the engineering spaces. Chief Tomich, feeling the ship beginning to lean to its side, ordered his sailors to evacuate.

Knowing that the ship was certainly going to capsize, Chief Tomich thought only of saving his crew. While his sailors were evacuating, he maintained his post, and began singlehandedly securing all the boilers to prevent an explosion. As the ship continued to capsize, Chief Tomich calmly stabilized and secured his boilers, preventing a massive explosion on board the ship. Shortly thereafter, *Utah* rolled, trapping Chief Tomich and fifty-seven others on board. By preventing the boilers from exploding, he saved the lives of hundreds of men on board and in the water nearby.

Because of his valor and concern for the lives of others, Chief Peter Tomich was posthumously awarded the Medal of Honor. USS *Tomich* (DE242) was commissioned and named in his honor in 1943. Because his next of kin could not be found, his medal was displayed aboard the USS *Tomich*, and, after decommissioning of the destroyer escort in 1974, was presented to the Senior Enlisted Academy at Newport, Rhode Island, where it now holds a place of honor at Tomich Hall, named in his honor.[4]

Chief Peterson's career was similar to that of Chief Tomich. He spent three years on active duty, left the Navy, but after five years on the beach, reenlisted as a fireman second-class in 1928. Over the next four years, he served on board the USS *Moody* and the USS *Trevor*, leaving *Trevor* as a watertender second-class. As his enlistment was coming to a close, Peterson extended for three more years. In October 1934 he transferred to the USS *Pruitt*, where he attained the rating of watertender first-class, and in February 1941 Peterson was appointed acting chief watertender on board the USS *Neceies*. In April 1941, he was transferred to the fleet oiler, USS *Neosho*, where he was permanently appointed chief watertender on 28 February 1942.

Chief Peterson was aboard the USS *Neosho* on 7 May 1942, when it was attacked by Japanese bombers. The *Neosho* had been operating in the South Pacific in support of USS *Yorktown* and USS *Lexington*. Escorted by USS *Sims*, *Neosho* had been detached from the main body of the fleet, when, operating independently, both were spotted by a Japanese aircraft. Both ships faced repeated attacks during the day. Around noon a large force of Japanese dive-bombers appeared and commenced heavy bombing runs on both ships. *Sims* sank within half an hour of its first direct hit, and *Neosho* was heavily damaged. Intense fires raged aboard the oiler, and Chief Peterson took charge of the repair party.

While others were abandoning ship, Chief Peterson remained aboard to close the bulkhead stop valves, preventing explosion of the fuel aboard. With all the members of the repair party injured, and himself gravely wounded, Chief Peterson ignored the extreme danger and succeeded in closing the valves without assistance. In doing so, he received additional burns that resulted in his death. The USS *Henley* rescued 109 survivors of the *Neosho* on 11 May 1942, due to Chief Peterson's self-sacrifice in saving his ship. Chief Peterson died two days later from his burns.

Chief Oscar Peterson was posthumously awarded the Medal of Honor, "for extraordinary courage and conspicuous heroism above and beyond the call of duty while in charge of a repair party during an attack on the U.S.S. *Neosho* by enemy Japanese aerial forces on May 7, 1942."[5]

Four chief petty officers and four heroes. But heroism is not confined to the history books; sometimes it is as close as the front page.

The small boys—the destroyers and cruisers that make up the muscle of carrier battle groups—are special. Perhaps no element in the surface warfare community has the cohesiveness and cachet of "tin can sailors," the guys who ride close to the water and are the first to go into harm's way. Chief Richard Costelow and Chief Andrew Triplett (limited duty ensign) were tin can men all the way.

Chief Electronics Technician Richard Costelow grew up in the small town of Morrisville, Pennsylvania. Known to his high school peers as hard-working and motivated, he gained a reputation as someone who gave 100 percent in everything he did. He graduated from Morrisville High School in 1983, and quickly went to work as an electronics repairman.

Chief Electrician (Ensign) Andrew Triplett grew up in Shuqualak, Mississippi, nearly a mile and a half from the nearest paved road. His parents raised him to value hard work and duty. These lessons were evident in the way he carried himself. His peers saw him as an ambitious, natural student, well liked by all. He made the honor roll, and stayed on it. His dream was to become an engineer, as he had a natural ability to fix things, although family resources prevented him from attending college.

Costelow enlisted in the Navy in April 1988. He graduated from Recruit Training Command at San Diego, trained as an electronics technician, and was transferred to his first tour of duty in Sigonella, Italy. He served in Sicily for two years, and because of his spotless service record, was then assigned to the White House Communication Agency, where he installed communications equipment for senior White House staff, the National Security Council, the Secret Service, and the president. After five years with the White House Communication Agency, he was recognized for his dedication and hard work. President Clinton described him as "a technology wizard who helped update the White House Communications system for this new century." Continuing his career, in January 1998 Costelow reported to the destroyer USS *Cole*.

In his twelve-year career as an enlisted sailor, Costelow had swiftly risen up the enlisted ranks, and on 16 September 2000 he was initiated as a chief electronics technician on board the USS *Cole*. Chief Costelow took great pride in his pinning, writing, "The process does not make Chiefs by accident, though some people may think that. There must be a reason why I have been chosen to lead. I must have the tools to lead. I DO have the tools to lead. I will use these tools to be successful in my new work, in order to train and shape the future of the Navy. I will do this with Honor, Courage and Commitment."[6]

Ensign Andrew Triplett joined the Navy just a few months after Costelow. Immediately after graduating from his all-black public high school in June 1987, he drove to Jackson, Mississippi, to enlist in the Navy at the age of seventeen. Starting in the engine rooms of ships like the USS *Sphinx*, he quickly absorbed the skills and knowledge of the engineman rating. In short order, he certified in diesel engine repair, air conditioning and refrigeration repair, and air compressor repair. Dedicated as he was to hard work and doing his duty, it was not long before he was noticed. Triplett never lost his love for the Navy; despite numerous opportunities in the private sector, he chose to stay with the Navy that he loved.

Reporting aboard USS *Ticonderoga* in 1994, Triplett soon gained a reputation as a natural leader. During his tour on the *Ticonderoga*, the ship won the Arleigh Burke Fleet Trophy for the most improved operational unit, and a Battle Efficiency Award. The *Ticonderoga's* captain attributed much of these successes to the dedication of Triplett. He notes that "it takes a real leader to get the troops to put out that effort. Triplett did that, with a very quiet confidence and leadership." Soon, Triplett was appointed engineering officer of the watch, where he demanded hard work from his shipmates. While demanding, he was also very outspoken on their behalf. The commanding officer and the entire wardroom encouraged him to apply for limited duty officer status, and, as a newly commissioned ensign, he transferred to the destroyer USS *Cole* in the spring of 1999. Younger junior officers were drawn to him because of his personality and experience. Yet, as an ensign, he still felt a bond with the engine crew, and worked closely with experienced petty officers and strikers alike to ensure that each had the wherewithal and tools to advance in their chosen ratings.[7]

Fate forever linked Chief Costelow and Ensign Triplett. On 12 October 2000, just one day before the Navy's two hundred twenty-fifth birthday, USS *Cole* (DDG-67), part of the USS *George Washington* battle group, detached and docked at the port of Aden, Yemen. On its way from the Mediterranean to the Arabian Sea to enforce sanctions against Iraq, *Cole* intended to refuel for the journey. At approximately 11:18 that morning, a small rubber boat laden with explosives pulled up next to the *Cole*. Seconds later, the explosives on the boat were detonated, shattering the destroyer's port side and devastating *Cole's* adjacent mess decks and engineering spaces.

Both Chief Costelow and Ensign Triplett, who was in the ship's laboratory testing the fuel that was being pumped on board, were among the seventeen sailors killed in the explosion. Costelow and Triplett were the only "khakis" to die in the infamous attack. Both gave their lives in defense of our nation's freedom, and both went gladly into harm's way to serve the Navy that they loved.

History may well record the attack on USS *Cole* as the opening salvo of a third, and most dangerous, world war. Less than a year later, the American homeland was attacked, and U.S. forces quickly deployed to crush our enemies in their fortress hideouts high in the Himalayas. Special forces would play a vital role in this conflict, and Navy SEALs were in the forefront.

Chief Hospital Corpsman Matthew Bourgeois was born in Illinois in 1967. His great-grandfather had fought in World War I; his grandfather served for three decades in the Navy; and an uncle fought in the Vietnam War. As a child, his interest in the military blossomed as he listened to the stories that his uncle would tell him about his years of service in the Vietnam War. In 1985 he joined the Florida National Guard, and in 1987 he enlisted in the Navy. After recruit training, realizing that he wanted to be best positioned to help shipmates in distress, he attended and graduated from the Navy's hospital corpsman school at Great Lakes, Illinois. Soon after, he volunteered for the elite Basic Underwater Demolitions/SEAL training program in San Diego. Although he found the training tough, he was inspired by his family's military history and graduated from BUD as a member of class 162 in 1988.

As a combat corpsman, Bourgeois was a member of SEAL teams on both coasts, and rapidly advanced in rating, while completing a tour of duty during the Persian Gulf War. Most recently assigned to Little Creek Amphibious Base, shortly after the terrorist attacks of September 11, 2001, Bourgeois was promoted to chief hospital corpsman and deployed to Afghanistan as part of Operation Enduring Freedom. His SEAL team struck al-Qaeda terrorist bases, forcing the removal of the Taliban regime in Afghanistan, and the disruption of the terrorist network. With only a few more weeks left before redeployment stateside, on 28 March 2002 he participated in special operations training in a remote area near Kandahar, where he was killed by enemy ordnance. He died in the field, leaving a wife and seven-month-old son.

Bourgeois is remembered as a family man, who would call his wife every night, and who shared a love of deer hunting and fishing with his family members. He knew that his job was dangerous, but he knew it was his job and he believed in what he was doing. He was proud to be a Navy SEAL. During his fourteen years in the Navy, Chief Bourgeois served his country and its people with pride and honor.[8]

How does one commemorate such valor? Medals can be struck, buildings renamed, names spoken in reverence in every chiefs mess. But tradition—

that human memory, which we hold and cherish—is passed on from generation to generation. Shortly before his death, Chief Richard Costelow wrote a paper as part of his CPO initiation. In many ways it was prescient. "If by some means that I can't do this any longer, it will be time for a new Chief to take my place. Who knows, maybe one that was in my charge." Chief Costelow had learned many of the traditions of the sea service and the chief petty officers mess during that initiation. He learned that Honor, Courage, and Commitment were not just buzzwords but concepts that have guided the Navy and its sailors through dangers and terrors afloat and ashore. As you read these words, sailors may be manning flight decks, battling raging storms, racing to complete airfields and forward bases, and engaging enemies of democracy and freedom on battlefields far and wide. And every one is led by a chief petty officer.

Chief Wylie:

I was aboard USS *Simpson,* a sister ship to the *Cole.* We were together in the Gulf, and had just parted company a few days before the incident at Aden. That was probably the most challenging time in my career. We were doing interdictions, which was basically boarding Iraqi tankers and freighters and inspecting them for contraband. Whenever we found it, we'd confiscate the ship, take it to a holding area, and keep them there until the governments got it all sorted out. We called our holding area "Area Comiskey" because they were all named after famous ballparks.

Now, the Iraqis have a nasty habit of trying to sink their ships once they are caught. And my job as a damage controlman was to keep the ship afloat. So, I basically went from ship to ship, doing more damage control stuff on Iraqi freighters than I've ever done on a Navy ship. I've dealt with the skin of the ship inside the tankers, where you can literally see 500 beams of light coming through the holes, there was that much rust and corrosion. I was in a major storm at sea, aboard one of the Iraqi freighters. When I arrived there we had 18 feet of water, and still rising, inside the engine room. We were completely out of power— the water was over the switchboards, it was over all the generators—

and the ship was listing pretty well. We had to use P100s to pump it out. The storm came up, and we were unable to leave the ship, we were aboard all that night.

So I spent a night aboard, and the wind and sea conditions were so terrible that we were making 5 knots, according to the GPS, and we were still at anchor. And what was interesting was that we were in the middle of a bunch of other Iraqi ships that were being held there, too. I remember distinctly watching waves crash over the pilothouse of one of those tankers—these little Arab tankers have only about 3 feet of freeboard anyway. And we were watching 12-foot waves going over the ship completely. And it got really exciting when two of our main deck covers came off, and water was just pouring into the hold. And not only us, but also five Iraqis ran out on deck, trying to put those covers back on, because we would have all died. We had a temporary generator that night, we at least had lights, and we had power going to a couple of plugs.

Now, all this was during Ramadan, so the Iraqis slept all day and were up all night, and one of the times, right before these big waves came over and took off the covers, we were standing in this galley, maybe a 20- by 20-foot space. We had the TV going, to find out what the hell was happening outside, because there was no way you wanted to be on that deck if you could help it. We're sitting there, watching TV with our Iraqi prisoners, the TV announces that George Bush has won the election back home, and the lights go off. Now, I'm standing in a room with about fifteen Iraqis who had already tried to scuttle their ship, who had already tried to escape once or twice, and whom we had had under guard for about four days. There was only one other of our guys in the room, so I was pretty nervous. I had my weapon, and at that point, I pulled it out, because I didn't want somebody to grab it out of my holster without me being able to see it. So I grabbed it out, and I had it in my hand, and I locked and loaded it, because I figured, "Well, here we go." And as I did, I dropped a shell on the deck. And this Iraqi kid on board, who must have heard the other guys call me by name, goes "Terry, Terry, you dropped a bullet." And he reaches over and picks it up and hands it back to me.

So, definitely not one of my greater moments, but without a doubt one of the hairier ones. We saved the ship, saved ourselves, saved the Iraqis, and made it home alive. But if anyone doesn't believe that there's a war going on out here, let them come and ride with us for a while.

Senior Chief Padmore:

Carriers can be scary places, too, no doubt about it. I was on the USS *America* (CV-66) back in 1984 or 1985. We had an old A7E Corsair— we call them the man-eaters—and it hit the round down during night recovery, and I was out there on deck, and I helped fight the fire. That scene, at night, flight deck on fire, jet parts flying everywhere, trying to get that pilot out, with jet fuel running into the scuppers—that was the scariest thing that I've ever seen. I've had things happen to me that might seem minor to others, but you ask a man up there if he wasn't scared; we all were, and I was, too.

Senior Chief Gentry:

Well, we work hard to prevent accidents from happening. Being an AB is a fun job, but you have to like the challenge. It's a very dynamic challenge on the flight deck. I've been in the Navy for over seventeen years; every day I get up it's something new, when you're on the flight deck. I have a lot of young men and women up there on "the roof"—I have a division of 173 people and about 120 of them are E-3 or below—and every day you have a new challenge with them. And they are young; their average age is about nineteen or twenty years old. When we're flying, we'll come up two hours prior for flight quarters, we'll do an FOD walk down, after that we'll bring out the yellow shirts, the leadership of the flight deck.

It doesn't make any difference if it's an E-2 who's brand new to the Navy or myself as an E-8, we'll review all the safety aspects, situational awareness and keeping your head up, we'll go through the events of the day, and discuss the day before, what we could change or do better, in the hope of having a safer day. Looking after those young sailors is the most important thing I do, every single day.

Even those whose duties keep them inside the "island" and away from the dangers presented by thundering aircraft bolting across the flight deck can have moments of excitement—or, often enough, sheer terror.

Chief McPherson:

I remember once when we nearly had a catastrophe. We were working one night, and the flight deck got fouled. And there were metal shards everywhere. These things never happen during slack times; no, we had a pattern full of planes. We had just started pushing the planes, because we were still doing the launch; that's how it got fouled. So we had three tankers overhead, with about fifteen planes heading toward the flight deck, and it gets fouled. And it's taking them forever to square away the deck, and I've got planes all over the sky, running out of fuel. The jets were running out of fuel, and the tankers were refueling them, and the tankers themselves were running out of fuel. So we called in an Air Force KC135, because pretty soon we'd be having airplanes dropping into the sea. We even sent the KC135 out to the marshal stack where we had planes backed up, to start tanking them there. And with all those planes, and all that chaos—you're not breaking any rules, but you're inventing your own as you go along, because there's no way you even put this kind of stuff into writing, you know.

And out of all that, we got every single aircraft back on deck that night safely. And you're pumped for hours after that, no way can you ever sleep. Everybody is in there, you know, wired. And just knowing that you brought them home safe—that's the rush.

It has been said that one difference between the Army and the Air Force is that in the Army, officers send their enlisted off to war; in the Air Force, the enlisted send the officers off to combat. In a very real sense, the same thing happens aboard aircraft carriers, as sailors watch their officers depart into the unknown.

Chief Grodski:

I was aboard the USS *Eisenhower* (CVN-69) back in 1998, and we were informed that we were about twenty-four hours away from launching an air strike. The armament came up in the hangar bay, and people were signing their names on bombs. I don't scare all that easily, but that was frightening to me. It was scary to me, not because of any danger to myself, but rather because it brought up many feelings for me. It brought up feelings of, well, these pilots I see every day, I may not see them tomorrow, you know? It also brought up a lot of moral issues for me. I've been in the Navy a long time, but like any sensible person, I am against killing and violence, yet here I am writing my name on a bomb that's going to go and land on someone's head. But mostly I worried about those pilots—the guys who were going in harm's way to complete our mission.

Chief Grodski shares that important trait of all good chief petty officers—an overriding concern for the well-being of shipmates.

Senior Chief Hospital Corpsman (AW/SW)
Marcus Jones, USS Normandy *(CG-60):*
Like Doc Bourgeois on the SEAL team, I'm an independent duty corpsman. I work for the navigator, but as you can imagine, we don't have a lot in common. I'm responsible for four hundred individuals on this ship, but my boss and I don't interact on a technical or medical level, hardly at all. I make darn sure, though, that before a corpsman accepts orders to this ship, I always invite him or her to come out and see that this isn't Naval Hospital *Normandy.* We have three corpsmen to take care of four hundred people, and we never know when we'll be operating independently away from the carriers or other big-deck ships with large medical departments. I never want to have a corpsman aboard who doesn't know what it's like out here—let them ride the ship before they make that decision.

Command Master Chief Pierce:
We're always shorthanded. Right now we have twenty-four chiefs on board. The normal complement is twenty-seven. But it's a very rewarding and challenging experience. The challenges are that there are so

many things going on; on a small ship we have to be fully flexible. Just today everyone expected the Unrep (Underway Replenishment) to happen this morning, and at 0-dark-30 last night, everything changed. So we got up, looking for the Unrep, and the schedule had changed by several hours. On small ships, we have to adjust. We're in three duty sections here, so it's go, go all the time, but you have to be prepared for the unexpected.

Chief Electrician's Mate Russell Lincoln (SW), USS Normandy:
Well, on these smaller ships, being shorthanded gets pretty rough at times, because we take care of propulsion, lighting, air conditioning when we get to hot areas, whatever. So, you are constantly trying to keep everything cool, and as an Aegis platform, lots of the gear needs a lot of cooling, so it's a never-ending job.

Chief Boatswain's Mate Ricky Brooks, USS Normandy:
Well, out here on one of the small boys, for me, it's very, very challenging. Being the only BMC on the ship, and the only deck khaki on the ship, I find the responsibilities are overwhelming. The days are long, you are expected to know everything that happens in the deck world, and to fix everything in the deck world, and it is a challenging tour, which is why I took it. My deck division is twenty-three people, and the First Lieutenant is right out of ROTC. He's a really good first lieutenant, but it's "what's this" or "how do we do that." And on a cruiser or destroyer, there really isn't a whole lot of time left over for "school of the ship," it's go out and do it.

Chief Electronics Warfare Technician Eddie Chambliss, USS Normandy:
It's extremely hard out here at times—it's man vs. machine. Small ships are workhorses, they are always ready, always on the go, and you're battling equipment that's highly technical, in a world that is not all that friendly, environmentally. In my world, as a warfare technician, when I push the button, I want to hear something go "whoosh." And on these smaller ships, with space and personnel limitations, it's a battle sometimes, no doubt about it.

Command Master Chief McCalip:

I'm a submariner, through and through. I'm also a Navy parachute jumper. And now I'm on the biggest, fastest, most efficient aircraft carrier ever built, and we're heading off to, well, who knows what? When we clear the Suez Canal tomorrow, and start launching planes over the beach, it's war—and I don't care what anyone else calls it, that's what we're doing. That flight deck will be going twenty-four, seven. Are people scared? Am I scared? I think you'd have to be a little crazy not to be. But we've trained to do this, and I know we've trained our people to do this. But you can be sure of one thing—whatever goes down, tomorrow, next week, next month—there'll be a chief leading his or her sailors, doing the right thing, the right way. Because that's what we do.

Fourteen

Chiefs Are What Chiefs Do

It was time to go home.

We'd been at sea for weeks, but when I awoke that July morning, change was in the air. As I opened my blue privacy curtain, I was greeted by the sight of spit-shined shoes where only scuffed work boots had been before. You can tell a lot about the plan of the day just by peeping out of a bottom rack.

"Hey, you're awake, Jack. We're about an hour out of Suda Bay," Eric Oitzman shouted from the narrow passageway leading to the forward ladder, "Looks like we'll have lines across in about two hours. Liberty will probably be called around 0900, I should imagine."

I thanked him for the update, rolled out of my rack, and, after a quick wash-up, headed toward the hangar deck. Over the weeks we'd been at sea, I'd appropriated a corner of the "mountain"—the large stack of inflatable boats, spare parts, and gawd-knows-what that filled the aft end of hangar bay three—as my "sea cabin." Perched on the edge of a wooden crate, I had

205

a clear view through both the starboard and portside elevator doors. I'd grown accustomed to the cobalt-blue Gulf Stream, the cold gray waves of the North Atlantic, and the green waters of the Mediterranean as we made our way from Virginia to Crete. After a while, it was the first place anyone looked for me if they wanted to chat.

I sat on my perch, watching the tiny white houses of Crete get ever larger, as the browns and tans of the rocky island gradually replaced the azure waters of the Aegean Sea. I'd forgotten how startling landfall could be: for weeks we'd been surrounded by water, the endless seascapes broken only by occasional glimpses of our escorting cruisers and destroyers. Lost in thought, I watched the blue and white flag of Greece fluttering in the warm breeze over the fleet landing stage. Out of the corner of my eye, I saw Scott Benning, clipboard in hand, making his way aft from hangar bay two.

"Well, we're here, anyway," he said. "Ever been to Crete?" I shook my head; one of the pleasures that I'd missed on active duty had been a Mediterranean cruise. I'd had to content myself with others' stories of great liberty ports—of Spain and Portugal, of Italy and Greece. Suda Bay was a fairly new addition to that list. On the northwest coast of Crete, it was only a few hours from the mouth of the Suez Canal. By tomorrow, I'd be on my way home—and *George Washington* would be steaming into harm's way. But first—ah, first!—there was liberty.

"Mike McCalip and I are thinking about renting a car and seeing a bit of the island," Scott said. "Want to come along with us? We'll shove off as soon as we get the last sailors ashore, and we ought to have a couple of hours before you have to catch the ferry to Athens. We'll probably head into Chania, the biggest town on this end of the island. If things go as planned, we ought to be across the brow by, oh, 1100 at the latest. I'll meet you down at his office a few minutes before eleven, okay?"

I readily agreed, and sat idly, watching Bob Heinrichs's boatswain's mates toss messenger lines toward the pier, followed quickly by thick mooring hawsers. Within the hour, the brow was in place, and there was a palpable air of excitement as everyone waited for the first liberty parties to be called away. Checking my watch, I headed below to the mess decks, and made my way toward the command master chief's office. Finding Mike in civilian clothes was as much of a shock as seeing houses and fields where only the sea had been before; my mental picture of Mike and every chief on board was in monochrome, and khaki at that.

"Hey, Scott tells me you're coming ashore with us. Outstanding! As soon as we get things squared away here, we'll go up to the Naval Support Activity. I've got a couple of things I need to do, and then we'll head off into town. We ought to be out of here in a minute, and we'll grab some lunch before we wander off into Chania, OK?"

I sat patiently, reading a three-week-old copy of *Navy Times*, while Mike attended to the business of getting five thousand sailors ashore for liberty. The phone rang constantly; urgent messages interrupted the phone calls; and visitors knocked loudly on the now closed door, interrupting even the urgent messages. "We need more buses"; "The base wants twenty more shore patrolmen"; "They've got plenty of beer for our guys at the fleet landing, but it's been sitting in the sun all day, and the iceman hasn't come yet." Mike fielded each issue like a shortstop-passing one problem to the MWR representative, another to the ship's galley ("Oh, maybe a ton of ice ought to do it, Chief, your guys can handle that, right?"), while other problems seemed to float in orbit, touching down only when the maelstrom had calmed, and then only for a moment. Scott Benning arrived and pitched in, but it was well past noon when the chaos abated and we finally had a chance to leave the ship. Mildly annoyed and hungry, I thought myself crazy to go on liberty with two guys who didn't know when the job stopped and liberty began. And then it hit me. This is what chiefs do.

It was nearly 1300 when we finally crossed the brow and found the rental car. We headed out past camouflaged sailors armed with shotguns and M-16s, sailors who would watch over *George Washington* as the ship lay silent, five thousand miles from home. I'd joked, on the way across, about how easy it was to spot the masters-at-arms aboard the ship; their camouflaged fatigues made them stand out clearly against the haze gray background of the nuclear carrier. But they blended perfectly into the hot, dry, dusty landscape of Crete, and, as we cleared the last checkpoint, we barely spotted Master Chief Greg Ciaccio as he distributed water to his sailors. "Looks like Chach is gonna be busy for the next day or so," McCalip remarked. "As long as he's got a single master-at-arms out here standing guard, he'll be out here alongside him. No liberty for him this trip, unfortunately; he'll be out here all day and all night looking after his troops." And that's what chiefs do.

In the searing heat, the underpowered Fiesta slowly climbed the narrow, twisting road between the fleet landing and the Naval Support Activity. "I know that you have to clear customs here," Mike remarked, "so while you're getting your passport in order over at base operations, Scott and I can stop off and get haircuts at the Navy Exchange." I laughed to myself; as the father of three sons I'd fought the haircut battle countless times, but if my three boys had hair as short and neat as Scott and Mike's, the barbers in my town would soon be out of business. Mike dropped me at base operations and wandered off to find the barbershop. Command Master Chief Tom Tribble of Naval Support Activity had arranged a messenger to carry my passport from the operations building to the commercial airport, and provided me with an escort to speedily clear Greek customs. Everything went perfectly. But, then again, that's what chiefs do.

My business completed, I walked along the single street of the Naval Support Activity, searching for my two liberty companions. I spotted commotion ahead; when I got close enough to see, I found Mike McCalip, newly shorn, accosting sailors and "suggesting," in no uncertain language, that they too avail themselves of a trip to the barber before heading out to town. "You know the grooming standards," I heard him say to one slightly hirsute sailor, "but more importantly, you want to give everyone a good impression of Americans and the *George Washington* when you hit the beach, now, don't you?" The airman—he couldn't be older than twenty—smiled, but only to be polite. Soon the shop was filled with young sailors off the *George Washington,* all on their way toward looking sharp and presentable when the shuttles dropped them off in Chania. They'd make a good impression, with but a gentle reminder from their seniors. Because that's what chiefs do.

It took us forever, it seemed, to get off the base. We headed off toward the post office, where Scott stopped a few sailors who were arguing among themselves and sorted out a quick problem between squadron mates. We stopped at the base gas station, and Mike, pumping gas, spotted a sailor across the street. "My god," he said, to no one in particular, "tell me that guy doesn't have an earring in his ear." He sprinted across the street to investigate, taking the keys, leaving Scott and myself stranded in the stifling car. In the distance we could see the sailor remove the offending ring and shove it in his pocket. Mike returned, and finally we set off toward Chania, where, half-starving, I steered us into the first taverna that I spotted on the crescent-shaped road ringing the inner harbor.

Enjoying the gentle breeze, we drank ouzo, ate fresh mushrooms and home-baked bread and told sea stories, until a large party of sailors arrived. Boisterous as sailors sometimes can be, it was clear that this was not the first taverna they had discovered since leaving ship, nor were the small complimentary glasses of ouzo set out by the genial host their first exposure of the day to the potent licorice-flavored drink. But one, more alert than his shipmates, spotted the three of us at the back of the taverna, and the noise level ratcheted down several decibels, returning the taverna to its accustomed role as a family gathering place for the local citizenry. Neither Scott nor Mike had said a word, but they didn't have to. And that's what chiefs do, too.

It was like that the remainder of the day. Open beer bottles on the street brought a stern stare from Mike; horseplay in a souvenir shop brought a gentle, but firm rebuke from Scott. We encountered some young officers on a back street, who told us enthusiastically about the gold and gems that were available "with special discounts for our American friends," and the three of us sighed, remembering perhaps a time on our own first overseas liberty, when all that glittered really was gold. Or so we thought, back then, until an older, wiser chief reminded us that, if you don't know jewels, it might be a good idea to know the jeweler. Chiefs are like that, sometimes.

The shadows grew long, and my departure time approached. I wanted to make one more stop, though, and Scott and Mike were amenable to the short detour. I'd mentioned earlier that whenever I'd gone overseas as a sailor or civilian, I'd try to visit any military cemetery I might find along the way. Scott had looked at me quizzically, but I told him that, on the odd chance I ever went to heaven, I thought it might be useful to have an advance party to help clear the way. I just wanted to stop in, I said, and see how the boys were getting along. Mike drove, and Scott navigated—no small feat when the road map, logically enough, was written in Greek.

We soon found the Commonwealth War Cemetery, just north of the Chania-Heraklion road. It's a quiet spot, secluded, on a gentle hillside sweeping down to the waters of the Aegean. A monument reads simply: "The land on which this cemetery stands is a gift of the Greek people, as the perpetual resting place of the sailors, soldiers and airmen who are honoured here." Sunset was near, and we were alone, as we walked the well-tended paths among the white marble headstones. "Lots of New Zealanders," Mike remarked, spotting the inscriptions of men who had come from Wellington and Auckland, Hastings and Christchurch, to fight and die alongside their British cousins at Maleme airfield in May 1941. "Fifth New Zealand Field Regiment; Twenty-second NZ Regiment; Twenty-seventh NZ Machine Gun Battalion," he read. "They came a long way to die, didn't they?"

A long way, indeed. And there were others there as well: Australian and Indian, South African and British, airmen and sailors, too. To one side, we found the resting-place of sailors from HMS *Fiji*, sunk at sea by German aircraft in the early hours of 23 May 1941. Out of ammunition, the cruiser had not given up without a fight; nearly twenty of the crew were later decorated for bravery, or mentioned posthumously in dispatches. Even the chaplain, Padre C. C. Turner, was awarded the Albert Medal, and later the George Cross, for his heroism in saving shipmates in the waters off the island's south coast.

Scott had stopped at one grave, a few yards away. He beckoned to us, and we joined him.

We stood there silently, sailors among sailors, lost in thought. I read the inscription at common grave 14-C-10-11:

Kenyon, Sidney, 78300,
Mecanician
[Chief Engine Room Artificer],
HMS Fiji, Royal Navy, 23.5.41,
Age 34
Caldmore, Walsall, Stratfordshire.

"He was a chief, " Mike said quietly, "he was one of us."

We lingered a moment in the fading light. Chief Kenyon was surrounded by shipmates, all safely ashore now, free from the terror and horror of that night, now sixty years past. *Fiji* fought bravely till its ammunition was expended, and *Fiji* died bravely, too. I didn't know Chief Kenyon, and no one fully knows the story of what happened on that terrible night below the cliffs of Crete. I don't know him, or his shipmates, or his story, but I know others like him, and I know this. I know that whatever happened that night, he died helping those who surround him now; leading, communicating, supporting. Because, you see, he was a chief petty officer. And that's what chiefs do.

Glossary

AIRLANT	Commander, Naval Air Forces, Atlantic.
AIRPAC	Commander, Naval Air Forces, Pacific.
Air traffic controller (AT)	Controls air space near ships and naval stations.
Airwing	Commander Air Wing Seventeen was embarked on USS *George Washington* (CVN-73).
Albert Medal	Royal Navy award founded by Queen Victoria in 1866 for sea-based acts of heroism.
Anchor frogs	Small clasps that secure the fouled anchor device to the uniform collar.
"Ask the chief"	Household phrase in the Navy, used when all other sources of information have proven futile.
Aviation boatswain's mate (AB)	Operates flight and hangar decks at sea and ashore.

Aviation maintenance administrationman (AZ)	Maintains records regarding aircraft maintenance.
Aviation ordnanceman (AO)	Handles, stows, maintains, and loads munitions for naval aircraft.
Aviation support equipment technician (AS)	Maintains aviation ground equipment.
Avionics electronics technician (AT)	Maintains the electronics systems aboard naval aircraft.
Balut	Fermented duck egg, a Tagalog delicacy.
Battle E	Designation annually awarded to ship or squadron showing best warfare preparation.
Blackshoe	Officer or enlisted in the surface or submarine warfare communities.
Blueshirt	Enlisted sailor in paygrades E1–E6. The term comes from the blue utility shirt worn as part of the working uniform.
Boatswain's mate (BM)	Responsible for marlinespike, deck, and small boat seamanship.
Brow	The gangway between ship and pier.
Bulkhead	Wall or partition aboard ship.
Butter bar	Gold collar device worn by ensigns (1) in the U.S. Navy.
"Can Do"	Unofficial motto of the U.S. Navy Seabees (construction forces).
Captain's Cup	Award presented to the ship or squadron winning local athletic competitions.
Charge book	Book of directions, suggestions, and maxims collected by newly selected chief petty officers.
CIC	Combat Information Center, the fighting heart of a warship.
CINCPACFLT	Commander in chief, Pacific Fleet.
CMC	Command master chief petty officer.
CNO	Chief of Naval Operations.
CNOCM	CNO-directed command master chief (major commands).
CO	Commanding officer.
COB	Chief of the boat. In the submarine community, equivalent to command master chief.

CPO	Chief petty officer.
Crackerjack	Traditional naval enlisted uniform (bellbottoms).
Cycle	To perform physical exercises ad infinitum, and often, ad nauseam.
Damage controlman (DC)	Responsible for firefighting, decontamination, and battle damage repair.
Deckplates	Term referring to areas where enlisted sailors work and live, used by extension to mean enlisted members of the Navy.
Dixie cup	Round, brimless hat worn by Navy enlisted (males) E1–E6.
Electrician's mate (EM)	Responsible for a ship's power generation and distribution.
Electronics technician (ET)	Maintains a wide variety of electronic equipment at sea and ashore.
Electronics warfare technician (EW)	Responsible for target detection and location, and prevention of enemy jamming and electronic surveillance.
Engineman (EN)	Responsible for diesel or gasoline engines, as well as refrigeration, air-conditioning, and distillation equipment at sea.
EOD	Explosive ordnance disposal.
Equipment operator (EO)	Operates heavy construction equipment in Public Works or Seabee units.
Fire controlman (FC)	Maintains the electrical and mechanical elements of surface-ship weapons systems.
"First and Finest"	Motto of USN Mobile Construction Battalion One. They really are the first and finest among Seabees.
FLTCM	Fleet command master chief.
Fo'c'sle	Forecastle; place where enlisted sailors live and work. (*See also* deck plates.)
FORCM	Force command master chief.
Fouled anchors	The rating insignia of a chief petty officer. Senior chief petty officers' anchors have a single star above the anchor, those of master chiefs have two stars.
George Cross	Royal Navy award given for great heroism or extraordinary bravery, British equivalent of U.S. Medal of Honor.

Goat locker	Sailor's familiar and usually apt nickname for CPO berthing.
Golden dragon	Sailor who has crossed the international dateline; ceremony commemorating the event.
Green shirts	Flight deck personnel responsible for catapults and arresting gear.
Gunny sergeant	Gunnery sergeant, USMC. Equivalent in rank and status to a chief petty officer.
Hospital corpsman (HM)	Provides health care to naval personnel and their families.
Information systems technician (IT)	Responsible for the Navy's command, control, communications, computer, and intelligence systems.
Interior communications electrician (IC)	Responsible for a ship's internal communications systems, including television, telephone, and video conferencing.
Journalist (JO)	Responsible for the Navy's internal media and external public relations and information.
Killeck anchor	Badge of authority worn by leading seamen in the Royal Navy.
Large deck ships	Generally, aircraft carriers and large amphibious ships.
LDO	Limited duty officer.
Machinist's mate (MM)	Responsible for the ship's main propulsion units on steam-powered systems (including nuclear power plants).
Marshall stack	Holding area for aircraft attempting to land on a carrier.
Master-at-arms (MA)	Responsible for force protection and internal order and discipline.
Master chief	Master chief petty officer (E-9).
MCPON	Master Chief Petty Officer of the Navy.
Mess	Berthing and dining area at sea.
Mess cook	Junior enlisted assigned to assist in food preparation; now called "food service assistant."
Mess management specialist (MS)	Responsible for Navy dining and berthing facilities.
Molder (ML)	Navy metallurgists, responsible for the manufacture of specially needed parts.

Mustangs	Officers directly commissioned from the enlisted community.
MWR	Morale Welfare and Recreation; formerly Special Services.
Navy counselor (NC)	Responsible for providing vocational guidance to Navy personnel and potential recruits.
NCM, NAM, FLOC	Naval awards, respectively: Navy Commendation Medal, Navy Achievement Medal, Flag Letter of Commendation.
NEC9580s	Navy enlisted classification for command master chief petty officers.
Nelson's eye	To turn a blind eye, to ignore. Lord Nelson was sightless in one eye.
North Island	Naval Air Station, San Diego, California.
Operations specialist (OS)	Responsible for radar, navigation, and communications equipment in a ship's combat information center or bridge.
Personnelman (PM)	Human relations specialist responsible for personnel record keeping.
Plebe summer	"Boot camp" for U.S. Naval Academy midshipmen.
Port Hueneme, California	Headquarters for Naval Construction Forces, Pacific.
Postal clerk (PC)	Provides all forms of postal services to personnel at sea and ashore.
Quarterdeck	Ceremonial entrance point to a ship or station. The term is used colloquially to refer to ships' officers generally.
Quartermaster (QM)	Responsible for the safe navigation of ships at sea.
Rack	Bunk or bed.
Radioman (RM)	The Navy's high-speed Morse code operators. The best and the brightest. Many think the skill obsolete, but true radiomen stand ready for duty when the sophisticated high-tech equipment fails, as it inevitably does.
Red shirts	Aviation ordnancemen aboard a carrier, responsible for bombs and aircraft armaments.
Religious program specialist (RP)	Assists chaplains with religious and morale-related services.

ROTC	Reserve Officer Training Corps, university-based officer training program.
Royal baby	Member of King Neptune's court during Shellback or Golden Dragon ceremonies, "third in command" after King Neptune and Queen Aphrodite.
SEA	Senior Enlisted Academy, located at Tomisch Hall, Newport Naval Station, Rhode Island.
Seabees	Naval Construction Forces. Their motto "We Build, We Fight" says it all.
Sea cabin	Commanding officer's stateroom when at sea, used when there is a need to be close to the action. Old wooden crates work well for embarked writers and reporters.
Senior chief	Senior chief petty officer (E-8).
Shellback	One who has crossed the equator on a warship.
Signalman (SM)	Responsible for visual signaling by flag or light; serves as lookout while at sea.
Slug	Newly selected chief petty officer who has not completed initiation ceremonies.
Small boys	Naval vessels smaller than cruisers.
Snipes	Members of the engineering ratings (hull technician, machinist's mate, and so forth).
Sonar technician (ST)	Responsible for sonar and other active and passive sound locating systems.
South Gedunk Sea	Mythical ocean, where the winds are gentle, seas calm, the coffee hot, and the master chief is always in a good mood. Rarely found.
Storekeeper (SK)	Maintains the Navy's supply and logistics systems at sea and ashore.
TQL	Total Quality Leadership; Navy version of W. Edwards Deming's Fourteen Points of Quality Control.
Unrep	Under way replenishment; an exercise at sea when a fleet supply ship or oiler transfers cargo or fuel to a warship while both are steaming, usually in excess of 20 knots. A very difficult and exciting evolution performed routinely by ships at sea.

Wardroom	Dining and berthing space for officers; collectively, the officers aboard ship.
Warrant	Commissioned officer, ranking between master chief petty officer and ensign. (Technically, warrant officers in grade W-1 are not commissioned but selected.)
WESTPAC	Western Pacific, area west of Hawaii.
XO	Executive officer, second in command of a naval unit.

Notes

Chapter 1. What Is a Chief Petty Officer?

1. Department of the Navy, Chief of Naval Training and Education, Chief Petty Officer Indoctrination, Document 38202, Part One.
2. Chief Warrant Officer Lester B. Tucker, USN (Ret.), "History of the Chief Petty Officer Grade," *Pull Together: Newsletter of the Naval Historical Foundation and the Naval Historical Center* 32, no. 1 (Spring–Summer 1993).
3. Regulating Petty Officer E. B. M. Springfield, RNR (Ret.). E-mail to author, 22 August 2002.

Chapter 2. In the Beginning

1. Tucker, "History of the Chief Petty Officer Grade."
2. *The Bluejacket's Manual*, 2nd ed. (Annapolis: Naval Institute Press, 1908).

Chapter 3. Making Chief

1. Department of the Navy, Bureau of Personnel, BUPERS Instruction 1430.16E, Manual for Advancement of Navy Personnel, 25 July 2001.

2. Ibid.

3. Department of the Navy, Chief of Naval Education and Training, Navedtra Document 38202-b, Chief Petty Officer Indoctrination Course, July 2001.

4. Department of the Navy, Office of the Master Chief Petty Officer of the Navy, *Direct Line* 16, no. 3 (May–June 1996).

5. Department of the Navy, Office of the Master Chief Petty Officer of the Navy, *Honoring Tradition: Collected Speeches of the Master Chief Petty Officer of the Navy* (1997), Navy Office of Information.

Chapter 4. Initiation

1. First Armored Division, Mental Health Services, Wiesbaden Germany, 2003.

2. Author's research conducted with 221 respondents to author's queries during May 2002. (www.goatlocker.org)

3. *From Annapolis to Scapa Flow: The Autobiography of Edward L. Beach, Sr.* (Annapolis: Naval Institute Press, 2003).

4. Department of the Navy, Office of the Secretary of the Navy, Secretary of the Navy Instruction Secnavinst. 1610.2, 10 October 1997.

5. Department of the Navy, Officer of the Master Chief Petty Officer of the Navy, *The Year 2000: Journey into the Chief Petty Officers Mess*, Naval Public Affairs Library, U.S. Naval Academy, Annapolis, Public Affairs.

Chapter 5. The Chief Petty Officers Mess

1. Department of the Navy, Office of the Master Chief Petty Officer of the Navy, *The Chief Petty Officer's Creed (Revised)*, Naval Public Affairs Library.

2. Adm. William Smyth, RN, *The Sailor's Wordbook* (London: Her Majesty's Stationery Office, 1867), 25–27.

3. Department of the Navy, Chief of Naval Training and Education, Chief Petty Officer Indoctrination, Document 38202B, Part Seven.

4. "Chief Petty Officer's Core Competencies: Worldwide Command Master Chief Petty Officer's Conference," Dallas, Texas, 25–28 June 2001.

5. Ibid.

6. Department of the Navy, Chief of Naval Training and Education, Chief Petty Officer Indoctrination, Document 38202, Section Two; and Department of the Navy, Chief of Naval Training and Education, Military Requirements for Chief Petty Officers, Document 12047, July 2000.

Chapter 6. Chiefs and Junior Officers

1. Department of the Navy, Chief of Naval Training and Education, Chief Petty Officer Indoctrination, Document 38202, Section Two.

2. Author John Reese, quoted by Senior Chief Aviation Electronics Technician (AW) Jack Reese. (www.goatlocker.org)

3. Remarks by Adm. J. M. (Mike) Boorda, chief of Naval Operations, at the commissioning of USS *Chief* (MCM-14), Norfolk, Virginia, 5 November 1994, Naval Public Affairs Library.

Chapter 7. Mustangs

1. Department of the Navy, Bureau of Naval Personnel, (PERS211), OPNAVINST 1420.1, Enlisted to Officer Commissioning Program Administrative Manual, Enlisted Briefing, 20 July 2002.

2. Bulletin board posting from "Gunner," 0826Z, 10 September 2002, on http://www.goatlocker.org. Permission to quote anonymously granted in a private e-mail message, 14 September 2002.

Chapter 8. Then and Now

1. Department of the Navy, Chief of Naval Information, Naval Public Affairs Library, "Enduring Freedom."

Chapter 9. Quality and Leadership

1. Capt. Donald C. Hefkin, USN, *The Navy's Quality Journey: Operational Implementation of TQL* (Washington, D.C.: Industrial College of the Armed Forces, National Defense University, 1993), appendix C.

Chapter 10. The Command Master Chief Petty Officer

1. Tucker, "History of the Chief Petty Officer Grade."

2. JO1 Charlotte D. (Roberts) Crist, USNR, *Winds of Change: The History of the Office of the Master Chief Petty Officer of the Navy* (Washington, D.C.: Jointly published by the Office of the Master Chief Petty Officer of the Navy and the Naval Historical Center, 1992).

3. Department of the Navy, Chief of Naval Operations, Fleet Force, CNO-Directed and Command Master Chief Program, Opnavinst 1306.2D, NOOD, 19 December 2000.

Chapter 11. The Master Chief Petty Officer of the Navy

1. Crist, *Winds of Change.*

Chapter 13. In Harm's Way

1. "Honoring Tradition, Master Chief Petty Officer of the Navy John Hagan, Commentary," *Naval Institute Proceedings* (December 1997).

2. "Congressional Medal of Honor: Heroes of Pearl Harbor"; Naval Historical Center, On Line Library of Images; "Doing the Impossible: Day of Infamy at Pearl Harbor."

3. Congressional Medal of Honor Society, "Full Citations of Living Recipients"; "Paradise Lost: The First Attack, Kaneohe Bay"; "John Finn: Medal of Honor Recipient."

4. USS *Utah* Battle Logs; "The Unclaimed Medal of Honor"; "The Pearl Harbor Attack, 07 December 1941, Ships Named for Individual Sailors," Naval Historical Center.

5. "Home of the Heroes: Medal of Honor Citations for America's Heroes"; "USS *O. V. Peterson* (DE152)"; U.S. Coast Guard, List of World War II Cutters.

6. Richard E. Costelow Memorial Page; Richard E. Costelow Memorial; Arlington National Cemetery Home Page.

7. Chief Petty Officer Andrew Triplett Memorial; "Just Starting to Live: Remembering Those Who Died on the USS *Cole*," ABC News; "USS *Cole* (DDG67) Returns to the Fleet," Navy Office of Information.

8. Mike Vasilinda, "Florida Native Killed by Land Mine," Capital News Service, Tallahassee, Florida, 28 March 2002.

Index

About the Author

J. F. Leahy is both a Navy and Coast Guard veteran. His service as a radioman included one combat tour with Mobile Construction Battalion One at Phu Bai and Da Nang, Vietnam, in 1969–70. He later completed his baccalaureate and graduate education as a civilian and then worked as a consultant and manager in a number of intelligence-gathering programs overseas.

Leahy retired in 2000 as senior manager of international operations at the Western Electric Company after nearly twenty-five years of continuous service. He is currently an adjunct professor of business at Franklin University's Ross School of Leadership and Management in Columbus, Ohio. In 2002 the Naval Institute published Leahy's first book, *Honor, Courage, Commitment: Navy Boot Camp.*